MULTICULTURAL EDUCATION SERIES

James A. Banks, Series Editor

(continued)

Forbidden Language

ENGLISH LEARNERS AND RESTRICTIVE LANGUAGE POLICIES

Edited by Patricia Gándara and Megan Hopkins

TEACHERS
COLLEGE
PRESS

Teachers College, Columbia University
New York and London

Published by Teachers College Press, 1234 Amsterdam Avenue, New York, NY 10027

Library of Congress Cataloging-in-Publication Data

Forbidden language : English learners and restrictive language policies / edited by Patricia Gándara, Megan Hopkins.

    p. cm.

Multicultural education series

Includes bibliographical references and index.

    ISBN 978-0-8077-5045-2 (pbk : alk. paper) — ISBN 978-0-8077-5046-9 (cloth : alk. paper)

    1. Hispanic Americans—Education.   2. Hispanic American students—Social conditions.   3. Language arts—United States.   4. Education, Bilingual—United States.   I. Gándara, Patricia C.   II. Hopkins, Megan.

    LC2672.4.F67 2009

    428.2'4—dc22

                                     2009039511

ISBN: 978-0-8077-5045-2 (paper)
ISBN: 978-0-8077-5046-9 (cloth)

Printed on acid-free paper
Manufactured in the United States of America

17   16   15   14   13   12   11   10   8   7   6   5   4   3   2   1

To the researchers who have so tirelessly sought the truth
and the students who have persevered in spite
of all the obstacles. PG

and

To Belén, José, Johana, and all of my former students
in Phoenix, Arizona. MH

Contents

Series Foreword

THE NATION'S deepening ethnic texture, interracial tension and conflict, and the increasing percentage of students who speak a first language other than English (Suárez-Orozco, Suárez-Orozco, & Todorova, 2008) make multicultural education imperative. Ethnic minorities made up 100 million of the total U.S. population of just over 300 million in 2006, and the U.S. Census Bureau (2009) projects that their share of the nation's population will increase from one-third in 2006 to 50% in 2042 (Roberts, 2008).

American classrooms are experiencing the largest influx of immigrant students since the beginning of the 20th century. About a million immigrants are making the United States their home each year (Martin & Midgley, 1999). Between 1997 and 2006, 9,105,162 immigrants entered the United States (U.S. Department of Homeland Security, 2007). Only 15% came from nations in Europe. Most came from nations in Asia, from Mexico, and from nations in Latin America, Central America, and the Caribbean (U.S. Department of Homeland Security, 2007). A large but undetermined number of undocumented immigrants also enter the United States each year. In 2007, the *New York Times* estimated that there were 12 million undocumented immigrants in the United States ("Immigration Sabotage," 2007). The influence of an increasingly ethnically diverse population on U.S. schools, colleges, and universities is and will continue to be enormous.

Schools in the United States are characterized by rich ethnic, cultural, linguistic, and religious diversity. U.S. schools are more diverse today than they have been since the early 1900s, when a flood of immigrants entered the United States from Southern, Central, and Eastern Europe. In the 30-year period between 1973 and 2004, the percentage of students of color in U.S. public schools increased from 22 to 43%. If current trends continue, students of color might equal or exceed the percentage of White students in U.S. public schools within one or two decades. Students of color already exceed the number of White students in six states: California, Hawaii, Louisiana, Mississippi, New Mexico, and Texas (Dillon, 2006).

Language and religious diversity is also increasing in the U.S. student population. In 2000, about 20% of the school-age population spoke a language other than English at home (U.S. Census Bureau, 2003). The Progressive Policy Institute (2008) estimated that 50 million Americans (out of 300 million) spoke a language other than English at home in 2008. Harvard professor Diana L. Eck (2001) calls the United States the "most religiously diverse nation on earth" (p. 4). Islam is now the fastest-growing religion in the United States, as well as in several European nations, such as France, the United Kingdom, and The Netherlands (Banks, 2009; Cesari, 2004). Most teachers now in the classroom and in teacher education programs are likely to have students from diverse ethnic, racial, linguistic, and religious groups in their classrooms during their careers. This is true for both inner-city and suburban teachers in the United States, as well as in many other Western nations (Banks, 2009).

An important goal of multicultural education is to improve race relations and to help all students acquire the knowledge, attitudes, and skills needed to participate in cross-cultural interactions and in personal, social, and civic action that will help make the United States more democratic and just. Multicultural education is consequently as important for middle-class White suburban students as it is for students of color who live in the inner city. Multicultural education fosters the public good and the overarching goals of the commonwealth.

The major purpose of the Multicultural Education Series is to provide preservice educators, practicing educators, graduate students, scholars, and policymakers with an interrelated and comprehensive set of books that summarizes and analyzes important research, theory, and practice related to the education of ethnic, racial, cultural, and linguistic groups in the United States and the education of mainstream students about diversity. The books in the series provide research, theoretical, and practical knowledge about the behaviors and learning characteristics of students of color, language minority students, and low-income students. They also provide knowledge about ways to improve academic achievement and race relations in educational settings.

The definition of multicultural education in the *Handbook of Research on Multicultural Education* (Banks & Banks, 2004) is used in the series: Multicultural education is "a field of study designed to increase educational equity for all students that incorporates, for this purpose, content, concepts, principles, theories, and paradigms from history, the social and behavioral sciences, and particularly from ethnic studies and women's studies" (p. xii). In the series, as in the *Handbook*, multicultural education is considered a metadiscipline.

The dimensions of multicultural education, developed by Banks (2004) and described in the *Handbook of Research on Multicultural Education*, provide the conceptual framework for the development of the publications in the series. Those dimensions are *content integration, the knowledge construction process, prejudice reduction, an equity pedagogy*, and *an empowering school culture and social structure*. To implement multicultural education effectively, teachers and administrators must attend to each of the five dimensions. They should use content from diverse groups when teaching concepts and skills, help students to understand how knowledge in the various disciplines is constructed, help students to develop positive intergroup attitudes and behaviors, and modify their teaching strategies so that students from different racial, cultural, linguistic, and social-class groups will experience equal educational opportunities. The total environment and culture of the school must also be transformed so that students from diverse groups will experience equal status in the culture and life of the school.

Although the five dimensions of multicultural education are highly interrelated, each requires deliberate attention and focus. Each publication in the series focuses on one or more of the dimensions, although each book deals with all of them to some extent because of the highly interrelated characteristics of the dimensions.

This engaging, well-researched, and informative book should be read and comprehended within the historical and social context in which the gains of the Civil Rights Movement of the 1960s and 1970s were overshadowed and undercut by the rise of the worldwide conservative and neoliberal movements, which became prominent and powerful in the 1980s (Friedman, 2005). The Civil Rights Movement in the United States echoed around the world and challenged democratic nation-states to close the gap between their ideals and realities. In response to the Civil Rights Movement, significant changes were made in the United States, including increased civic, political, social, and cultural rights for ethnic groups of color, such as African Americans, Hispanics, Asian Americans, and Native Americans. Rights were also expanded for other groups, such as women, people with disabilities, speakers of languages other than English, and people with different sexual orientations.

The Civil Rights Movement stimulated ethnic revitalization movements around the world and politically empowered groups such as Australian Aborigines, Blacks and Asians in England (Tomlinson, 2009), Catholics in Northern Ireland (Dooley, 1998), and Blacks and Indigenous groups in Brazil (Gonçalves e Silva, 2004). These groups demanded that the institutions within their societies—such as schools, colleges, and universities—incorporate their histories, cultures, languages, and identities and grant them structural inclusion. Nations in many parts of the world responded to these demands differently. Immigrant nations such as the United States, Canada, and Australia developed myriad multicultural reforms and philosophies of multiculturalism (Banks, 2009). Nations such as France, Germany, and Switzerland resisted multiculturalism and remained strongly assimilationist (Minkenberg, 2008). In the 2000s, the assimilationist ideology weakened in Germany (Luchtenberg, 2004), but remained tenacious in France (Lemaire, 2009) and Switzerland (Minkenberg, 2008).

One of the most important consequences of the Civil Rights Movement in the United States was the eradication of the immigration policy that severely restricted the immigration of people from nations in Latin America, Asia, the Caribbean, and Africa. The Immigration Act of 1965, which became effective in 1968, substantially changed the sources of U. S. immigration. Prior to 1968, most immigrants to the United States came from Europe. Today, most come from Latin America, Asia, and the Caribbean. A significant number are also African. The European immigrants were primarily White and Christian, whereas most of the immigrants entering the United States today are non-White and have many different religious affiliations, including Islam, Buddhism, Hinduism, and Sikhism (Barnes, 2007).

Since the 1980s, several developments have eclipsed the gains of the Civil Rights Movement and ushered in a new wave of conservatism, neoliberalism, assimilationism, and xenophobia. These developments include the rise of political conservatism that resulted in the presidential elections of Ronald Reagan and George H. W. and George W. Bush, and the response to the Muslim fundamentalism epitomized by the 9/11 attack on the United States, the bombing of four commuter trains in Madrid on March 11, 2004, and the bombing of the London transportation system on July 7, 2005. The increase of immigration in the United States and around the world is another development that triggered the rise of conservatism and neoliberalism. The United States is experiencing its largest wave of immigration since the turn of the 20th century (Roberts, 2008).

This adroit and lucid book compellingly describes the depressing consequences of English-only and restrictive language policies on students, teachers, and schools. The restrictive language policies that were approved by voters in California, Arizona, and Massachusetts were manifestations of the neoliberalism, conservatism, and xenophobia that gripped the country in the early 2000s and that are still powerful and intractable forces in the United States and the rest of the world. Neoliberals advocate "social cohesion" in Canada and "community cohesion" in the United Kingdom. In both Canada and the United Kingdom, conservatives and neoliberals contend that social and community cohesion are essential because of the divisiveness wrought by immigration and diversity. As Tomlinson (2009) writes:

> There were many suggestions that a once cohesive British society had been fractured by the presence of racial and ethnic groups and the arrival of newer economic migrants, refugees, and asylum seekers. . . . A major political reaction was to focus on concepts of *community cohesion* and *integration* into an undefined "British" society, with little acknowledgement that the society had always been divided along lines of social class, wealth, gender, race, religion, and region. (p. 121; italics added)

Tomlinson's astute observation can be used to explain the conservative movement in the United States and why its advocates mounted a searing attack on bilingual education in U.S. schools. The contributors to this illuminating book use empirical and persuasive language to describe the educational harm and problems caused by misguided conservative educational policies that targeted immigrant groups, language diversity, and school reform designed to use the cultural strengths of students and the rich funds of knowledge in their families and communities (on education tapping cultural capital, see Moll & González, 2004). The restrictive language policies initiated in California, Arizona, and Massachusetts have not only failed to attain their alleged goal of closing the achievement gap and significantly improving the English language skills of language minority students, they have caused confusion and uncertainty among teachers and school administrators. Some evidence indicates that these policies have in some cases increased educational inequality for English language learners.

This significant and needed book goes beyond describing the complex, nuanced, and unfortunate effects of restrictive language policies on educational policy, teaching, and learning. It provides a philosophical rationale for implementing multilingual policies and school reforms that avoid a subtractive approach to language education (see Valenzuela, 1999), effectively utilize the cultural capital of diverse language groups, and enrich the nation by increasing its linguistic capital in a diverse world in which competency in more than one language is a cultural and economic asset. Part III of this book describes promising ways to implement language programs and policies that foster language diversity and build upon the strengths and cultural capital of English language learners. Effective multilingual interventions include dual language programs in which language minority students and students whose first language is English learn two languages. Evidence indicates that dual language programs foster effective language learning by both groups of students as well as positive intergroup attitudes (Bikle, Billings, & Hakuta, 2004).

Patricia Gándara and Megan Hopkins skillfully edited this comprehensive, coherent, and timely book. I hope it will be widely and thoughtfully read by policymakers, teachers, administrators, students, and other citizens who are committed to making our schools safe and affirming places for all children and youth, including those who have the gift of speaking more than one language.

—James A. Banks

REFERENCES

Banks, J. A. (2004). Multicultural education: Historical development, dimensions, and practice. In J. A. Banks & C.A.M. Banks (Eds.), *Handbook of research on multicultural education* (2nd ed., pp. 3–29). San Francisco: Jossey-Bass.

Banks, J. A. (Ed.). (2009). *The Routledge international companion to multicultural education.* New York and London: Routledge.

Banks, J. A., & Banks, C.A.M. (Eds.). (2004). *Handbook of research on multicultural education* (2nd ed.). San Francisco: Jossey-Bass.

Barnes, I. (2007). *World religions.* London: Cartographica Press.

Bikle, K., Billings, S., & Hakuta, K. (2004). Trends in two-way immersion research. In J. A. Banks & C.A.M. Banks (Eds.), *Handbook of research on multicultural education* (2nd ed., pp. 589–604). San Francisco: Jossey-Bass.

Cesari, J. (2004). *When Islam and democracy meet: Muslims in Europe and the United States.* New York: Pelgrave Macmillan.

Dillon, S. (2006, August 27). In schools across U. S., the melting pot overflows. *New York Times*, pp. A7 & 16.

Dooley, B. (1998). *Black and green: The fight for civil rights in Northern Ireland and Black America.* London: Pluto Press.

Eck, D. L. (2001). *A new religious America: How a "Christian country" has become the world's most religiously diverse nation.* New York: HarperSanFrancisco.

Friedman, M. (2005). *The neoconservative revolution: Jewish intellectuals and the shaping of public policy.* New York: Cambridge University Press.

Gonçalves e Silva, P. (2004). Citizenship and education in Brazil: The contribution of Indian Peoples and Blacks in the struggle for citizenship and recognition. In J. A. Banks (Ed.), *Diversity and citizenship education: Global perspectives* (pp. 185–214). San Francisco: Jossey-Bass.

Immigration sabotage [Editorial]. (2007, June 4). *New York Times*, p. A22.

Lemaire, E. (2009). Education, integration, and citizenship in France. In J. A. Banks (Ed.), *The Routledge international companion to multicultural education* (pp. 323–333). New York and London: Routledge.

Luchtenberg, S. (2004). Ethnic diversity and citizenship education in Germany. In J. A. Banks (Ed.), *Diversity and citizenship education: Global perspectives* (pp. 245–271). San Francisco: Jossey-Bass.

Martin, P., & Midgley, E. (1999). Immigration to the United States. *Population Bulletin*, 54 (2), pp. 1–44. Washington, D.C.: Population Reference Bureau.

Minkenberg, M. (2008). Religious legacies and the politics of multiculturalism: A comparative analysis of integration policies in Western democracies. In A. C. d'Appollonia & S. Reich (Eds.), *Immigration, integration, and security: America and Europe in comparative perspective* (pp. 44–66). Pittsburgh, PA: University of Pittsburgh Press.

Moll, L. C., & González, N. (2004). Engaging life: A funds-of-knowledge approach to multicultural education. In J. A. Banks & C.A.M. Banks (Eds.), *Handbook of research on multicultural education* (2nd ed., pp. 699–715). San Francisco: Jossey-Bass.

Progressive Policy Institute (2008). *50 million Americans speak languages other than English at home.* Retrieved September 2, 2008, from http://www.ppionline.org/ppi_ci.cfm?knlgAreaID=108&subsecID=900003&contentID=254619

Roberts, S. (2008, August 14). A generation away, minorities may become the majority in U.S. *New York Times*, pp. A1 & A18.

Tomlinson, S. (2009). Multicultural education in the United Kingdom. In J. A. Banks (Ed.), *The Routledge international companion to multicultural education* (pp. 121–133). New York and London: Routledge.

Suárez-Orozco, C., Suárez-Orozco, M. M., & Todorova, I. (2008). *Learning a new land: Immigrant students in American society.* Cambridge, MA: Harvard University Press.

U.S. Census Bureau. (2003, October). *Language use and English-speaking ability: 2000.* Retrieved September 2, 2008, from http://www.census.gov/prod/2003pubs/c2kbr-29.pdf

U.S. Census Bureau. (2009). *The 2009 statistical abstract: The national data book.* Retrieved August 31, 2009, from http://www.census.gov/prod/compendia/statab/2009edition .html

U.S. Department of Homeland Security. (2007). *Yearbook of immigration statistics, 2006.* Retrieved August 11, 2009, from http://www.dhs.gov/files/statistics/publications/ ,ook.shtm

Valenzuela, A. (1999). *Substractive schooling: U.S.–Mexican youth and the politics of caring.* Albany: State University of New York Press.

Acknowledgments

W E WISH TO thank Stanley Johnson, Danny Martinez, Dianna Moreno, and Genevieve Siegel-Hawley, graduate students at UCLA, for their help during the early stages of this project, without which the book would never have happened. We are grateful for the support of the Linguistic Minority Research Institute in initially bringing the researchers included in this volume together. We would also like to thank Wendy Schwartz and Brian Ellerbeck at Teachers College Press for their care and expertise in the review and publication of this manuscript, and James Banks for his hearty encouragement and endorsement of the need to bring this book into being.

A Note on Usage

THE TERM *Limited English Proficient* (*LEP*) is used in various databases and in various statutes and policy statements; it is also sometimes used by educators. The term *English learner* (*EL*) is used throughout this volume as a general category that includes students identified as LEP.

Introduction

THIS BOOK PRESENTS new research on the impact of English-only policies on English learner (EL) students and their teachers in the United States. Three states—California, Arizona, and Massachusetts—have passed these restrictive language policies in the past 10 years, seriously curtailing the use of bilingual instruction. One of the primary goals of this book is to determine the effects of restricting the use of children's primary language in the classroom on student outcomes as well as on teachers' abilities to meet their EL students' needs. A second important goal of the volume is to consider to what extent such policies align with empirical research on English-only and bilingual instruction. A third goal is to determine what recommendations for policy can be drawn from this new body of research and to suggest alternative policy options. Finally, we examine the legal issues inherent in establishing policies that require schools to implement programs that do not appear to meet the courts' mandate to show success over time. This book is intended for individuals whose work concerns or involves English learners, a group of students who represent a significant and growing population in U.S. schools. Teachers, teacher educators, researchers, school administrators, and policymakers alike will find this volume a tremendous resource that deepens and challenges current understandings of the instruction of English learners.

The volume is organized into four parts. The two chapters in Part I offer an overview of English learners and language policy in education in the United States. Chapter 1, written by the volume's editors, surveys current demographics on and the growth of the population of English learners in schools across the nation. The reader will also find a review of EL academic achievement in this chapter, in addition to information related to how EL students are identified and how their English proficiency is assessed. In Chapter 2, a small collection of experts in the field provide a brief history of language policy in education in the United States, with particular emphasis on the conflicting assumptions about how EL students can best be educated and incorporated into schools and society. The political climates that lead to restrictive language policies in California, Arizona, and Massachusetts are described in this chapter, and the components of these policies are detailed to provide a context for the studies presented here.

The six chapters in Part II bring together a set of recent empirical studies, examining new and never-before-analyzed national and state-level data to determine the scope of impact of English-only policies on students and teachers. The first three chapters of this part (Chapters 3, 4, and 5) examine student academic outcomes in the aftermath of the passage of restrictive language policies in California, Arizona, and Massachusetts, respectively, and find no evidence for narrowing of achievement gaps between EL and non-EL students beyond third grade or of more rapid advancement in English for English learners. After a minimum of 5 years, English learners appear to maintain the same relative (and very low) position academically compared to their English-speaking peers in all three states. In Chapter 3, Wentworth and her colleagues examine the impact of California's English-only law, Proposition 227, on the state's English learners since its passage in 1998. They find, consistent with an earlier 5-year study of the impact of Proposition 227 on outcomes for California's ELs, that there has been no discernible closing of the achievement gaps for these students, although there is some evidence that the first cohort of students studied may have actually experienced educational harm (demonstrated in their lower achievement scores) as a result of the confusion that ensued after the passage of the law. Mahoney and her colleagues, the authors of Chapter 4, relate similar findings for Arizona, where its English-only law, Proposition 203, was voted in 2 years after the California mandate. The researchers find that, over time and across grades, Arizona's reclassified English learners—those who have "graduated" from the English-only program, Structured English Immersion (SEI)—appear to be losing ground when compared to English speakers. Mahoney and her colleagues argue that Proposition 203 has not met the "third prong" of a test established by the Fifth Circuit Court of Appeals in *Castañeda v. Pickard* (1981) that a program implemented by school districts to assist ELs must demonstrate its effectiveness after a period of time. In Chapter 5, Uriarte and her colleagues add another dimension in their assessment of the outcomes for English learners after the passage of Massachusetts' English-only policy, Question 2, in 2002. In addition to finding that the gaps in academic outcomes between ELs and native English speakers have not narrowed and in some cases have widened, the authors also document an increase in student dropout, especially at middle school, which they suggest is due, in part, to the reduced options for primary-language instruction. The researchers also find an initial reduction in the numbers of students identified as English learners, but they find no evidence that students are learning English any faster.

The next three chapters in this part (Chapters 6, 7, and 8) each take on another aspect of policy impact. In Chapter 6, researchers Rumberger and Tran examine National Assessment of Educational Progress (NAEP) data for students in the restrictive language policy states with others that do not have such policies in an attempt to explain why it may be that these initiatives have so little effect on closing achievement gaps. Looking across states, they find a pattern of smaller achievement gaps between EL and non-EL students at grade 4 in those states with large EL populations that offer a bilingual program, when compared to the states with English-only policies. Through more detailed analyses, the authors also find that the composition of the students in the schools accounts for more of the variance in EL student performance than the programs schools offer and that EL students are very heavily segregated into schools with large numbers of EL students. This finding suggests that one of the most important policies that could affect outcomes for EL students is to reduce their isolation and to integrate them with other nonpoor and non-EL students. Next, Artiles and his colleagues, in Chapter 7, pursue the question of whether the introduction of restrictive language policies has had an impact on special education placement in Arizona and California. They find a varying pattern, with relatively little or uneven impact overall; however, when they examine specific special education categories, they find evidence that more EL students may be identified for special education in Arizona because of the lack of appropriate services available for students under Proposition 203. In Chapter 8, the final chapter of this part, de Jong and her colleagues examine the impact of restrictive language policies on the preparation and the work of teachers in Arizona and Massachusetts. In Arizona, the researchers find that teacher preparation practices ostensibly aligned to the provisions of Proposition 203 to teach students through English immersion, in fact, reduce both the breadth and depth of the training that most teachers of EL students receive and fail to address how teachers can instruct the 4-hour block of English language instruction that is now mandated by the state. They find especially troubling that the authority to design new teacher preparation programs has been usurped by the Arizona Department of Education, such that faculty must submit their syllabi to the state for review, which is unprecedented in higher education. In Massachusetts, de Jong and colleagues find that the policy removes tools that teachers have been trained to use with English learner students and fails to provide adequate alternatives, causing some teachers in the state to feel stressed and incompetent.

Given that the conclusion from Part II appears to be that restrictive language policies have failed to deliver on their promise, and in fact may be creating new inequalities in the schools and in society, Part III provides a review of the empirical research on alternative instructional strategies that have been shown to enhance outcomes for EL students. In Chapter 9, based on a multiyear study commissioned by the U.S. Department of Education, August and her colleagues provide an extensive review of the research comparing results from English-only and bilingual education programs. They find that the research yields consistent agreement that primary-language instruction, or instruction in the primary and secondary language simultaneously, results in superior outcomes compared to English-only instruction in improving the English reading achievement of English learners. The authors thus challenge the instructional model adopted in Arizona for the state's ELs that requires 4 hours of daily English language development instruction, warning of the potentially detrimental effects on students if this practice continues. They also cite the literature on the benefits of being bilingual, including cognitive flexibility, family cohesion, and increased self-esteem. The authors of Chapter 10, Morales and Aldana, advance this argument by demonstrating the positive intergroup relations that can be cultivated in bilingual education programs. Morales and Aldana, noting that bilingual education is often treated as though it were a single type of program, provide a taxonomy of programs that incorporate students' primary language, from early-exit bilingual to two-way dual-immersion programs, and discuss the political potential of dual-language models that promote bilingualism and biliteracy for English learners *as well as* English-dominant students. Then, in Chapter 11, Linton and Franklin describe how 12 school districts in California and Massachusetts have maintained dual-immersion programs or have implemented new such programs in the wake of restrictive language policies. While some schools and districts, particularly in California, interpreted the policy as "no bilingual education" and dismantled their programs, others had an opposite response, resulting in dramatic growth of dual-language programs in California post–Proposition 227, often at the impetus of parents seeking an enriched education for their monolingual children.

Finally, Part IV outlines the legal frameworks in which restrictive language policies operate and the potential legal options for addressing the instructional needs of English learners. In Chapter 12, Losen compares results from the National Assessment of Educational Progress (NAEP) in states with restrictive language policies to those without and finds that achievement scores have declined in states with restrictive policies relative to others. Losen, a legal scholar, also critiques the potential impact of the 2009 *Horne v. Flores* Supreme Court decision and reviews the ways in which opportunity to learn has been precluded for EL students by inadequate funding and the failure to meet basic civil rights protections. He argues that there is likely still a basis in *Castañeda v. Pickard* (1981) and in the Equal Educational Opportunity Act for legally challenging these policies. Gándara and Orfield conclude the volume in Chapter 13 and advocate for school districts and states to develop a new vision for language policy, both within and beyond the classroom, that views non-English languages as potential assets rather than impediments to learning.

The intent of this book is to motivate the reassessment of educational goals and policies for English learners in the United States. Current policy supports a goal for English learners to achieve a minimal level of functioning in English in order to be quickly mainstreamed into classes where they too often fail. This volume suggests that a more worthy goal might be to work toward developing multilingual, culturally adept citizens who can prosper and contribute to our increasingly global society. As such, the chapters in this book call on educators, researchers, policymakers, and even registered voters to weigh the evidence and reconsider the path restrictive language policies are leading us down and to create new and better learning opportunities for English learners—and for all our nation's students.

PART I

English Learners and Restrictive Language Policies

The Changing Linguistic Landscape
of the United States

Patricia Gándara and Megan Hopkins

ONE IN FIVE students in the United States is the child of an immigrant, and most of these students speak a language other than English at home (Capps et al., 2005). Half of these students—about 10% of all students—do not speak English well enough to be considered fluent English speakers (Batalova, 2006). These students, commonly referred to as English learners (ELs), perform at lower levels on virtually every measure from achievement scores to graduation rates than almost any other category of students. And, while the general student population in the United States grew just 2.6% between 1995 and 2005, the EL student population grew 56% (Batalova, Fix, & Murray, 2007). Increasingly, then, the academic achievement of English learners is affecting the overall education level of the nation.

Some have argued that the languages spoken by these students are resources that should be nurtured and preserved as students learn English. Others have asserted that since English is the language of the land, students should learn English as rapidly as possible by being immersed in it and that home languages should be kept at home. The debates that have raged over policies for the instruction of English learners have done little to help these students achieve, and they remain among the most vulnerable students in our schools. Given their large and growing presence in American schools, the education of EL students is an increasingly urgent concern.

Since the 1965 change in immigration policy, removing the caps on immigration from specific groups and privileging family unification as the main rationale for gaining legal status, there has been a dramatic increase in immigration, particularly from the Pacific Rim–Asia and Latin America (see Figure 1.1). America's wars abroad have also resulted in influxes of refugees from Southeast Asia and Central America over the last several decades.

Even more dramatic than the shift in overall immigration demographics is the change in public school enrollments. Today, U.S. public schools serve a very different population than they did during the 1960s (see Table 1.1). At that time, about 80% of students were White. Today they are barely more than 50%, and they are a minority of students in all of the nation's large urban districts.

Although virtually all of the languages on the globe are spoken somewhere in the United States, 85% of students speak one of only five. Figure 1.2 shows the most common languages spoken by children in U.S. schools. Given the source of recent immigration, it is no surprise that the top five languages spoken among immigrants are Spanish, Vietnamese, Hmong, Chinese (Cantonese), and Korean. It is notable that more than three-fourths of all English learners speak only one language: Spanish. That so many ELs speak the same language is important because it means that the overwhelming majority of students who do not speak English can be instructed in their native language with relatively little additional burden on the schools.

Figure 1.1. Foreign-born U.S. population by world region of birth, 1960–2000 (millions).

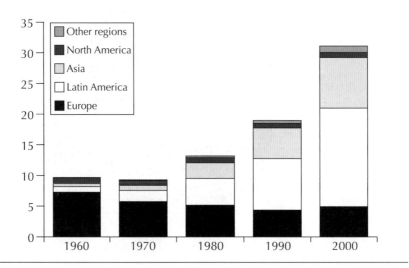

Note: The "Other regions" category includes Africa and Oceania.
Source: Data obtained from the Migration Policy Institute.

Table 1.1. Public school enrollment by race/ethnicity, 1968–2005 (millions).

Race/Ethnicity	1968	1980	1996	2005	Change
White	34.7	29.2	29.1	27.7	–7.0/–20%
Black	6.3	6.4	7.7	8.4	+2.1/33%
Latino	2	3.2	6.4	9.6	+7.6/380%

Source: From *Historic Reversals, Accelerating Desegregation and the Need for New Integration Strategies,* by G. Orfield and C. Lee, 2007. Los Angeles, CA: Civil Rights Project/Proyecto Derechos (www.civilrightsproject.ucla.edu). Copyright © 2007 by Civil Rights Project/Proyecto Derechos. Reprinted with permission.

Although the great majority of English learners speak only a few languages, these students present a new challenge in some parts of the country. Until relatively recently, the overwhelming majority of English learners were clustered in traditional immigrant-receiving or formerly Mexican-held territories: the Southwest, California, Florida, New York/New Jersey, and Chicago, Illinois. However, in recent years there has been a shift as well in the communities to which new

Figure 1.2. Language backgrounds of English learners in the United States, 2000–2001.

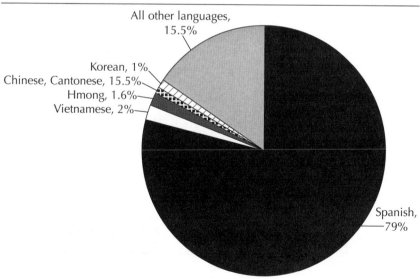

Note: Percentages do not total 100 due to rounding.
Source: Adapted from National Clearinghouse for English Language Acquisition, 2006a.

immigrants have migrated. The most rapid growth in English learners is now occurring in some of the southern states—Georgia, Alabama, Arkansas, and Tennessee, for example—where poultry processing, furniture and carpet manufacturing, housing construction, and service-sector jobs have drawn them (see Figure 1.3). These jobs are low paying and back breaking, attracting individuals with few other occupational options.

EDUCATIONAL CHALLENGES FOR ENGLISH LEARNER STUDENTS

Although English learners are increasingly dispersed across the nation, they are not equally distributed across schools. Seventy percent of the nation's EL students attend just 10% of the nation's schools (de Cohen, Deterding, & Clewell, 2005). These schools tend to be in urban areas with high concentrations of minority and economically disadvantaged students. English learners thus tend to be highly segregated from English-speaking students, attending schools with very high percentages of students like themselves, where the opportunity to hear good models of English and interact with peers who are native speakers are minimal.

Because the United States is an immigrant nation, English learners have always had a presence in this country. However, the last time that the United States

Figure 1.3. Growth in the U.S. English learner population,1995–2005.

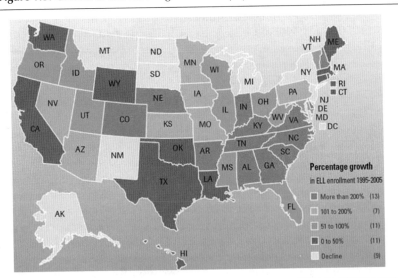

Source: From Education Week's *Quality Counts.* Reprinted with permission from Editorial Projects in Education and Education Week. Vol. 28, No. 17, January 8, 2009.

had such a large influx of immigrants speaking non-English languages, at the turn of the 20th century, they entered in a very different economy and a world in which only about 6% of youth actually received a high school diploma (Lemann, 2000). Today, a high school diploma is the bare minimum educational requirement for virtually any kind of stable employment. Yet data show that Latino students who have not fully mastered English by high school have only about a 40% chance at best of completing high school and acquiring a diploma with their agemates (Jammal & Duong, 2007). Data from the Los Angeles schools in 2007 showed that only 27% of EL students who began the ninth grade graduated 4 years later from the district, suggesting that in large urban centers the dropout rate may be considerably higher.

Finishing high school has become an even more daunting task in recent years with the advent of high school exit exams. To date, 23 states require students to pass exit exams in order to graduate from high school (Cech, 2009). These high-stakes exams prevent EL students who have successfully completed all high school coursework, but cannot pass the English-only test, from getting a diploma. Even completing the required coursework is an obstacle for many EL students, because they spend so much of their high school careers in classes learning English instead of in subject-area classes (Center on Education Policy, 2006). A few states allow students to take exit exams in some subject areas in their native languages; however, students must still pass the English language arts exam to receive their diplomas. There are thus large gaps in high school exit exam pass rates between EL students and all other students. In California, for example, while 74% of non-EL students passed the math exit exam on the first try in 2004, only 49% of EL students passed on the first try. Similarly, 75% of non-EL students passed the reading exam on the first try, while only 39% of ELs passed. These large gaps exist for every state that requires an exit exam (Center on Education Policy, 2006).

English learner students struggle in school more than any other group of students except those who have been identified for special education. From the time they enter school at kindergarten until they are in high school, *if* they continue on to high school, they fall far behind other children on virtually all academic measures. Figures 1.4 and 1.5 show the large and persistent gaps between EL students and their non-EL counterparts in math and reading at both fourth and eighth grades.

The disastrously low academic achievement of these students has, in recent years, made them a focus of attention for education reformers and a convenient object of attention for some individuals who have used their plight to push English-only instructional policies in the states. One argument that has been used is that if these students are denied instruction in their native language, they will be forced to abandon "the crutch" of native language, and learn English more rapidly. Further, although a significant body of research refutes the assertion,

Figure 1.4. National Assessment of Educational Progress (NAEP) results for English learners versus non–English learners in fourth-grade, 2000–2007.

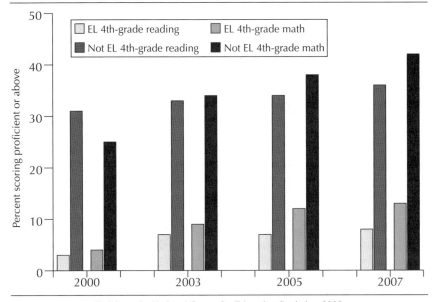

Source: Data compiled from the National Center for Education Statistics, 2008.

this more rapid transition to English is then supposed to result in better academic achievement. Three states—California, Arizona, and Massachusetts—passed ballot initiatives based on these arguments. However, as more evidence has mounted that these state referenda have not been the panacea for English learners that they were promised to be, more recently two states—Colorado and Oregon—have rejected such initiatives.

Nonetheless, in a sagging economy, the issues of immigration and the children of immigration are politically volatile, and these students often find themselves used as political pawns. For example, a growing problem exists for young people who were brought to this country by immigrant parents at very young ages, often before they were even cognizant of their birthplace, and find themselves ineligible for higher education (because they must pay extremely high foreign-student fees and/or are ineligible for any student financial aid) even though they have excelled academically and have never known another country or sometimes even another language. Being anti-immigrant and in favor of English-only policies wins votes in many economically battered areas, and so these young people are often denied access to postsecondary education and told to "go home" when in reality they have never known another home. It is important to point out, how-

Figure 1.5. National Assessment of Educational Progress (NAEP) results for English learners versus non–English learners in eighth-grade, 2003–2007.

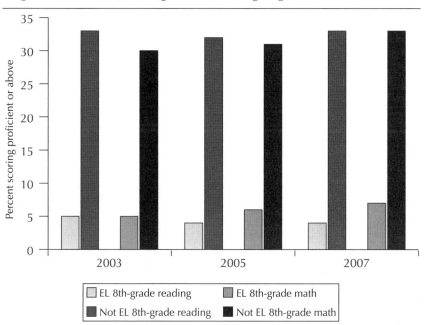

Source: Data compiled from the National Center for Education Statistics, 2008.

ever, that upwards of 80% of English learners in U.S. schools were actually born in the United States and are U.S. citizens with all the rights and privileges of any other U.S. citizen. And, among the far fewer students who lack proper documentation, even they are guaranteed the same K–12 education as native-born students. In 1982, the Supreme Court, in the case *Plyler v. Doe*, established that undocumented students brought to this country by their parents are eligible for full access to K–12 schooling in the United States.

BECOMING AND UN-BECOMING AN ENGLISH LEARNER

The issues of how students are deemed English learners and how they are judged to have learned sufficient English to be mainstreamed into regular school classes are intimately tied to the controversies surrounding language of instruction and the effectiveness of different approaches to instructing English learners. One reason that policies that simply immerse students in English do not always yield the hoped-for results is that learning English turns out to be much more complicated than it seems. Most non-native speakers learn to communicate in English relatively rapidly, especially in school settings where there are many English speakers. However, simply being able to communicate basic information or needs in English does not prepare students to excel in school, and most schools require that students achieve a proficiency in the language, and often in core subject-matter knowledge, that is considerably more extensive than basic communication.

To excel, or even survive academically in school, students must be able to understand a specialized vocabulary (e.g., words such as *summarize* or *analyze* are not generally used on the playground), comprehend complex written text, write essays that are well structured and coherent, make oral presentations on academic topics, and especially pass examinations that are written in a form of English that is often meant to challenge the language skills of native English speakers. If they cannot do these things, they will fail. Moreover, if they have missed out on lessons in history, social studies, science, and math because they could not understand them in English, they are far behind their peers in knowing the material that is tested and cannot hope to pass grade-level exams. Without significant academic intervention, and more time to acquire all that has been missed, these children then fall farther and farther behind as the years go by.

All states have developed tests of English language proficiency that measure English learners' progress in listening, speaking, reading, and writing English, as a requirement of the No Child Left Behind Act (NCLB) (Zehr, 2009). These English-language-proficiency (ELP) assessments are used in every state and the District of Columbia as screening tests to help determine whether or not a student receives the designation "English learner." The use of the state's ELP assessment as the sole criterion to determine program placement can be problematic, however, when a single cutoff score decides whether or not a student should be transitioned out of an EL program. For example, if the cutoff score is 500, and students score 499, they are still designated English learners; however, if they score 501, they are redesignated fluent English proficient (R-FEP). A 2-point difference could make all the difference for children in terms of the language and academic support they receive (if transitioned out of the EL program too early, adequate supports may not be in place for students to succeed in a mainstream classroom). Of course, students do not magically convert from being limited in English to being fluent English speakers overnight. Becoming a fluent English speaker is a process that occurs over a period of time and requires different types and levels of support throughout that period.

Almost all states include a home-language survey as well to determine the languages students speak at home (EPE Research Center, 2009). These surveys are normally used to trigger a more elaborate evaluation of language proficiency if warranted. Other measures include teacher judgment, state or local tests (not the ELP assessment), parent or student interviews, and student grades. There is little uniformity, however, across states or even school districts in how English learners are designated, how their progress is measured, or how they are redesignated as English speakers. When the support they are provided hinges on these measures, such discrepancies can have serious repercussions for EL students. Thus, there are substantial differences across the states in the students that are identified as English learners and in the services that are provided for them.

TEACHERS OF ENGLISH LEARNERS

The success of English learner students depends on the support they receive in learning English as well as in learning their academic subjects. Providing this support to students is by no means easy, as teachers of ELs must essentially do double the work (e.g., teaching academic English and science at the same time) and must be checking for understanding, often without being able to communicate with students. Most teachers have not been adequately trained to address these complex demands. English learners are more likely than any other group of students to be taught by a teacher who lacks appropriate teaching credentials (Gándara, Maxwell-Jolly, & Rumberger, 2008). As of 2000, 41% of U.S. teachers had taught English learner students, but only 13% had received any specialized training on how to teach them (National Center for Education Statistics, 2002). According to a 2003 national survey (Zehler et al., 2003), only 5% of teachers of EL students nationwide had a bilingual certification.

The need for certified teachers to teach English learners is acute and continues to grow, particularly in states and locales that for the first time are experiencing the presence of EL populations. As demographics continue to shift, states and school districts must grapple with how best to provide programs for EL students and how to train teachers who may have never before worked with this population. Table 1.2 shows the current certified teacher–EL student ratio in Title III language-instruction programs (which includes bilingual and English-only instructional programs) and the percent of additional certified teachers needed for Title III in the next 5 years for states with the fastest-growing EL populations and for states with the densest EL student populations.

The numbers in the table show the tremendous challenge some states face in finding teachers to serve their EL populations. For example, in Tennessee, a state with one of the fastest-growing EL student populations, the current student–certified teacher ratio is respectable, at 1:27; however, due to the growing numbers of EL students, the state projects needing 2.5 times the current number of EL certified teachers in the next 5 years. In Nevada, a state with one of the densest populations of EL students, the student–certified teacher ratio is abysmal at 1:128, with an additional 27.4% of teachers needed over the next 5 years.

Table 1.2. Certified teacher-to-student ratio and teachers needed for EL students, 2006–2007.

	EL Students per Certified Title III Teacher (n)	Additional Certified Teachers Needed for Title III in Next 5 Years, as Share of Current Teachers (%)
Fastest-growing EL population (more than 200%)		
Alabama	86	10.2
Arkansas	19	66.5
Colorado	17	48.4
Georgia	31	50.1
Indiana	26	62.0
Kentucky	3	6.3
Nebraska	43	34.7
North Carolina	20	25.2
South Carolina	55	60.9
Tennessee	27	150.0
Virginia	49	64.8
Densest population of EL students		
Arizona	16	14.3
California	—	—
Nevada	128	27.4
New Mexico	7	11.3
Oregon	466	—
Texas	31	58.3
Utah	28	199.8

Note: Colorado has one of the fastest-growing and the densest EL student populations.

Sources: From National Clearinghouse for English Language Acquisition, 2006b; Viadero, 2009.

While there is considerable consensus that many more well-prepared teachers are needed, a recent survey of 5,300 educators in California demonstrated that many of the teachers of English learners in that state felt unprepared to meet the challenge of teaching them, even when they held specialized credentials (Gándara, Maxwell-Jolly, & Driscoll, 2005). The underpreparation of teachers results in part because there is not a strong consensus of what constitutes a "highly qualified" or even reasonably prepared teacher for EL students. Of course, much depends on the goals of the program in which they are teaching—a bilingual or dual-language classroom requires skills above and beyond what would be required for an English as Second Language (ESL) class. Wong Fillmore and Snow (2005) argue that all teachers of EL students need extensive knowledge of first- and second-language acquisition as well as how to explicitly teach about language. Others have argued for a host of additional competencies, including an understanding of how to plan, implement, and manage instruction aligned with English Language Development standards and the resources needed to execute effective instruction; a knowledge of appropriate assessments for EL students and an attentiveness to the biases embedded in some standardized tests; an awareness of the history of EL issues and the motivation to advocate on students' behalf; and a sensitivity to cultural differences and a willingness to incorporate students' culture into the curriculum (Téllez & Waxman, 2006). Of course, teachers of English learners should also be responsive to the diversity within the EL population; there is no "one size fits all" model for teaching such a diverse group of students (García & Stritikus, 2006). At a minimum, however, teachers must feel that they are prepared and should be able to demonstrate success with these students, things that many of the California teachers surveyed did not believe was true for them.

Although researchers have outlined some of the critical competencies for teachers of English learners, there is still much to be learned about what kind of teacher is best suited to work with these students and how best to recruit and retain these teachers (Gándara & Maxwell-Jolly, 2006). It has been suggested that teachers who are from similar communities or who share similar backgrounds with EL students may be best suited to understand the needs of this population and the most likely to continue teaching in these communities. Yet the teaching force remains largely White and middle-class, suggesting the need to expand the teacher pool by recruiting and providing incentives for teacher candidates from underrepresented communities. Moreover, as the nation diversifies, teachers will increasingly be required to meet the needs of many different types of students in their classrooms, and there is no evidence that simply being from one minority group necessarily increases teachers' sensitivity to all others.

Aside from needing adequate preparation and continuing support, teachers of ELs are more likely than other teachers to report that they do not have adequate school facilities or educational materials, which only adds to the difficulty of their job (Gándara & Maxwell-Jolly, 2006). Given the large and increasing number of ELs in U.S. public schools, it behooves the educational community—and the nation as a whole—to improve the educational environments and opportunities for these students and their teachers. Failing to do so will put the entire education system at risk. For example, in California, with one-third of the nation's English learners, the overwhelming majority of schools in Program Improvement status for failing to meet No Child Left Behind benchmarks are schools with high proportions of English learners. As the percent of students required to meet academic proficiency under NCLB continues to rise, all schools with significant numbers of EL students will face this fate.

REFERENCES

Batalova, J. (2006). Spotlight on limited English proficient students in the United States. *Migration Information Source.* Retrieved January 5, 2009, from http://www.migrationinformation.org/USfocus/display.cfm?id=373#8

Batalova, J., Fix, M., & Murray, J. (2007). *Measures of change: The demography and literacy of adolescent English learners—A report to the Carnegie Corporation of New York.* Washington, D.C.: Migration Policy Institute.

Capps, R., Fix, M., Murray, J., Ost, J., Passel, J. S., & Herwantoro, S. (2005). The new demography of America's schools: Immigration and the No Child Left Behind Act. Washington, DC: Urban Institute. Retrieved on January 10, 2009, from http://www.urban.org/url.cfm?ID=311230

Cech, S. J. (2009). Elusive diplomas: Graduation hurdles prove high for ELLs. *Education Week, 28*(17), 36.

Center on Education Policy. (2006). High school exit exams: Special problems affecting English language learners. *Exit exams policy brief.* Washington, DC: Center on Education Policy. Retrieved October 21, 2008, from http://www.cep-dc.org/index.cfm?fuseaction=page.viewPage&pageID=567&nodeID=1

de Cohen, C. C., Deterding, N., & Clewell, B. C. (2005). Who's left behind? Immigrant children in high and low LEP schools. Washington, DC: Urban Institute. Retrieved May 18, 2009, from http://www.urban.org/url.cfm?ID=411231

EPE Research Center. (2009). Identifying English-language learners. Retrieved January 5, 2009, from http://www.edweek.org/ew/articles/2009/01/08/17screening.h28.html?r=796094003

Gándara, P., & Maxwell-Jolly, J. (2006). Critical issues in developing the teacher corps for English learners. In In K. Téllez & H. C. Waxman (Eds.), *Preparing quality educators for English language learners: Research, policies, and practices* (pp. 99–120). Mahwah, NJ: Erlbaum.

Gándara, P., Maxwell-Jolly, J., & Driscoll, A. (2005). *Listening to teachers of English language learners: A survey of California teachers' challenges, experiences, and professional development needs.* Santa Cruz, CA: Center for the Future of Teaching and Learning.

Gándara, P., Maxwell-Jolly, J., & Rumberger, R. W. (2008). *Resource needs for English learners: Getting down to policy recommendations.* Santa Barbara, CA: University of California Linguistic Minority Research Institute.

García, E. E., & Stritikus, T. (2006). Proposition 227 in California: Issues for the preparation of quality teachers for linguistically and culturally diverse students. In K. Téllez & H. C. Waxman (Eds.), *Preparing quality educators for English language learners: Research, policies, and practices* (pp. 45–69). Mahwah, NJ: Erlbaum.

Jammal, S., & Duong, T. (2007). *Language rights: An integration agenda for immigrant communities.* Washington, DC: MALDEF/Asian American Justice Center/Migration Policy Institute. Retrieved November 15, 2008, from http://www.migrationinformation.org/integration/language_portal/files/Language_Rights_Briefing_Book.pdf

Lemann, N. (2000). *The big test: The secret history of the American meritocracy.* New York: Farrar, Straus, & Giroux.

Maxwell, L. A. (2009). Shifting landscape: Immigration transforms communities. *Education Week*, *28*(17), 10.

Migration Policy Institute. (2007). U.S. historical immigration trends, MPI Data Hub. Retrieved January 14, 2009, from http://www.migrationinformation.org/datahub/historicaltrends.cfm

National Center for Education Statistics. (2002). *Schools and staffing survey: 1999–2000*. Retrieved January 10, 2009, from http://nces.ed.gov/pubs2002/2002313/pdf

National Center for Education Statistics. (2008). *The nation's report card: NAEP data explorer*. Retrieved January 29, 2009, from http://nces.ed.gov/nationsreportcard/naepdata

National Clearinghouse for English Language Acquisition. (2006a). Data on languages spoken by U.S. students. Washington, DC: Author. Retrieved January 15, 2009, from http://www.ncela.gwu.edu/stats/4_toplanguages/languages.html

National Clearinghouse for English Language Acquisition. (2006b). The growing numbers of Limited English Proficient students 1995/96–2005/06. Retrieved January 18, 2009, from www.ncela.gwu.edu/policy/states/reports/statedata/2002LEP/Growing_LEP02.03.pdf

Téllez, K., & Waxman, H. C. (Eds.). (2006). *Preparing quality educators for English language learners: Research, policies, and practices*. Mahwah, NJ: Erlbaum.

Viadero, D. (2009). Delving deep: Research hones focus on ELLs. *Education Week*, *28*(17), 26.

Wong Fillmore, L., & Snow, C. (2005). What teachers need to know about language. In C. T. Adger, C. E. Snow, & D. Christian (Eds.), *What teachers need to know about language* (pp. 7–54). Washington, DC: Center for Applied Linguistics.

Zehler, A. M., Fleischman, H. L., Hopstock, P. J., Stephenson, T. G., Pendzick, M. L., & Sapru, S. (2003). *Descriptive study of services to LEP students and LEP students with disabilities* (Vol. I). Washington, DC: U.S. Department of Education, Office of English Language Acquisition, Language Enhancement, and Academic Achievement of Limited English Proficient Students (OELA).

Zehr, M. A. (2009). The right place: Screening students proves to be crucial. *Education Week*, *28*(17), 30–34.

CHAPTER 2

Forbidden Language:
A Brief History of U.S. Language Policy

Patricia Gándara, Daniel Losen, Diane August,
Miren Uriarte, M. Cecilia Gómez, and Megan Hopkins

UNLIKE OTHER multicultural nations, which have pursued policies supporting multilingualism, the United States has consistently sought to maintain the primacy of English both in educational settings and in public life. The European Union (EU), America's primary global cultural and economic competitor, for example, has embraced multilingualism at the institutional and educational level in its declarations. It has a policy of institutional multilingualism with 23 official languages, as of the last official declaration (Europa, 2008), that supports the promotion of a linguistically and culturally diverse Europe through language learning and intercultural dialogue. Such a language policy aims, first of all, for communication with citizens and heads of government in their mother tongues.

Although the EU does not have an official lingua franca, scholars find that, for pragmatic reasons, it has been using a more restricted set of working languages (e.g., English, French, German) when operating internally. In educational terms, the language policy supports the "mother tongue plus two foreign languages" principle for every EU citizen. The study of English, which is seen as necessary for participating in the international community, and the study of local and community languages are also addressed. The EU emphasizes multilingualism (for nation-states), plurilingualism (for EU citizens), and cultural diversity for pragmatic, economic, political, and ideological reasons. (Plurilingualism, in which multiple different languages are spoken by subgroups in the population, is distinguished from multilingualism, in which the population speaks more than one language.) However, even this seemingly enlightened approach to language policy distinguishes between indigenous languages and those of new immigrants.

Many countries, such as those in the EU, distinguish in their language policies between indigenous minority languages (languages spoken by natives of the land) and immigrant languages (those that come with newer arrivals). In such cases, indigenous languages are often given a preferred status, at least statutorily, if not in actual practice. For example, the EU provides special status for regional and minority languages that have traditionally been spoken within a nation-state but not necessarily for newer immigrant languages (Gándara & Gómez, 2009). In fact, in parts of the EU, there have even been concerted efforts to revive endangered native languages, such as with Gaelic in Ireland and the Basque language in Spain.

LANGUAGE POLICIES IN THE UNITED STATES

In reality, the United States has no official language policy. It only has laws that provide non–English speaking students a right to acquire the English language and to have access to an equitable education while they are doing so.

Some protections have been provided for indigenous languages in the United States; however, these protections have been weak, and American Indian languages have been becoming extinct at an alarming rate. It has been estimated that of the 175 American Indian languages still spoken today, only 20 will survive to mid-century (Crawford, 2004). Spanish holds a unique role in the United States that places it nearer to an indigenous language than to an immigrant language. While English-only advocates frequently characterize the use of Spanish as "un-American" and cast it as a language of immigrants, in fact, Spanish was spoken in about one-third of what would become the United States long before the Pilgrims arrived on its eastern shores. And Puerto Ricans, who are U.S. citizens and inhabit large communities in several parts of the U.S. mainland, speak Spanish as their birthright. Thus, in spite of local laws and initiatives that seek to outlaw the use of Spanish in the public sphere, it has a longer history in the United States than does English. Notwithstanding the Treaty of Guadalupe Hidalgo in 1848, which extended the right to speak the Spanish language in those territories forcibly taken by the United States in the Mexican-American War, U.S. law does not provide any special protection for the use of Spanish within its borders.

Non-English language loss among immigrants is also accelerating. Spanish-speaking immigrants—and their children—are actually acquiring English at a more rapid rate than previous generations and simultaneously losing their ability to speak Spanish more quickly (Tienda & Mitchell, 2006). A recent survey by the Pew Hispanic Center (2002) found that by the second generation, only 4% of Hispanics counted themselves as Spanish-dominant, down from 72% in the first generation.

Not surprisingly, then, the United States has been described as "a graveyard for languages" (Rumbaut, Massey, & Bean, 2006, p. 448). Nonetheless, an extreme concern for the survival of English as the official language of the United States has driven many policies for educating English learners.

What may seem an irrational idea—that English would ever lose its hegemony in U.S. culture given its clear world dominance—is actually a proxy for concern about social and economic opportunity. In a multilingual state, language becomes a critical marker of social and political status. Schmidt (2000), in fact, argues that "the dispute [over language policies] is essentially a disagreement over the meanings and uses of group identity in the public life of the nation-state, and not language as such" (p. 47). Minority languages are always culturally subordinated to the majority or "official" language and thus so are their speakers. Such cultural subordination always carries economic consequences. In sum, the stakes are very high for language policies, as they shape the core identity of groups of people and determine their social, educational, and economic opportunities.

EDUCATING ENGLISH LEARNERS IN THE UNITED STATES

The United States historically has had a weak commitment to the education of its English learners. The use of non-English languages for instructional purposes in the United States has been controversial since the early 18th century, with alternating cycles of acceptance and rejection depending on the relationship of the United States with the countries from which immigrants came and their levels of immigration. Moreover, given that the federal government has never had an actual language policy (only a series of policies about language and education), the states have also diverged from one another and from the federal government in the policies they have implemented. Ovando (2003) characterizes the 18th and 19th centuries in the United States as "inconsistent and contradictory regarding the ideology, policies, and politics of language diversity" (pp. 3–4). He asserts that, "though some states published official documents in minority languages, the U.S. Congress consistently refused to do so. Some states authorized bilingual education while others mandated English-only instruction. . . . Responses to language diversity were shaped by the changing localized political, social, and economic forces rather than by systematic ideas about language itself" (pp. 3–4). Overall, however, he characterizes the period between 1700 and 1880 as tolerant toward non-English, immigrant language use in part because if people did not like their neighbors, they could "keep clearing the land and move" (p. 4).

During the 19th century, large numbers of immigrants arrived in the United States believing that they could maintain their native language while concurrently participating in U.S. society. By the second half of the 19th century, bilingual or non-English instruction was provided in many public and private schools: "German in Pennsylvania, Maryland, Ohio, Indiana, Illinois, Missouri, Nebraska, Colorado, and Oregon; Swedish, Norwegian, and Danish in Wisconsin, Illinois, Minnesota, Iowa, North and South Dakota, Nebraska, and Washington; Dutch in Michigan; Polish and Italian in Wisconsin; Czech in Texas; French in Louisiana; and Spanish in the Southwest" (Kloss, 1977/1998, cited in Ovando, 2003, p. 4).

However, the period spanning the 1880s to the 1960s was a turning point in which a number of repressive policies were promulgated, but for different reasons. They included repressive Indian language policies mandated by the U.S. government as a means to "civilize" Indians and contain them on reservations, which is described by some scholars as "a campaign of linguistic genocide" (Crawford, 1995, p. 26). The best-documented examples are the compulsory boarding schools for Native American children (Deyhle & Swisher, 1997). In essence, the ideology, policies, and practices that made English-speaking synonymous with "being a student" were honed in a period when the federal government forced American Indian children to attend boarding schools far from their families and tribes. While enrolled, students were punished severely in these restricted institutions for use of their native language or observance of their native religious practices (Deyhle & Swisher, 1997). As historical and current data show, these regulations in no way guaranteed academic success, integration, or successful biculturalism for the children enrolled. This history provides the most cautionary instance where the suppression of a first language was defined as critical to achieving full American citizenship, yet the version of English (and the practices that supported the acquisition process) supplied was impoverished at best. The current marginalization and low academic achievement of many Native American communities is testament to the costs of this forced trade.

The rise of European nationalism at the turn of the 20th century also created fear on the part of U.S. citizens that these ideologies would be imported to the United States, prompting calls for the assimilation of immigrant populations (Ovando, 2003). English-only school laws were adopted in Illinois and Wisconsin in 1889, and the Naturalization Act of 1906 required immigrants to speak English before they could become naturalized U.S. citizens. This stance toward immigrants continued into the 20th century, fueled by World War I. The teaching of German as a foreign language was curtailed; the Bureaus of Naturalization and Education sponsored bills that "provided for substantial federal aid to states, on a dollar-matching basis, to finance the teaching of English" (Higham, 1992, p. 82), and by 1923, the legislatures of 34 states had dictated English-only instructional policies in all private and public schools (Kloss, 1977/1998). A push toward homogeneity continued during the first half of the 20th century. This push was spurred by many factors, including the standardization and bureaucratization of urban schools (Tyack, 1974), the need for national unity during the two world wars, and the desire to centralize and solidify national gains around unified goals for the country (Gonzalez, 1975).

It was during this period, moreover, that many schools took a "sink or swim" approach to the instruction of recent immigrants in which it was up to the immigrant student to adapt to English-only instruction. No doubt as a result, in 1911, the U.S. Immigration Service found that 77% of Italian, 60% of Russian, and 51% of German immigrant children were one or more grade levels behind in school compared to 28% of American-born White children (Kloss, 1977/1998).

The enforced trade of first languages for English was implicated in two foundational education law cases decided in the 1920s. These cases came about as the result of a belief established in law that immigrants needed to be either excluded entirely from the mainstream of American society or controlled by being compelled to attend public school, where English was the only language of instruction. In *Meyer v. Nebraska* (1923), the Supreme Court struck down a law barring public and private schoolteachers from teaching in a language other than English, with violators subject to criminal penalties. The Court's decision served to protect immigrant children from a state statute born of animosity toward foreigners (in this case Germans). In the second case, *Pierce v. Society of Sisters* (1925), the central legal question was whether compulsory education laws precluded parents from choosing a nonpublic (parochial) school for their children's education. The Court found in favor of the parents' right to choose their children's school, but the case was the result of a referendum campaign of the Ku Klux Klan in which one of its leaders argued, "Somehow these mongrel hordes must be Americanized; failing that, the only remedy is deportation" (Yudof, Kirp, Levin, & Moran, 2002). In each case, the parents' right to choose was upheld as a shield against attempts by the state government to use compulsory English-only instruction to strip the children of foreign-born residents of their culture. All the same, during the 1920s, "the laws of twenty-two states prohibited non-English language instruction in elementary education" (Myhill, 2004, p. 400). It is noteworthy that the United States continues to consider linguistic assimilation of immigrants, or the achievement of English monolingualism, as the final step in the multigenerational assimilation process.

LANGUAGE RIGHTS VERSUS ENGLISH ONLY

The Civil Rights Act of 1964 ushered in a new era of rights for English learner students based on Title VI of the Act, which forbids discrimination based on national origin, interpreted to include language. Shortly thereafter, in 1968, the first federal policy designed to address the needs of students who had "limited English proficiency" was passed as Title VII of the Elementary and Secondary Education Act (ESEA), also known as the Bilingual Education Act (BEA). The act, however, carried no funding and was largely symbolic. Thus, the "bilingual" law did not actually encourage bilingualism in its original language. Rather, it was inextricably associated with the War on Poverty legislation and was, from the beginning, a compensatory program to remediate the language deficits of economically poor limited English speakers. In 1969, $7.5 million in funding was added to the act, sufficient to serve just 27,000 children (Castellanos, 1983). It was not until 1974 that another case reached the Supreme Court that would spell out students' rights to access education regardless of their primary language. *Lau v. Nichols* (1974) recognized the right of linguistic minority students to have access to the same curriculum as English-speaking students and made it incumbent on the schools to facilitate that access through whatever effective means they chose, including bilingual education. Immediately following this decision in 1974, the Bilingual Education Act was renewed with a strong mandate to help children to learn in their primary language while they also acquired English; this time, the act carried substantially enhanced funding. This positive climate surrounding bilingual education, however, was short lived.

The 1975 Lau Remedies and the Lau Compliance Reviews, promulgated by the U.S. Department of Education, followed soon after the *Lau* decision and provided the regulatory framework for the implementation of the decision. The Lau Remedies established how school districts should assess and instruct English learners (ELs) and required schools to offer bilingual education to students who were not proficient in English when it could be demonstrated that their civil rights had been violated. The remedies, which were widely viewed as supporting primary language maintenance, were only guidelines and lacked the legal status of federal regulations, though in the political environment of the mid-1970s and following on *Lau*, the Office for Civil Rights (OCR) enforced them.

But the honeymoon was short. The end of the 1970s and the 1980s saw an increase in opposition to bilingual education. In 1978, Title VII was reauthorized, and the amendments excluded the native-language-maintenance component of the bilingual programs. Funding for bilingual education was cut by 25%. Federal funding would support only transitional bilingual education (TBE) programs, and there was an increase in seats for English speakers, ostensibly to serve as language models for English learners. The growth of the foreign-born population, especially of Spanish speakers, and the challenges faced by non-English-speaking minorities met with the rise of conservative forces in the U.S. government and in groups leading the English-only movement. The movement redefined bilingual education as a barrier to cultural assimilation and citizen participation and successfully lobbied for the closure of bilingual education programs in several states. It put forth a series of arguments for English-only education: (1) that language diversity can lead a nation into ethnic and political conflict and separation (erroneously likened to the situation of Quebec within Canada), (2) that the English language is the "social glue" that unites all Americans, and (3) that the new immigrants refused to learn English and were not assimilating as fast as before (Crawford, 2004). The English-only movement had anti-immigration and nativist political goals that were similar to those of the Americanization movement of the early 20th century (Wiley & Wright, 2004).

Starting in 1981, the English-only movement, led by a former senator from California, S. I. Hayakawa, and a Michigan physician who had founded an anti-immigration lobby, tried to introduce several constitutional amendments to make English the official language of the country. Even though they were unsuccessful at the federal level, up to 23 states passed similar measures (Wiley & Wright, 2004). Their political agenda was incorporated into the policy of the Reagan administration, and in 1984, the BEA was reauthorized with modest funding for developmental bilingual education and a guarantee that at least 25% of funds would be allocated to "special alternative" (all-English) programs (Crawford, 2004).

The antibilingual and antimulticultural tenor of the times continued to build through the 1980s, 1990s, and 2000s, with increasing immigration, rising numbers of ELs, and a "close the borders" mentality gripping the nation. Arthur Schlesinger, a well-known historian and self-admitted political liberal sounded an alarm in 1991 with the publication of *The Disuniting of America: Reflections on a Multicultural Society.* In a related essay, he lamented that with the new immigration of the 20th century, "a cult of ethnicity had erupted" whose only result could be "the fragmentation, resegregation, and tribalization of American life" (Schlesinger, 1991, p. 20). With the Democrats moving away from support of the bilingual education legislation, the future of federal education policy was bound to shift.

In 1994, Title VII of ESEA, newly named Improving America's School Act (IASA), was reauthorized, and this time the cap on English-only programs was effectively removed. Any district that claimed it could not mount a bilingual program was authorized to proceed with English-only education. And, finally, with the reauthorization of the legislation under the new title of No Child Left Behind (NCLB), all references to any bilingual instruction were removed. The former Office of Bilingual Education was renamed the Office of English Language Acquisition, Language Enhancement, and Academic Achievement for Limited English Proficient Students. The eradication of any mandate to support the development of native languages, or support academic instruction through native languages, was complete (Gándara, Moran, & García, 2004).

RESTRICTIVE LANGUAGE POLICIES: CALIFORNIA, ARIZONA, AND MASSACHUSETTS

While immigrants have never been especially warmly welcomed into this country, recent steep increases in immigration, especially from Latin America, have incited strong anti-immigrant feelings and punitive legislation. California and Arizona, two states with particularly high percentages of new immigrants, have been especially fertile sites for anti-immigrant activity. In 1994, California voters passed Proposition 187, barring most undocumented immigrants from any public services, including schooling. That law was ultimately vacated by the state's supreme court, but in 1998, Californians passed another referendum, Proposition 227, the intent of which was to bar the use of primary languages for the instruction of English learners, who, by and large, are the children of immigrants. The passage of the initiative, which also allowed citizens to sue teachers if they were found not to be in compliance with the barring of primary-language instruction, had an almost immediate effect of reducing the number of students receiving such instruction from about 29% of English learners to about 8%.

During the same period, Arizonans attempted to pass a series of increasingly restrictive measures against immigrants, and in 2000, Arizona followed California's lead with an anti–bilingual instruction law of its own: Proposition 203. Proposition 203 was modeled on the California initiative but included provisions that made it even more difficult for parents to seek waivers to opt out of the prescribed Structured English Immersion (SEI) program. In 2004, the state also passed a highly restrictive referendum barring undocumented immigrants from any kind of public social services and made it a crime to fail to report any application for services by an undocumented person.

Effective September 2006, Arizona created stricter regulations on the implementation of its English-only educational policy. Under the authority of Laws 2006, Chapter 4, an Arizona Task Force was established and charged with developing and adopting "research-based" methods of Structured English Immersion programs to be used in school districts and charter schools in Arizona. Arizona Revised Statutes 15-756.01 require that the models include a minimum of 4 hours a day of English Language Development (ELD) for the first year in which a pupil is classified as an English learner. (Full text for the law regarding the responsibilities of the Arizona Task Force and the development of the SEI model is located in Title 15, Chapter 7, Article 3.1: English Language Education for Children in Public Schools.) However, current Arizona policy provides that students remain in Structured English Immersion classrooms until they score as proficient on the Arizona English Language Learner Assessment (AZELLA), which is the state's English language proficiency test. The Task Force defined English language development in Structured English Immersion classes as separate from content-area instruction, where "the content of the ELD emphasizes the English language itself" (Arizona Task Force, 2007). Students are to be grouped with other students of the same proficiency level, and the Task Force has specified the number of minutes to be spent on each element of language and literacy instruction, with different time allotments at each level of proficiency. Thus, EL students in Arizona are segregated into classrooms with no exposure to English-dominant peers for 80% of the schoolday (4 hours), and the instruction they receive focuses on learning English over learning subject matter (e.g., math, science, social studies).

In 2002, Massachusetts also passed an anti–bilingual education initiative. However, in the case of Massachusetts, the law was modified to allow for the operation of two-way dual-language programs that had garnered an important political constituency, particularly in the Cambridge public schools. This fact has to some extent complicated analyses of data from Massachusetts. Nonetheless, by 2003, three entire states, as well as many local districts, had either moved away from primary-language instruction or banned its use altogether. A national survey of programs for English learners conducted by Development Associates in Washington, D.C., found that in the period between 1992 and 2002, there was a decline from 59% to only 37% of EL students receiving some educational services in their primary language (Zehler et al., 2003).

The ostensible impetus behind the host of English-only initiatives was to better promote English learning for English learner students. The California law was the model for the Arizona and Massachusetts laws, which both include similar language in their preambles:

(d) Whereas, The public schools of California currently do a poor job of educating immigrant children, wasting programs whose failure over the past two decades is demonstrated by the current high drop-out rates and low English literacy levels of many immigrant children;

(e) Whereas, Young immigrant children can easily acquire full fluency in a new language, such as English, if they are heavily exposed to that language in the classroom at an early age. . . . (Chapter 3, Article 1 added to Part I of the California Education Code)

The preamble to the proposed law suggests that, by its passage, (1) the state will spend ("waste") less money on the education of English learners; (2) the changes the law mandates will raise their English literacy levels; and (3) imposition of Structured English Immersion will help them to acquire full fluency in English more quickly. Certainly these were the promises made by the proponents of Proposition 227 on the campaign trail. Many observers, however, saw it as part of a larger assault on immigrant children and their families.

The voters in California, Arizona, and Massachusetts replaced a wide-ranging set of bilingual programs with Structured English Immersion programs that have as their main purpose to expedite the learning of the English language. Unlike transitional bilingual education (TBE, the most popular form of bilingual instruction in the pre–English-only era), which relies on the English learners' own language to facilitate the learning of academic subjects as they master English, the SEI model is based on the concept that the English language is acquired quickly when taught through meaningful content and effective interaction. SEI programs rely on the use of simple English in the classroom to impart academic content, using students' native languages only to assist them in completing tasks or to answer a question, if at all. The initiatives in all three states require that English learners "normally" be placed in SEI programs for no longer than 1 year and then transition into mainstream classrooms. This provision, however, has been especially troublesome, as very few students are proficient enough in English within 1 year to survive academically in mainstream classrooms. A 5-year study of the implementation of Proposition 227 in California, commissioned by its Department of Education, found that the "probability of an EL being redesignated to fluent English proficient status *after 10 years* [emphasis added] in California" was less than 40% (Parrish et al., 2006, p. ix). Hence, what should be done with all the children who were not proficient in English but had exceeded their time allotted for SEI? The answer to this question appears to be as varied as the variations of the programs that resulted from the new law.

Aside from the conceptual changes that restrictive language policies enforce, they also represent a shift in the practices of districts and schools. Implementation in California and Arizona, which preceded the Massachusetts referendum, was marked by a lack of specificity about what the law allowed and a lack of clear operational definitions of instructional approaches, leaving districts and schools to interpret the law and develop practice essentially on their own. The results have been that districts and schools differ widely in the types of programs available to ELs, depending in large part on the districts' and the schools' attitude toward bilingual education.

California, for example, exhibited tremendous variation in the program models implemented as a result of Proposition 227 (Parrish et al., 2006). Gándara and colleagues (2000) and Gándara (2000) reported on analyses of the impact of the new law in California and observed that the districts' decisions on how to handle parents' right to request waivers of SEI (i.e., to request a bilingual program instead) made a profound difference in the type of programs districts offered. On the one hand, in the immediate aftermath of the passage of Proposition 227, districts that had strong bilingual education programs often supported parents' rights to request waivers, and in many ways, their practice was not changed. On the other hand, in those districts with a lukewarm or negative attitude toward bilingual education, there tended to be less commitment to enforcing parental waiver rights in these districts; thus, primary-language programs declined, and SEI programs proliferated. With the advent of increased high-stakes testing under NCLB, additional pressure was placed on schools to get students quickly into English-only programs, and further erosion in the programs occurred (Zehr, 2007).

In the case of Arizona's Proposition 203, during the first 2 years of implementation, parents were allowed to waive participation in SEI, resulting in the presence of a wide variety of offerings for children. In 2003, stricter enforcement of the waiver provisions began, narrowing the school districts' options. Wright and Pu (2005) observed that in the first 2 years of implementation, there was a small reduction in the gap between ELs and others in the results of the Arizona Instrument to Measure Standards (AIMS) and the Stanford Achievement Test,

Ninth Edition (SAT-9) in 2002 and 2003; this gap widened in 2004, the first year of the new, stricter enforcement of English-only education programs. The authors argued that improvement in test scores between 2002 and 2003 was due to greater flexibility for schools in offering English as a Second Language (ESL) and bilingual education, while the decline of scores in 2004 corresponded to a period of forced closure for most bilingual programs and mandates for English-only instruction for ELs.

The confusion and the changes in policy implementation have had their harshest effects on instruction at the classroom level because the SEI-required changes have coincided with the demands posed by other education reform efforts in the state, such as the implementation of accountability regimes (Gándara, 2000). Some report a deterioration of teaching practice when SEI forces instruction that is devoid of a context familiar to the student and that focuses exclusively on learning English language sounds, or where oral fluency trumps literacy in order to ensure adequate performance on English language tests (Gutiérrez, Baquedano-Lopez, & Asato, 2000). Gándara (2000) reported that teachers in California expressed "fear" and "confusion" about how to shape their instruction so that it met accountability standards while keeping to the spirit—and staying away from the teacher sanctions—of Proposition 227. This trepidation was echoed in Wright and Choi's (2006) Arizona study, which showed that teachers felt confused about what is and is not allowed in SEI classes according to the new laws.

THE NATIONAL SENTIMENT TOWARD LANGUAGE

The "fear of harm to America" from non-English speakers and the languages they speak still plays a potent role in our discourse regarding both immigration and the education of English learners. In April 2006, in the midst of a press conference about overhauling U.S. immigration laws, President George W. Bush responded to a question regarding a Spanish language recording of the Star Spangled Banner by a British producer who said he wanted to honor America's immigrants. Bush said, "One of the things that's very important is, when we debate this issue, that we not lose our national soul. . . . I think people who want to be a citizen of this country ought to learn English, and they ought to learn to sing the national anthem in English" (quoted in MacAskill, 2006). The fact that the president was willing to sacrifice his earlier support of bilingual education and resistance to English-only instruction in return for a modicum of flexibility in immigration policy suggests how our historical intolerance toward non-English speakers on our soil, and in our institutions, still influences the course of immigration and education policy. Furthermore, it suggests the deep connections for many U.S. residents between the right to citizenship and monolingual English-speaking—at least in the public sphere, be it in schooling or in singing the national anthem.

In short, across the last century, the United States has developed into a culture in which the category of citizen (and by extension, student) has been defined in terms of having a primary allegiance to speaking only in English. This is a matter of choice and values, rather than of logic or necessity, as other cultures, as we have noted, view multilingualism as a natural and desirable attribute of citizens worth supporting through education and other policies. Thus, in the United States, the systems for describing the language skills of non-native speakers focus exclusively on their mastery of English, hence terms like *Limited English Proficient* (LEP) and *Fluent English Proficient* (FEP). Yet, in terms of success in school and other types of formal learning, what matters is not only who can and elects to communicate in English, but also who acquires and controls the resources of cognitive academic discourses—the languages students need to thrive in mathematics, history, or literature classes and the linguistic interactions of discussion, questioning, doing research, and offering and seeking help (Gee, 1996). To the extent that this activity occurs in English only, native speakers of the language will almost always hold an advantage over English learners.

Whether in a period of relative beneficence regarding English learners, such as during the civil rights period of the 1960s and early 1970s, or in more ungenerous times, we have never served the students who are not native English speakers well. We have never produced enough well-trained teachers to teach these students, and we have never supported the dissemination of curricula that would allow them to acquire English while also excelling academically in another language. The fixation on one research question—Is bilingual or English-only instruction superior?—has meant that other, far more important questions, like how to teach reading to English learners or how to assess their strengths across more than one language, have not been provided with sufficient research support. Policy has been made in a relative knowledge vacuum. The chapters that follow attempt to help fill this void and provide both empirical analyses of the effects of particular language policies on student learning and schooling conditions as well as an examination of the research bases for pursuing alternative policies.

REFERENCES

Arizona Task Force. (2007). Structured English Immersion models of the Arizona English Language Learners Task Force. Retrieved October 21, 2008, from https://ade.state.az.us/ELLTaskForce/SEIModels9-15-07.pdf

Castellanos, D. (1983). *The best of two worlds: Bilingual-bicultural education in the U.S.* Trenton, NJ: New Jersey State Department of Education.

Crawford, J. (1995). *Bilingual education: History, politics, theory, and practice* (3rd ed.). Los Angeles: Bilingual Educational Services.

Crawford, J. (2004). *Educating English learners: Language diversity in the classroom* (5th ed.). Los Angeles: Bilingual Educational Services.

Deyhle, D., & Swisher, K. (1997). Research in American Indian and Alaska Native education: From assimilation to self-determination. *Review of Research in Education*, *22*, 113–194.

Europa. (2008). *Languages of Europe*. Retrieved January 30, 2009, from http://ec.europa .eu/education/languages/languages-of-europe/index_en.htm

Gándara, P. (2000). In the aftermath of the storm: English learners in the post 227 era. *Bilingual Research Journal*, *24*(1&2), 1–13.

Gándara, P., & Gómez, M. C. (2009). Language policy in education. In B. Schneider, G. Sykes, & D. Plank (Eds.), *AERA handbook on educational policy research* (pp. 581–595). Washington, DC: American Educational Research Association.

Gándara, P., Maxwell-Jolly, J., García, E., Asato, J., Gutiérrez, K., Stritikus, T., & Curry, J. (2000). *The initial impact of Proposition 227 on the instruction of English language learners*. Davis: University of California, Linguistic Minority Research Institute, Education Policy Center.

Gándara, P., Moran, R., & García, E. (2004). Legacy of Brown, Lau and language policy in the United States. *Review of Research in Education*, *28*, 27–46.

Gee, J. P. (1996). *Social linguistics and literacies: Ideology in discourses*. London: Taylor & Francis.

Gonzalez, J. M. (1975). Coming of age in bilingual/bicultural education: A historical perspective. *Inequality in Education*, *19*, 5–17.

Gutiérrez, K., Baquedano-Lopez, P., & Asato, J. (2000). "English for the children": The new literacy of the old world order, language policy and educational reform. *Bilingual Research Journal*, *24*(1–2), 87–112.

Higham, J. (1992). Crusade for Americanization. In J. Crawford (Ed.), *Language loyalties: A source book on the official English controversy* (pp. 72–85). Chicago: University of Chicago Press.

Kloss, H. (1998). *The American bilingual tradition*. Washington, DC: Delta Systems & Center for Applied Linguistics. (Original work published 1977)

Lau v. Nichols, 414 U.S. 563 (1974).

MacAskill, E. (2006 April 29). Bush objects to Spanish version of US anthem. *The Guardian*. Retrieved January 29, 2009, from http://www.guardian.co.uk/world/2006/apr/ 29/usa.spain

Meyer v. Nebraska, 262 U.S. 390 (1923).

Myhill, W. (2004). The state of public education and the needs of English language learners in the era of "No Child Left Behind." *Journal of Gender, Race & Justice*, *8*, 393–448.

Ovando, C. J. (2003). Bilingual education in the United States: Historical development and current issues. *Bilingual Research Journal*, *27*(1), 1–24.

Parrish, T. B., Merickel, A., Perez. M, Linquanti, R., Socia, M., Spain, A., Speroni, C., Esra, P., Brock, L., & Delancey, D. (2006). *Effects of the implementation of Proposition 227 on the education of English learners, K–12: Findings from a five-year evaluation*. Palo Alto, CA: American Institutes for Research and WestEd.

Pew Hispanic Center. (2002). *Pew Hispanic Center/Kaiser Family Foundation 2002 National Survey of Latinos*. Retrieved September 23, 2007, from http://pewhispanic .org/reports/report.php?ReportID=15

Pierce v. Society of Sisters, 268 U.S. 510 (1925).

Rumbaut, R., Massey, D., & Bean, F. D. (2006). Linguistic life expectancies: Immigrant language retention in southern California. *Population and Development Review, 32,* 447–460.

Schlesinger, A. (1991). The cult of ethnicity, good and bad. *Time, 138,* 20.

Schmidt, R. (2000). *Language policy and identity politics in the United States.* Philadelphia: Temple University Press.

Tienda, M., & Mitchell, F. (2006). *Multiple origins, uncertain destinies: Hispanics and the American future.* Washington, DC: National Academy of Sciences.

Tyack, D. B. (1974). *The one best system: A history of American urban education.* Cambridge, MA: Harvard University Press.

Wiley, T. G., & Wright, W. E. (2004). Against the undertow: Language-minority education policy and politics in the "age of accountability." *Educational Policy, 18*(1), 142–168.

Wright, W. E., & Choi, D. (2006). The impact of language and high-stakes testing policies on elementary school English language learners in Arizona. *Education Policy Analysis Archives, 14*(13). Retrieved February 3, 2009, from http://epaa.asu.edu/epaa/v14n13/

Wright, W. E., & Pu, C. (2005). *Academic achievement of English language learners in post Proposition 203 Arizona.* Tempe, AZ: Arizona State University, Education Policy Studies Laboratory, Language Policy Research Unit.

Yudof, M., Kirp, D., Levin, B., & Moran, R. (2002). *Education policy and the law and policy* (4th ed.). Belmont, CA: Wadsworth.

Zehler, A. M., Fleischman, H. L., Hopstock, P. J., Stephenson, T. G., Pendzick, M. L., & Sapru, S. (2003). *Descriptive study of services to LEP students and LEP students with disabilities. Vol. 1: Research report.* Arlington, VA: Development Associates, Inc. Retrieved April 10, 2008, from: http://www.ncela.gwu.edu/resabout/research/descriptivestudyfiles/voll_research_fulltxt.pdf

Zehr, M. A. (2007). NCLB seen a damper on bilingual programs. *Education Week, 26*(36), 5, 12.

PART II

Evidence on Outcomes
of Restrictive Language Policies

Proposition 227 in California:
A Long-Term Appraisal of Its Impact
on English Learner Student Achievement

Laura Wentworth, Nathan Pellegrin,
Karen Thompson, and Kenji Hakuta

IN JUNE 1998, California voters passed Proposition 227 (hereafter Prop 227), a law requiring public schools to conduct instruction "overwhelmingly" in English. With over 1.5 million students in California classified as English learners, the law affected one-fourth of California students and over one-third of English learners in the United States (California State Department of Education, 2008a; Hoffman & Sable, 2006). The law especially impacted English learners receiving instruction in bilingual programs. Since the passage of Prop 227, the percentage of English learners receiving primary-language instruction has decreased from 29.1% in 1997–1998 to 5.6% in 2006–2007 (California State Department of Education, 2008b, 2008c). This chapter examines the impact of Proposition 227 on educational outcomes for California's 1.5 million English learners. Building on prior research (Parrish, Pérez, Merickel, & Linquanti, 2006), we compare English learner and English-only student achievement by grade level, using data from the California Standards Test from 2003 to 2007.

Prop 227 drastically changed California's policies for educating English learners. Before Prop 227 passed, districts had control over the instructional methods they used to educate their English learners. However, under Prop 227, English-only instruction was mandated for all English learners unless parents signed a waiver otherwise. Prop 227 stipulated that English learners be placed in Structured

English Immersion (SEI) classes in which instruction was required to be "overwhelmingly in English." Once students acquired a "good working knowledge of English," students transferred to mainstream classrooms.

For almost 10 years now, school districts and, more importantly, English learners have felt the impact of Prop 227's policy change. A number of research reports have attempted to analyze the impact of Prop 227 with varying methods and findings (e.g., Butler, Orr, Gutiérrez, & Hakuta, 2000; Gándara et al., 2000; Parrish et al., 2006). In most cases, the reports relied on achievement data that straddled three different standardized tests; the Stanford Achievement Test, Ninth Edition (SAT-9); the California Achievement Tests, Sixth Edition Survey (CAT-6); and the California Standards Test (CST). Building on the findings from the state-mandated report conducted by Parrish and colleagues (2006), this chapter uses 5 years of CST data to examine Prop 227's impact on English learner achievement.

BACKGROUND

Many studies have addressed the impact of Prop 227 on English learners. Some studies showed the rapid decline in the number of students receiving instruction in their primary language (Gándara et al., 2000; Parrish et al., 2006). Other studies found wide variability in the implementation of the new policy, including variability in districts' use of waivers, in teachers' instructional responses, and in community attitudes towards Prop 227 (Gándara, 2000; Gándara et al., 2000; Maxwell-Jolly, 2000). Studies investigating the relationship between Prop 227 and student achievement found a variety of results. For example, some studies found that the achievement gap between native English speakers and English learners still existed and that Prop 227 did not increase the rate of English learners' reclassification as Fluent English Proficient (Butler et al., 2000; Gándara, 2000; Grissom, 2004).

Parrish and colleagues' (2006) study constitutes the largest, most thorough, and most recent examination of Prop 227's impact. Commissioned by the California Department of Education, the study lasted 5 years. It covered a broad range of topics, including the impact of Prop 227 on English learner achievement, the overall implementation of Prop 227, promising practices for English learners, issues around the reclassification of English learners, and the support of English acquisition in the community.

The study focused heavily on investigating possible changes in the achievement gap between English learners and non-English learners following Prop 227's implementation. The authors analyzed the test scores of students in all four language proficiency groups, as defined by the state: English learners (ELs); former English learners who have been redesignated as Fluent English Proficient (RFEPs); students who speak only English (EOs); and students who speak another language in addition to English but were initially classified as fluent in English when they entered school (IFEPs). To track achievement for these four language proficiency groups, Parrish and colleagues calculated achievement scores based on data from the Stanford Achievement Test, Ninth Edition (SAT-9) from 1997 through 2002 and on data from the California Standards Tests (CST) from 2002 through 2004. The authors addressed the challenge of having different tests with different scales by using a metric-free measure to gauge gains over time.

From their analysis, Parrish and colleagues (2006) found a slight decrease in the performance gap between native English speakers and English learners in the years following Prop 227's implementation, but, in general, the performance gap remained constant in most subject areas for most grades. When students who were former English learners were included in the English learner cohort, the performance gap remained. Also, the study looked at state and district data in the Los Angeles Unified School District to examine English learner performance under different instructional models, including bilingual and English-only programs. This analysis found little to no evidence of differences in performance for English learners by model of instruction. Our study builds on Parrish and colleagues' (2006) methods and findings regarding Prop 227's impact on English learner achievement.

ANALYSIS OF LONG-TERM TEST SCORE TRENDS IN CALIFORNIA FOLLOWING PROP 227

Prop 227 intended to improve academic outcomes for English learners through the elimination or reduction of bilingual education programs. Voters passed the initiative in June 1998, and the law took effect immediately, impacting instruction beginning in the fall of 1998. Figure 3.1 shows the years of Prop 227's impact, as well as the various standardized tests used in the state testing program over time. In this figure, we can see the successive cohorts of students who experienced these policies and the years in which the state administered different standardized tests. The dotted line in Figure 3.1 separates pre- and post-227 cohorts. All students above the dotted line entered school after Prop 227 was passed, whereas those below the dotted line had various amounts of schooling prior to Prop 227, depending on their grade levels when Prop 227 took effect.

Using available CST data from the 5-year period from 2003 to 2007, we examined student achievement separately by grade-level slices. We sought to answer the following question: How did English learner achievement compare to the achievement of other students following the passage of Prop 227? For each district, we estimated test score trend lines separately for ELs and for EOs at each grade level. Comparing ELs to EOs within the same district serves as a control for district-level effects. Of particular interest was whether the ELs and EOs showed different test score trends.

Figure 3.1. Grade-level slices included in analysis.

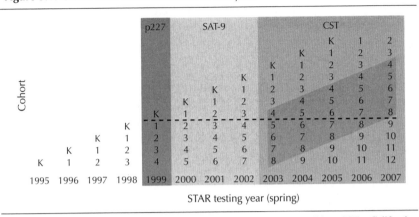

STAR testing year (spring)

Notes: p227 = Proposition 227; SAT-9 = Stanford Achievement Test, 9th Edition; CST = California Standards Test. Cohort panel shows grade level by year of CST testing, marking the year when Proposition 227 was implemented, and the state testing program that was in place during each year. All students in cells above the dotted line entered school after Prop 227 was implemented. Note that all students in the eighth-grade slice entered school before or during the year that Prop 227 took effect.

For the analysis, a data set was created from the public state research data files, using districts as the unit of analysis. Our selection criteria required districts to have data for all subgroups, years, and tests relevant to our analysis. Across the state research files, 359 of the state's 1,131 districts met these criteria and were included in our analysis. We incorporated both current and former English learners into the English learner subgroup (ELs + RFEPs). The English-only subgroup consisted of students who were never classified as English learners (EOs + IFEPs).

Using regression analysis, averaging across districts, we found a general positive trend in test scores for both ELs and EOs at all grade levels from 2003 to 2007. However, as Figure 3.2 illustrates, ELs showed greater achievement gains than EOs at some grade levels (grades 3, 5, 6, and 7). At other grade levels, ELs showed smaller achievement gains than EOs (grades 2, 4, and 8) over time. Statistical tests showed that the differences in EL and EO test score trends were significant at all but one grade level (grade 4). (A complete description of our analysis strategy is beyond the scope of the present volume; a technical version of this paper can be found on the UCLA Civil Rights Project/Proyecto Derechos Civiles website.)

ELs and EOs at grades 6 and 8 show the greatest difference in test score trends. Furthermore, EL and EO test score trends at these grade levels show opposite patterns. The grade 8 results merit particular consideration since every cohort in this grade level was enrolled in school the year that Prop 227 took effect (see Figure 3.1). Therefore, we might expect to observe Prop 227's greatest impact with this grade-level slice. The results for the eighth-grade slice show smaller achieve-

Figure 3.2. District trends on CST ELA, by English proficiency group.

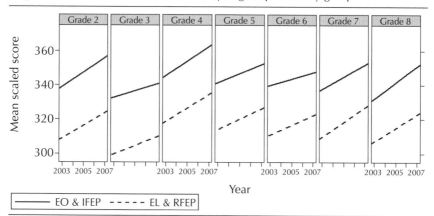

Notes: Linear regression was used to obtain a slope of the CST score on year of testing, separately for the EO and EL groups. The slopes for the EO and EL groups represent the average change in each group's mean CST score over time. There are two obvious and expected characteristics of the slopes that nevertheless need to be noted. First, the slopes are positive across all grade levels and for both the EO and EL groups, indicating that CST scores for both groups rose over time. Second, there is a gap in the mean scores of the EO and EL groups on the order of 20--30 CST points. But our focus of interest is whether the slopes of the test score trend lines for EOs and ELs represent the change in each group's mean CST scores over time. The differences in slopes can be seen in the extent to which the slopes are not parallel. Positive slope differences means that the EL slope exceeded the EO slope, while a negative slope difference means that the EO slope exceeded the EL slope. Positive slope differences were found for grades 3, 5, 6, and 7. Negative slope differences were found for grades 2, 4, and 8. For complete statistical results, see the UCLA Civil Rights Project/Proyecto Derechos Civiles Web site (www.civilrightsproject.ucla.edu).

ment gains for ELs than EOs over time. If more widespread bilingual education was beneficial for ELs and Prop 227 caused a harmful disruption, we might expect to see smaller achievement gains for ELs than for EOs over time. Therefore, the eighth-grade results appear to be consistent with the notion that Prop 227 was harmful for ELs. Furthermore, this apparent harm is detectable downstream in students' educational careers, after considerable time has elapsed.

The grade 6 results show the opposite pattern, with a greater increase in test scores over time for EL students relative to EO students. These results appear to be consistent with the notion that Prop 227 was beneficial for ELs. As we see at sixth grade, if in fact more widespread bilingual education was harmful for ELs and Prop 227 actually benefited this group, we might expect to see greater achievement gains for ELs than for EOs over time. However, a key difference between the sixth-grade and eighth-grade slices is that the sixth-grade slice includes two cohorts that were not enrolled in school when Prop 227 took effect, while all cohorts in the eighth-grade slice were enrolled in school when Prop 227 took effect.

Furthermore, no student in the sixth-grade slice experienced more than 2 years of bilingual education. Advocates of bilingual education might argue that 2 years is insufficient for these programs to benefit student achievement. The pattern we see at sixth grade may be influenced by the fact that no student in this group experienced bilingual education as it was intended.

Examining Differences in Instructional Services for ELs Among Districts

To further shed light on the impact of Prop 227, we analyzed data at grades 6 and 8 more closely. Specifically, we identified school districts where ELs were performing much better or worse over time relative to EO students, and we examined their reported instructional services for ELs both before and after Prop 227.

There is considerable variability in the difference between EL and EO test score trends across districts. From this distribution of districts, we selected the top 20 and bottom 20 districts, in terms of test score trend differences, at both sixth and eighth grades. We gathered data about the number of ELs receiving different instructional services for each district at four points in time: 1997–1998 (the year Prop 227 passed), 1998–1999 (the year Prop 227 was implemented), 2002–2003 (the first year the CST was administered), and 2006–2007 (the most recent year for which data were available). While these data provide important information about instructional services provided to English learners districtwide at particular points in time, they have significant limitations. First, we do not have student-level data. Second, we do not know the length of time for which particular English learners may have received particular services. Furthermore, since the instructional services data are not broken down by grade level, we cannot assess what percentage of a district's English learners received particular instructional services at specific grade levels.

Since Prop 227 attempted to improve educational outcomes for English learners by limiting their enrollment in bilingual programs, we were particularly interested in the percentages of ELs that were listed as "Receiving Academic Subjects Through the Primary Language" for the top 20 and bottom 20 districts over time. Past research has used the percentage of English learners listed in this category as a proxy for the percentage of English learners enrolled in bilingual programs (e.g., Parrish et al., 2006). We will continue this practice.

As is evident in Figures 3.3 and 3.4, the most striking feature of districts' instructional services for ELs is the sharp decline in the percentage of English learners who received academic subjects through their primary language over time. This trend occurs at the state level and for both the top 20 and bottom 20 districts at sixth and eighth grades. While Parrish and colleagues (2006) documented this trend from 1997–1998 through 2003–2004, our data show that the percentage of

Figure 3.3. Share of ELs receiving academic subjects through L1, sixth grade: Top 20 and bottom 20 means compared to state total.

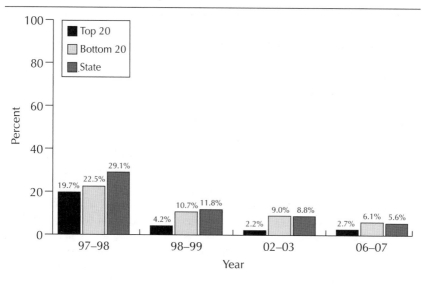

Figure 3.4. Share of ELs receiving academic subjects through L1, eighth grade: Top 20 and bottom 20 means compared to state total.

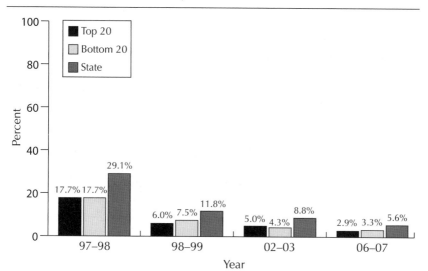

ELs receiving academic subjects in their primary language has continued to drop, from a statewide average of 29.1% in 1997–1998 before the passage of Prop 227 to a statewide average of 5.6% in 2006–2007. While there are differences in the means of the top 20 and bottom 20 districts at both grade levels, these differences are not statistically significant. Analysis of the available data suggests that districts that differ in the test score trends of their EL students compared to their EO students do not differ significantly in terms of the instructional services they provide to English learners, as measured by the state data system.

Examining Differences in Descriptive Characteristics Among Districts

We collected information about a variety of district characteristics, including total enrollment; percentage of students in the district that are classified as English learners; percentage of students who receive a free or reduced lunch; percentage of teachers who are fully credentialed; percentage of schools in the district that made their Academic Performance Index (API) goals under California's accountability system; percentage of students in the district that scored proficient or above on the English Language Arts (ELA) section of the CST; percentage of students in the district that scored proficient or above on the math section of the CST; and whether the district met its Adequate Yearly Progress Goals, as defined by No Child Left Behind. Figures 3.5 and 3.6 display the means for the top 20 and bottom 20 districts for each of these variables at sixth grade and eighth grade, respectively.

We found no statistically significant differences between the top 20 and bottom 20 districts at sixth and eighth grades for any of the variables we analyzed. This suggests that differences in test score trends for the top 20 and bottom 20

Figure 3.5. Descriptive characteristics of top 20/bottom 20 districts, sixth grade.

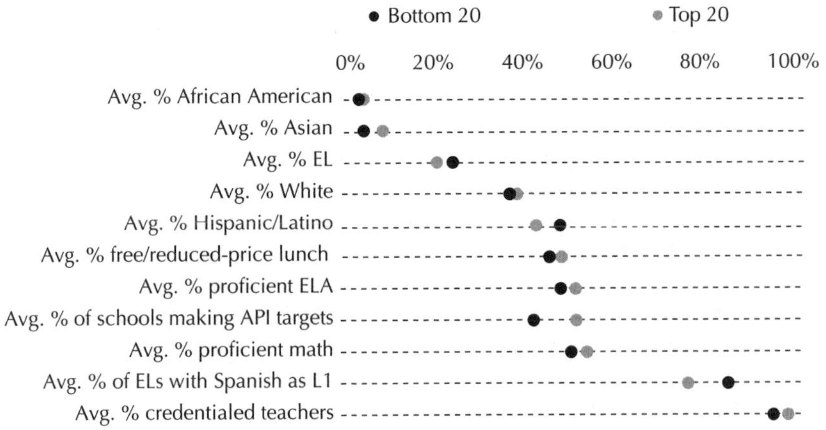

Figure 3.6. Descriptive characteristics of top 20/bottom 20 districts, eighth grade.

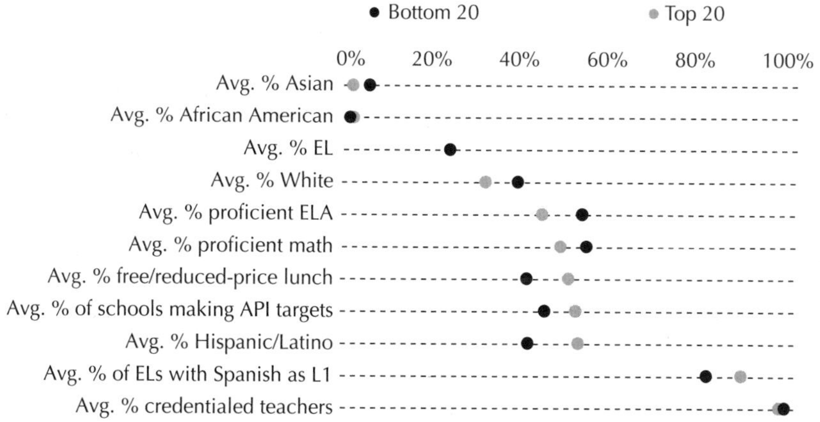

districts cannot be explained by differences in districts' descriptive characteristics. Again, caution must be exercised when interpreting these findings. We collected the descriptive data only for the 2006–2007 schoolyear, and districts' descriptive characteristics may have changed over time. While the top 20 and bottom 20 districts at sixth and eighth grades do not appear to differ significantly in their descriptive characteristics for the 2006–2007 schoolyear, it is conceivable that significant differences in particular characteristics may have existed at other points in time.

DISCUSSION AND POLICY IMPLICATIONS

Given our findings, has Prop 227 improved educational outcomes for English learners? While limitations in available data temper our ability to answer this question definitively, it is clear that, on average, students in California, including English learners, have shown increases in standardized test scores since Prop 227's passage. However, many factors, besides any possible effects of Prop 227, are likely influencing this change in CST scores. For example, under No Child Left Behind and California's accountability system, schools and districts have federal and state CST performance targets and face sanctions if students' scores do not improve each year. Given the shifting, intertwined policy landscape, it is difficult to tie these general achievement trends to Prop 227. Furthermore, the significant achievement gap between English learners and English-only students, while perhaps closing slightly at some grade levels and widening slightly at others, remains consistent and substantial.

What could explain the conflicting test score trends at different grade levels? The Parrish and colleagues (2006) analysis of the effects of Prop 227 included this summary of its findings:

> We conclude that Prop 227 focused on the wrong issue. It does not appear to be the model of instruction employed, or at least not the name given to it, but rather other factors that are much more operative in distinguishing between failure and success with ELs. (p. xii)

Our results support that conclusion. Available statistics about the instructional services offered for English learners by a district did not predict how trends for the performance of the district's ELs on the CST compared to the trends for its EOs.

What distinguishes districts in which the achievement gap between ELs and EOs narrowed from districts in which it widened? What might explain the differences in the comparative achievement trends of ELs and EOs at sixth and eighth grades? Why do we see an achievement gap between ELs and EOs that appears to be narrowing at sixth grade but widening at eighth grade?

Establishing definitive answers to these questions is impossible, but prior research may suggest possible interpretations. First, some studies suggest that it is not the particular type of instructional program that determines English learners' educational outcomes but rather the program's implementation (e.g., Gold, 2006; Parrish et al., 2006; Williams, Hakuta, Haertel, et al., 2007). While districts in our analysis had instructional services for ELs that appeared similar on paper, their programs for ELs may have differed on dimensions not captured by the state data system, such as quality of instruction, expectations for students, instructional leadership, use of assessment, and linkages between home and school.

Second, the initial implementation of any major policy shift, particularly one as far-reaching and as abruptly implemented as Prop 227, likely causes upheaval, regardless of the merits of the program. The implementation of Prop 227 was further complicated by initial widespread uncertainty about the law's requirements. For example, approximately half of the 153 schools surveyed by Parrish and colleagues (2002) reported that they needed additional guidance from the state regarding what instructional arrangements were permissible under Prop 227.

The eighth-grade slice in our sample was comprised of students who were in kindergarten through fourth grades when Prop 227 took effect. The confusion surrounding the law's implementation likely affected many students in this eighth-grade slice. The students who were kindergarteners during the first year of implementation possibly entered schools in which there was confusion about waivers, about the amount of primary-language instruction that was allowed, and about what "Structured English Immersion" meant. Meanwhile, the other students in the grade 8 data slice, who entered grades 1, 2, 3, or 4 during the year that Prop

227 took effect, may have been pulled out of bilingual programs that their districts eliminated.

The sixth-grade slice in our sample, meanwhile, consisted of two cohorts of students not yet enrolled in school when Prop 227 took effect, plus three cohorts of students in kindergarten, first, or second grades that year. Given the findings of Parrish and colleagues (2002) regarding the challenges schools encountered in implementing Prop 227, it is likely that by the time the two later cohorts entered school, confusion over Prop 227 had subsided and districts were more likely to have the coherent, consistent programs in place—bilingual or not—necessary for English learners to experience academic success. Thus, the seemingly contradictory findings of a widening of the achievement gap between ELs and EOs at eighth grade and the closing of this gap at sixth grade may be associated with implementation effects and program coherence rather than the benefits of one instructional program over another.

Yet how does this theory align with August, Goldenberg, and Rueda's (Chapter 9, this volume) findings about the positive effects of reading instruction in students' primary languages on reading achievement in English? If reading instruction in students' primary languages leads to higher achievement in English reading, why do English learners at all grade levels not show test score trend lines consistent with the hypothesis that Prop 227 caused harm? Although we cannot answer this question definitively, it is important to remember that, as August and colleagues (Chapter 9, this volume) point out, the positive effects of primary-language instruction are small to moderate in size. Furthermore, perhaps the positive effects of primary-language instruction are also limited in duration, given the prevalence of transitional rather than maintenance models and the fact that any positive effects in the early grades may be obscured by the powerful effects of school quality as students advance in their schooling careers. Maybe by the time students are in middle school, having experienced a coherent instructional program—bilingual or not—matters more for students' academic achievement than the effects of bilingual education in the early elementary grades. An additional difference between this study and that of August and colleagues is that the research they reviewed focuses on smaller-scale studies with high-quality program implementation. However, large-scale studies such as ours include many programs with wide variation in implementation quality, making clear conclusions about the relative effectiveness of different program models more difficult to draw. Therefore, we see no contradiction between our findings and those of August and colleagues. On balance, it seems fairly clear that the sledgehammer approach to dismantling bilingual education in California disrupted any coherence that may have existed in the system, harmed students in the immediate term, and on average created no overall benefit. Draconian educational policy changes as embodied in Prop 227, it would appear, are best avoided, tempting as they might be for policymakers.

Given the many questions that remain, future research could seek further detailed information about what specific practices at the district, school, and classroom level are associated with educational success for English learners. Specifically, building on our findings, researchers could conduct in-depth case studies comparing specific districts in which the gap between ELs and EOs is closing to those in which it is widening. These case studies could seek to determine differences in districts' practices possibly associated with achievement trends for EL students but not captured by information in the state data system.

In conclusion, while definitive statements about the impact of Prop 227 remain elusive, it is clear that current and former English learners are not achieving the same levels of academic success as their peers who enter school already knowing English. While this achievement gap appears to have closed slightly at some grade levels and widened slightly at others over the last 5 years, we do not see a clear association between the implementation of Prop 227 and consistent achievement gains for English learners relative to English-only students. If we aim to meet the challenge of closing this achievement gap and enabling all of California's more than 6 million public school students to experience academic success, we urgently need further research on effective policies and instructional practices for English learner students.

REFERENCES

Butler, Y. G., Orr, J. E., Gutiérrez, M. B., & Hakuta, K. (2000). Inadequate conclusions from an inadequate assessment: What can SAT-9 scores tell us about the impact of Proposition 227 in California. *Bilingual Research Journal, 24*(1&2), 141–154.

California State Department of Education. (2008a). Report: Number of English learners by language, 2006–07. *Dataquest*. Retrieved February 5, 2008, from http://data1 .cde.ca.gov/dataquest/LEPbyLang1.asp?cChoice=LepbyLang1&cYear=200607& cLevel=State&cTopic=LC&myTimeFrame=S&submit1=Submit

California State Department of Education. (2008b). Report: English learners, instructional settings and services, 2006–07. *Dataquest*. Retrieved February 5, 2008, from http://data1.cde.ca.gov/dataquest/ElP2_State.asp?RptYear=2006–07&RptType =ELPart2_1a

California State Department of Education. (2008c). Part II English learner (EL) students, 1997–98, number of English learner students receiving instructional services. *Dataquest*. Retrieved February 5, 2008, from http://data1.cde.ca.gov/dataquest/oElPart2_1 .asp?RptYear=1997–98&RptType=ELPart2_1a

Gándara, P. (2000). In the aftermath of the storm: English learners in the post-227 era. *Bilingual Research Journal, 24*(1–2).

Gándara, P., Maxwell-Jolly, J., Stritikus, T., Curry, J., García, E., Asato, J., & Gutiérrez, K. (2000). *The initial effects of Proposition 227 on English learners*. Santa Barbara: University of California, Linguistic Minority Research Institute.

Gold, N. (2006). *Successful bilingual schools: Six effective programs in California.* San Diego, CA: San Diego County Office of Education.

Grissom, J. B. (2004). Reclassification of English learners. *Education Policy Analysis Archives, 12*(36). Retrieved January 27, 2008, from http://epaa.asu.edu/epaa/v12n36/

Hoffman, L., & Sable, J. (2006). *Public elementary and secondary students, staff, schools, and school districts: School year 2003–04* (NCES Publication No. 2006-307). Washington DC: U.S. Department of Education, National Center for Education Statistics.

Maxwell-Jolly, J. (2000). Factors influencing implementation of mandated policy change: Proposition 227 in seven northern California school districts. *Bilingual Research Journal, 24,* (1–2), 37–56.

Parrish, T., Linquanti, R., Merickel, A., Quick, H. E., Laird, J., & Esra, P. (2002). *Effects of the implementation of Proposition 227 on the education of English learners, K–12: Year 2 report.* Palo Alto, CA: American Institutes for Research.

Parrish, T., Pérez, M., Merickel, A., & Linquanti, R. (2006). *Effects of the implementation of Proposition 227 on the education of English learners, K–12: Findings from a five-year evaluation.* Palo Alto, CA: American Institutes for Research.

Williams, T., Hakuta, K., Haertel, E., et al. (2007). *Similar English learner students, different results: Why do some schools do better? A follow-up analysis based on a large-scale survey of California elementary schools serving low-income and EL students.* Mountain View, CA: EdSource.

Castañeda's Third Prong:
Evaluating the Achievement of Arizona's English Learners Under Restrictive Language Policy

Kate Mahoney, Jeff MacSwan, Tom Haladyna, and David García

P ROPOSITION 203 was voted into law in 2000, placing severe restrictions on bilingual education in the state of Arizona. As in California, the law requires English-only instruction in the state's public schools; more specifically, it promotes the use of a Structured English Immersion instructional model. (See Chapter 2 for additional discussion.) This chapter evaluates the achievement of Arizona's English learners (ELs) before and after the implementation of Proposition 203 to determine whether English-only programs meet the "third prong" test of *Castañeda v. Pickard* (1981), a test that requires a program for ELs to demonstrate its effectiveness.

The Equal Educational Opportunities Act (EEOA) of 1974 was interpreted by the Fifth Circuit Court of Appeals in *Castañeda v. Pickard* (1981) to require school districts to take "appropriate action to overcome language barriers that impede equal participation by its students in its instructional programs" (Section 1703(f)). In so doing, the court established a famous three-part test for determining whether a school district has taken appropriate actions to overcome language barriers confronting ELs: (1) The district (or local educational agency) must pursue a program informed by an educational theory recognized as sound by experts in the field; (2) the programs and practices actually used by the district must be a reasonable reflection of the educational theory adopted; and (3) after a trial period, the success of the program in overcoming the language barriers that confront students must be demonstrable.

Court rulings in both Arizona and California permitted the implementation of English-only instructional programs based on expert testimony—provided by Christine Rossel, a professor of political science at Boston University, and others— that the programs reflected a valid educational theory, contrary to the majority view among educational researchers (Crawford, 2004). To the best of our knowledge, there has been no challenge brought against an educational agency on the basis of *Castañeda*'s third prong (T. Hogan, personal communication, May 2007). This is a surprising fact since the third prong is in many respects the most empirically testable of the three and lends itself to evidence-based evaluations of the viability of the English-only instructional model.

With *Castañeda*'s third prong in mind, we built on prior research that investigates the effectiveness of Arizona's English-only policies (for a summary, see Mahoney, Thompson, & MacSwan, 2004) by using statewide, student-level data to evaluate differences in the academic achievement of reclassified English learners before and since the implementation of Arizona's current restrictive language policy, Proposition 203. The question we asked is whether statewide assessment data suggest that the current English-only policy context in Arizona for ELs has satisfied *Castañeda*'s third prong, that is, whether language barriers have been overcome for ELs in the state. First, we review Arizona's policy context. Then we investigate two important questions designed to evaluate the achievement of ELs in Arizona under Proposition 203.

THE ARIZONA POLICY CONTEXT

There are currently an estimated 130,000 ELs in Arizona public schools, representing about one out of every seven children enrolled in public schools. Two events, the *Flores v. State of Arizona* ruling in 2000 and the voter-approved Proposition 203 in the same year, drastically altered the legal and educational landscape in Arizona for ELs. The *Flores* case imposed a number of mandates on the state superintendent of public instruction related to identifying and providing appropriate services and assessments for ELs, while Proposition 203 changed state laws governing the required services and assessments for ELs, mandating that "all children in Arizona public schools shall be taught English by being taught in English" (Arizona Revised Statutes § 15-752).

Passage of Proposition 203 in 2000 limited the type of educational programs available to ELs in Arizona. The federal Bilingual Education Act (BEA) of 1968 and the U.S. Supreme Court case of *Lau v. Nichols* (1974) allowed districts flexibility to choose from a variety of program models for educating ELs. Proposition 203 ended that flexibility in the state by repealing relevant sections of the Arizona state statutes, replacing them with a requirement that all ELs in the state be taught using Structured English Immersion (SEI). However, Proposition 203 actually requires bilingual education under appropriate conditions. Nonetheless, the state superintendent of public instruction has interpreted and implemented the law as a strict SEI mandate with essentially no bilingual education programs permitted. Table 4.1 shows the proportion of students enrolled in Arizona EL programs before and after Proposition 203. It shows a clear decline in enrollment in bilingual education co-occurring with the passage of Proposition 203 and an almost complete takeover of English-only programs in ensuing years. For example, in 1997, 32% of ELs were enrolled in bilingual education programs, but by 2004, only 5% were. At the same time, in 1997, 57% of ELs were enrolled in English-only programs, whereas by 2004, that percentage had increased to 94%.

In 1992, Miriam Flores sued the state of Arizona in Federal District Court, accusing it of failing to provide her and other EL children with an effective educational program. Flores alleged that she and other ELs were not achieving English proficiency and were not making adequate academic progress. Citing the EEOA of 1974, plaintiffs in the class action complained of underqualified teachers, inadequate processes for identifying and monitoring ELs, and a lack of funding for programs.

After winding through the federal court system, the *Flores* case resulted in a Consent Order, approved July 31, 2000, requiring the Arizona Department of Education (ADE) to provide detailed procedures to address the majority of complaints against the state. The Consent Order changed the process for monitoring the progress of ELs. In addition to new requirements for monitoring whole districts, the Consent Order required an evaluation of students every 2 years following their exit from EL status, with the evaluation to include reading, writing, math, and academic content-area skills for the purpose of determining whether ELs were performing satisfactorily compared to other students of the same age or grade level in the state.

The June 25, 2009, ruling by the Supreme Court in *Horne v. Flores* affirmed that the EEOA requires the state to meet the special needs of English learners, but remanded the case to the federal district court. The remand asked the court to examine whether Arizona had met its obligation to these students with a Structured English Immersion program consisting of 4 hours of daily English drill, by complying generally with the requirements of NCLB, by introducing some "structural management reforms" in the Nogales School District (the initial defendant in the case), and/or by providing some additional funding for all students in Arizona schools.

The 2006 law further required that a Task Force be appointed to develop a "scientifically based" instructional model. What emerged from the Task Force was a program of instruction that includes 4 hours of daily intensive instruction focused on English language development. "The model," as it is called, imposes unconventional methods on EL teachers and is heavily geared toward discrete-

Table 4.1. Number and share of tested students enrolled in bilingual education (BE) and English-only (EO) programs before and after Proposition 203.

	1997	1998	1999	2000
BEFORE PROPOSITION 203				
Bilingual Education	12,704 (32.31%)	13,288 (30.17%)	9,708 (22.2%)	10,237 (20.91%)
English-Only	22,454 (57.1%)	26,590 (60.38%)	29,281 (66.98%)	33,441 (68.31%)
Individual Education Plan (IEP)	4,163 (10.59%)	4,163 (9.45%)	4,730 (10.82%)	5,247 (10.77%)
Total	39,321	44,041	43,719	48,952

	2001	2002	2003	2004
AFTER PROPOSITION 203				
Bilingual Education	10,249 (20.85%)	9,373 (10.7%)	10,167 (10.24%)	5,147 (5.61%)
English-Only	34,290 (69.75%)	78,178 (89.29%)	89,030 (89.75%)	86,636 (94.39%)
Individual Education Plan (IEP)	4,620 (9.4%)			
Total	10,249 (20.85%)	9,373 (10.7%)	10,167 (10.24%)	5,147 (5.61%)

Notes: Bilingual education programs consisted of traditional bilingual K–6, secondary bilingual 7–12 before Proposition 203, and transitional bilingual education with waiver, bilingual/bicultural with waiver, bilingual/bicultural K–12 and dual language with waiver after Proposition 203. English-only programs consisted of English as a Second Language before Proposition 203 and Structured English Immersion and Mainstream English Classroom after Proposition 203. Individual Education Plan as a program option for ELs became unavailable after Proposition 203.

skill instruction. For a critical review of the state's model and its scientific merits, see Krashen, Rolstad, and MacSwan (2007) and August, Goldenberg, and Rueda (Chapter 9, this volume).

The evaluation of the academic achievement of ELs was further complicated by the introduction of No Child Left Behind (NCLB) and the passage of Proposition 203 because they dramatically changed state assessment policies in Arizona. In the 2004–2005 academic year, state assessment policy changed such that only a single measure, a language proficiency test, would be used for reclassification decisions. In prior years, Arizona districts had been permitted to select one of four language proficiency tests—the Language Assessment Scales (LAS), the IDEA Proficiency Test (IPT), the Woodcock-Muñoz Language Survey (WMLS), or the Woodcock Language Proficiency Battery (WLPB)—and were required to use student results on the language proficiency test in conjunction with a score on the Stanford Achievement Test, Ninth Edition (SAT-9), a standardized test of academic achievement, to make reclassification decisions. Hence, along with reducing the language proficiency tests to a single statewide assessment, Arizona policy also shifted away from incorporating multiple indicators for measuring the progress of ELs by eliminating the academic achievement assessment. Beginning in 2005, the reclassification process for ELs in Arizona relied solely on the Stanford English Language Proficiency (SELP) Test. Mahoney, Haladyna, and MacSwan (in press) studied the effects of these changes in assessment policy and found that at the same time the reclassification rate rose, more ELs were not succeeding in the mainstream curriculum. In 2006, the Arizona Department of Education changed the proficiency test to the Arizona English Language Learner Assessment (AZELLA), an augmented version of the SELP.

Given the shifts to more restrictive instructional models and more permissive assessment policies and use of instrumentation, we conducted a study that addresses two specific research questions in an effort to evaluate the outcomes of current state policies. Our specific research questions were: (1) How does the academic achievement among reclassified ELs (FEPs)—students who were formerly ELs and then tested at proficient levels on an English language exam—before the passage of Proposition 203 (1997–2000) compare to the academic achievement among similar students in the years immediately after the passage of the proposition (2001–2004)? (2) How did reclassified ELs perform relative to the Arizona State Standards in the later years (2002–2006)?

There are scant data about ELs that transcend the time periods before and since Proposition 203, so research question 1 is a unique opportunity to evaluate Proposition 203–related education policies by comparing similar student cohorts over time. Research question 2 provides a portrait of the academic performance of ELs since Proposition 203 but in this case does not include a comparison group of non-EL students.

RESEARCH QUESTION 1: A COMPARISON OF STUDENT LEARNING BEFORE AND AFTER PROPOSITION 203

Method

To answer the first question, data from similar cohorts of students were compared using SAT-9 scores. The SAT-9 is a national test that reflects national curriculum content standards. Each test record included key questions about students, namely, the student's primary language and whether the student participated in an English learner program. Primary language indicates the student's home language. The response options include English, Spanish, Navajo, and other. EL program participation refers to classification status, and students were coded as either EL or fluent English proficient (FEP). ELs are students enrolled in a special language program. FEPs are reclassified ELs, or students who have met reclassification criteria as required per state policy, such as reaching a certain level of language proficiency as measured by a language proficiency test. Students whose primary language was English and who were not coded as either EL or FEP were coded as English proficient (EP). Individual student SAT-9 records were linked across years based on student names and dates of birth. The student matches were verified using class rosters from selected school districts. On average, 89% of all eligible student records were matched across adjacent years.

The study compared two similar student cohorts, one before the passage of Proposition 203 and the other after its passage. The pre–Proposition 203 sample included students who attended Arizona public schools from 1997 to 2000; the post–Proposition 203 sample included students who attended Arizona schools from 2001 to 2004. For each time period, individual test records were tracked across grades and academic years to create student groups (see Figure 4.1).

Each student cohort was subdivided into one of the following three language classification groups based on the student's primary language and membership in an EL program:

Figure 4.1. Illustration of student cohorts in Arizona, pre–Proposition 203.

1997	1998	1999	2000
3	3	3	3
4	4	4	4
5	5	5	5
6	6	6	6
7	7	7	7
8	8	8	8
9	9	9	9

1. *EP*. The student's primary language was English, and the student was never placed in an EL program (neither EL nor FEP).
2. *FEP-3*. The student was coded as EL in the first year of our data set and coded as FEP the remaining 3 years.
3 *FEP-2*. The student was coded as EL in the first and second year of the database and coded as FEP the remaining 2 years.

The success of Arizona's Structured English Immersion (SEI) program was evaluated by comparing the mean SAT-9 scale scores (total reading and total mathematics) by language classification group across time periods. As a longitudinal analysis, the academic achievement over time is represented as changes in scale scores for the same cohorts of students as they progressed through grade levels. Scale scores were chosen as the metric of academic achievement because these scores are linear and span all grade levels of the SAT-9. The selection of a test score metric is important because the metric can influence the conclusions drawn from educational research (Seltzer, Frank, & Bryk, 1994). (For further discussion of the use of SAT-9 scaled scores in the context of EL program evaluation, see Thompson, DiCerbo, Mahoney, & MacSwan, 2002.)

Results: Student Gains Before and After Proposition 203 Were Nearly Identical

Very large samples of students were used for all three cohorts. For example, the FEP-3 group had 4,481 students pre–Proposition 203 and 5,017 students post, the FEP-2 group had 2,093 pre and 1,741 post, and the EP had 12,411 pre and 18,389 post. The composition of the three student groups differ ($X^2 = 3.96$, $df = 1$, $p < .05$), and the most notable difference is an increase in the post–Proposition 203 cohort. The increase reflects the state's increasing enrollments of EL students during the years under study.

The primary groups of interest for comparison are the fluent English proficient (FEP) students in the pre– and post–Proposition 203 periods, or those students who were at one point classified as ELs. The EP group, students never classified as ELs, was included as a reference point to benchmark the findings for the FEP student groups. Our first research question was explored in terms of two more narrowly focused questions. First, at what academic level did FEP students initially perform pre–Proposition 203 as compared to post? Second, how did the academic gains of FEP students compare before and after Proposition 203? Recall that FEP scores are the focus of this study; therefore, comparisons between pre– and post–Proposition 203 are made during the years a student was classified as FEP. For FEP-3, comparison years included 1998–2000 before Proposition 203 and 2002–2004 after. Because the FEP-2 group had one less year as reclassifed students (FEPs), comparion years included 1999–2000 before Proposition 203 and

2003–2004 after. EP group comparisons were made during the same years to provide a reference point.

Reading: Where Did the Student Groups Start? The starting point for all student groups was higher after Proposition 203 (see Table 4.2). The mean reading score for the FEP-3 group was 649 before and 655 (a 6-point increase) after Proposition 203; during the same years, the EP group increased by 3 points. The FEP-2 group showed a similar increase of 655 before and 660 after (a 5-point increase); again, as a reference point, the EP group increased 3 points.

Reading: How Much Did the Student Groups Gain? Gains in academic achievement before Proposition 203 were nearly identical to gains after Proposition 203 for all student groups. When comparing the FEP-3 student group before Proposition 203 to after, 25 points were gained before and 24 after. As a reference point to FEP-3, during the same years, the EP cohort gained 23 points before and 23 points after. The FEP-2 student group gained 11 points before and

Table 4.2. Mean reading and math scaled scores for all groups before and after Proposition 203.

	1997	1998	1999	2000	Total Gain
BEFORE PROPOSITION 203					
Reading					
EP	635	655	669	678	
FEP-3yr	628	649	665	674	25
FEP-2yr	616	639	655	666	11
Math					
EP	623	647	663	675	
FEP-3yr	618	644	660	673	29
FEP-2yr	608	635	652	664	12
	2001	2002	2003	2004	Total Gain
AFTER PROPOSITION 203					
Reading					
EP	639	658	672	681	
FEP-3yr	636	655	669	679	24
FEP-2yr	625	644	660	672	12
Math					
EP	634	655	671	682	
FEP-3yr	633	654	670	681	27
FEP-2yr	628	650	667	679	12

Notes: The shaded cells indicate the cohort was still classified as EL in those years. Only FEP scores are included in this analysis.

12 points after. And, as a reference point to FEP-2, during those same years, the EP student group gained 9 points before and 10 points after.

Mathematics: Where Did the Student Groups Start? The mathematics results parallel the reading results. The starting points for all student groups were higher after Proposition 203 (see Table 4.2). The mean math score for the FEP-3 group was 644 before and 654 after Proposition 203 (a 10-point difference); as a reference point, the EP group increased by 8 points during the same years. The FEP-2 group showed a larger increase, with 652 before and 667 after (a 15-point difference); the EP group increased by 8 points during the same years.

Mathematics: How Much Did the Student Groups Gain? Like reading, gains in academic achievement before Proposition 203 were nearly identical to gains after Proposition 203 for all student groups. When comparing the FEP-3 student group before Proposition 203 to after, 29 points were gained before and 27 points after. As a reference point to FEP-3 during the same years, the EP group gained 28 points before and 27 points after. The FEP-2 group gained 12 points before and 12 points after. And, as a reference point to FEP-2 during the same years, the EP group gained 12 points before and 11 points after.

RESEARCH QUESTION 2: ARE ARIZONA STUDENTS MEETING STANDARDS OF LEARNING AFTER PROPOSITION 203?

Method

The data for the analysis addressing the second research question come from a statewide, student-level database of student scores for Arizona's Instrument to Measure Standards (AIMS). The AIMS, designed to measure Arizona's content standards, is administered annually. Prior to 2005, grades 3, 5, 8, and 10 were tested in mathematics, reading, and writing; grades 4, 6, and 7 were included in the testing program beginning in 2005 to meet NCLB testing requirements. Because this analysis begins in 2002, when only grades 3, 5, and 8 were tested, and to maintain consistency across the 5-year period from 2002 to 2006 referenced earlier, only grades 3, 5, and 8 are included in this analysis. Proficiency levels on the AIMS (rendered as falls far below, approaches, meets, and exceeds the standard) were examined for FEPs each academic year from 2002 to 2006, all post–Proposition 203 years. This research design is cross-sectional; that is, a different group of students was evaluated each year. Because AIMS is Arizona's state standardized achievement measure and is designed to be aligned to the state's content standards, it seemed to be an appropriate measure of how well ELs perform in school with regard to the state's content standards.

Students coded as EL for all 4 years were excluded from the sample for three reasons. First, these students have varying levels of reading proficiency in English (Abedi & Lord, 2001). For example, if mathematics is being measured, reading proficiency affects students' performance (on word problems in particular) and distorts their true mathematics achievement. Second, the reliability of test scores is higher for students with higher levels of English proficiency than for students with lower levels of English proficiency since limited English proficiency is a source of error in an academic achievement test written in English (Thompson et al., 2002). Third, the *Flores* Consent Order requires that students be evaluated in each of the 2 years following their reclassification from an EL program. For the purpose of our analysis, the EP group—never classified as EL—serves as the comparison group.

Results: The Achievement of Fifth- and Eighth-Grade FEP Students Declines After Proposition 203

For the results of this research question, we focus on the percentage of students passing the AIMS test. The difference in the percentage of students passing AIMS between the student populations was statistically significant ($p < .0001$), in part because the sample sizes were extremely large and the smallest difference became significant. Therefore, we focus on effect size, defined here as the simple percentage-point difference for students passing the AIMS.

Reading. Table 4.3 shows the percentage of students passing the AIMS reading test for the two populations—EP and FEP—for grades 3, 5, and 8. The AIMS includes four performance levels, and "passing" the assessment is operationally defined as scoring at the highest two levels (meets or exceeds standards). As shown in Table 4.3, the difference between FEP and EP groups for students in grade 3 continues to narrow and reverses by 2006. However, the trends for grades 5 and 8 are very different. For fifth graders, the difference between EP and FEP students fluctuates with no discernible pattern or trend, ranging from a 4- to 10-percentage-point difference between the groups. For eighth graders, the percentages of students passing reading show very large differences across all years, with the difference between the percentage of EPs and FEPs who pass the AIMS growing over time.

Mathematics. Results for FEP and EP pass rates on the AIMS in mathematics follows the same pattern as reading. The difference in percentage passing for grade 3 EP and FEP students was 6% in 2002, then slowly diminished, and then became negative. In grade 5, the effects, or the difference between the percentage of EP and FEP students passing the AIMS, varied between 4 and 8 percentage-points, with EP students outperforming FEP students, although no difference was observed in 2006. In grade 8, effects were very large, with a large

Table 4.3. Percentage of EP and FEP students passing reading test on the AIMS.

	2002		*2003*		*2004*		*2005*		*2006*	
	%	N	%	N	%	N	%	N	%	N
Grade 3										
EP	75	52,645	74	53,295	70	55,235	71	61,436	73	61,974
FEP	69	3,718	72	5,279	70	4,542	75	3,340	74	5,023
Effect	6		2		0		−4		−1	
Grade 5										
EP	59	57,662	57	56,710	54	56,171	73	62,334	74	63,765
FEP	50	4,774	53	6,263	47	5,803	63	5,037	68	6,451
Effect	9		4		7		10		6	
Grade 8										
EP	54	57,487	53	56,908	51	58,788	68	65,441	68	66,122
FEP	40	3,716	44	6,443	39	5,957	54	3,972	53	5,166
Effect	14		9		12		14		15	

(13) percentage-point difference in 2005 and 2006, favoring English proficient (EP) students (see Table 4.4).

SUMMARY OF FINDINGS

The two research questions evaluate Proposition 203 in different ways. For research question 1, the analysis involved a well-known standardized achievement test based on national content standards. For research question 2, the analysis involved a test tied to Arizona's content standards and is therefore arguably a stronger indication of how students perform relative to Arizona-specific content standards. Furthermore, the design of question 1 was different from that of question 2. While question 1 followed two cohorts of students over years, question 2 used a cross-sectional approach of students with like backgrounds. Questions 1 and 2 involved different time periods—pre– and post–Proposition 203 in the case of research question 1 but only post–Proposition 203 in the case of question 2. In addition, data relevant to question 2 were disaggregated at the grade level, whereas data analyzed for question 1 were not. Question 1 was addressed by noting the academic gains of cohorts of FEP and EP students across years before and after Proposition 203 was passed, while question 2 was answered by noting differences in the percentage of students passing the mathematics and reading portions of the AIMS for a 4-year period following Proposition 203.

Table 4.4. Percentage of EP and FEP students passing mathematics test on the AIMS.

	2002		2003		2004		2005		2006	
	%	N	%	N	%	N	%	N	%	N
Grade 3										
EP	63	52,639	65	53,364	63	55,170	75	61,436	77	61,974
FEP	57	3,709	63	5,269	60	4,545	82	3,340	81	5,023
Effect	6		2		3		−7		−4	
Grade 5										
EP	46	57,114	49	56,151	49	56,097	72	62,334	73	63,765
FEP	38	4,733	45	6,225	41	5,800	68	5,037	73	6,451
Effect	8		4		8		4		0	
Grade 8										
EP	21	57,327	21	56,766	27	58,735	64	65,441	64	66,122
FEP	10	3,702	14	6,435	18	5,952	50	3,972	51	5,166
Effect	11		7		9		13		13	

The data for question 1 showed that all student groups—two FEP (reclassified ELs) groups and one EP (never classified as ELs) group—increased scores on the SAT-9 from before to after Proposition 203. A rise in test scores over time is to be expected. However, when specific gain was analyzed, the gain experienced before Proposition 203 was nearly identical to the gain after Proposition 203. The data presented for question 2, which pertain to the post–Proposition 203 policy context and could not be evaluated relative to the pre–Proposition 203 context, showed large gains for third graders but a dramatic deterioration in achievement for fifth and eighth graders.

DISCUSSION AND CONCLUSIONS

Recall that *Castañeda v. Pickard* (1981) established a three-part test for determining whether a school district had taken appropriate action to overcome language barriers confronting ELs. The focus of this study was the third prong—that, after a trial period, the success of the program implemented to help ELs overcome language barriers must be demonstrable.

As the enrollment in bilingual education programs decreased, we saw very little difference in the way FEPs performed before and after Proposition 203. Between 1997 and 2000, enrollment in bilingual education programs had already dropped from about 32% to about 20%, and it continued to taper off until it hit about 5% in 2004. An important limitation of our data is the lack of a reliable indicator of EL program membership for the reclassified students we tracked. We were not able to focus our analysis on students according to which program (English-only or bilingual, for instance) they had participated in; we only know that program participation shifted across the years from mostly English-only (about 68%) to almost entirely English-only (about 95%). Thus our data only permit us to examine student outcomes in these general policy contexts.

To situate our results in a broader research context, we note that many recent large-scale evaluations on the relative effectiveness of programs for ELs show that children in bilingual education programs do better on standardized achievement tests, in English, than do children educated through English-only programs (Francis, Lesaux, & August, 2006; Genesse, Lindholm-Leary, Saunders, & Christian, 2005; Rolstad, Mahoney, & Glass, 2005a, 2008; Slavin & Cheung, 2005). Indeed, Rolstad, Mahoney, and Glass (2005b) conducted an analysis of program effectiveness studies in Arizona and found that in a meta-analysis of more controlled studies, bilingual programs dramatically outperformed English-only approaches. These facts lead us to believe that the advantage children had in bilingual programs is suppressed in our analysis for question 1 in part by the diversity of the cohort in terms of program treatment—only a small minority, 32%, ever participated in bilingual programs—and that the potential positive effects of such programs appear to have tapered off as the state enacted restrictive policies affecting ELs. These policies became progressively more and more restrictive regarding the use of children's native language in schools during the Horne (as in *Horne v. Flores*) administration, as discussed earlier in this chapter.

A very interesting pattern is observed regarding data analyzed for question 2 as well. Recall that question 2 is addressed with cross-sectional data and does not therefore represent growth over time for the same cohort of students. These data give us a sense of how well students performed after reclassification to fluent English status for the years 2002 through 2006 in grades 3, 5, and 8. Note that by 2002, nearly 90% of all ELs were reported to be in English-only programs, with an increase to nearly 95% by 2004 (see Table 4.1). Thus these data represent a climate in which the use of children's native language for instructional purposes was severely restricted in the state.

Results show that reclassified children in grade 3 moved from a 6-percentage-point gap with English proficient students in 2002 to essential parity by 2006 in both reading (where they were 1 percentage point ahead) and mathematics (4 percentage points ahead). The slope is consistently downward for reading, with some variability for mathematics. However, for children in grades 5 and 8, the results are strikingly different. In grade 5, the gap between the EP and FEP students varies from 4 to 10 percentage points, with no discernible direction. The gap is appreciably higher in grade 8, where it ranges from 9 to 15 percentage points.

The observed effect may increase as the grades advance for a variety of reasons. First, there are important aspects of reading and mathematics in the third-grade curriculum that may be much more easily taught to EL students as they are learning English in years prior to reclassification, such as basic decoding and computing skills. The frequently noted "fourth-grade slump" is argued to follow from a transition from "learning to read" in grades K through 3, where there is a focus on decoding skills, to "reading to learn" in grades 4 through 12, where reading comprehension plays an increasingly significant role (Chall, Jacobs, & Baldwin, 1990). Furthermore, it has been found that EL children enrolled in English-only programs often do well initially, with performance tapering off in subsequent years (Ramirez, Yuen, Ramey, & Pasta, 1991); this observation is consistent with the theory that responding to the demands of the regular school curriculum becomes increasingly difficult as children advance through the grades, as early deficits resulting from incomprehensible instruction make it more and more difficult to keep up (Krashen, 1996).

However, the question at hand is this: Has Arizona enacted policies for educating ELs that allow them to overcome language barriers? Reclassification of ELs to fluent-English status is an indication that they are believed to be ready to participate in the regular school curriculum. In our study of reclassified ELs, we cannot address whether ELs did better before or after the passage of Proposition 203; however, with regard to the post–Proposition 203 context, we found that ELs suffer a persistent and dramatic achievement gap. Since the AIMS test is aligned with the state standards, which define the state's curriculum, we conclude that language barriers facing English learners in the state have not been removed. In our view, therefore, the state has failed to meet the *Castañeda* standard.

REFERENCES

Abedi, J., & Lord, C. (2001). The language factor in mathematics test. *Applied Measurement in Education, 14*(3), 219–234.

Chall, J. S., Jacobs, V. A., & Baldwin, L. (1990). *The reading crisis: Why poor children fall behind.* Cambridge, MA: Harvard University Press.

Crawford, J. (2004). *Educating English learners: Language diversity in the classroom* (5th ed.). Los Angeles: Bilingual Educational Services.

Flores v. Arizona, 48 F. Supp. 2d 937 (D. Ariz. 1999).

Francis, D., Lesaux, N., & August, D. (2006). Language of instruction. In D. August & T. Shanahan (Eds.), *Developing literacy in second language learners* (pp. 365–413). Mahwah, NJ: Erlbaum.

Genesse, F., Lindholm-Leary, K., Saunders, W., & Christian, D. (2005). English language learners in U.S. schools: An overview of research findings. *Journal of Education for Students Placed at Risk, 10*(4), 363–385.

Krashen, S. (1996). *Under attack: The case against bilingual education.* Culver City, CA: Language Education Associates.

Krashen, S., Rolstad, K., & MacSwan, J. (2007). Review of "Research summary and bibliography for Structured English Immersion programs" of the Arizona English Language Learners Task Force. Takoma Park, MD: Institute for Language Education and Policy. Retrieved September 6, 2008, from http://www.elladvocates.org/documents/AZ/Krashen_Rolstad_MacSwan_review.pdf

Mahoney, K., Haladyna, T., & MacSwan, J. (in press). The need for multiple measures in reclassification decisions: A validity study of the Stanford English Language Proficiency Test (SELP). In J. S. Lee, T. G. Wiley, & R. Rumberger (Eds.), *The education of language minority immigrants in the USA*. Bristol, UK: Multilingual Matters.

Mahoney, K., Thompson, M., & MacSwan, J. (2004). The condition of English language learners in Arizona, 2004. In A. Molnar (Ed.), *The condition of preK–12 education in Arizona, 2004* (pp. 1–27). Tempe, AZ: Education Policy Research Laboratory, Arizona State University. Retrieved September 17, 2008, from http://epsl.asu.edu/aepi/EPSL-0405-106-AEPI.pdf

Ramirez, J. D., Yuen, S., Ramey, D., & Pasta, D. (1991). *Longitudinal study of structured English immersion strategy, early-exit and late-exit bilingual education programs for language minority children* (Final Report Vols. 1 & 2). San Mateo, CA: Aguirre International. (ERIC Document Reproduction Service No. ED 330216).

Rolstad, K., Mahoney, K., & Glass, G. V. (2005a). The big picture: A meta-analysis of program effectiveness research on English language learners. *Educational Policy, 19*(4), 572–594.

Rolstad, K., Mahoney, K., & Glass, G. V. (2005b). Weighing the evidence: A meta-analysis of bilingual education in Arizona. *Bilingual Research Journal, 29*(1), 43–67.

Rolstad, K., Mahoney, K., & Glass, G. V. (2008). The big picture in bilingual education: A meta-analysis corrected for Gersten's coding error. *Journal of Educational Research & Policy Studies, 8*(2), 1–15.

Seltzer, M. H., Frank, K. A., & Bryk, A. S. (1994). The metric matters: The sensitivity of conclusions about growth in student achievement to choice of metric. *Educational Evaluation and Policy Analysis, 16*(1), 41–49.

Slavin, R., & Cheung, A. (2005). A synthesis of research of reading instruction for English language learners. *Review of Educational Research, 75*(2), 247–284.

Thompson, M. S., DiCerbo, K., Mahoney, K. S., & MacSwan, J. (2002). ¿Éxito en California? A validity critique of language program evaluations and analysis of English learner test scores. *Education Policy Analysis Archives, 10*(7), entire issue. Retrieved October 12, 2008, from http://epaa.asu.edu/epaa/v10n7/

CHAPTER 5

Impact of Restrictive Language Policies on Engagement and Academic Achievement of English Learners in Boston Public Schools

Miren Uriarte, Rosann Tung, Nicole Lavan, and Virginia Diez

IN NOVEMBER 2002, the voters of Massachusetts overwhelmingly approved Referendum Question 2. It became law as Chapter 386 of the Acts of 2002 in December and was implemented across the state in the fall of 2003. Chapter 386 stipulates Sheltered English Immersion as the method of English language acquisition, in which most classroom instruction is in English but with a curriculum and a presentation appropriate for English learners (ELs) (Commonwealth of Massachusetts, 2002). Under the slogan "English for the Children," the referendum ended transitional bilingual education (TBE) as the primary program available throughout the state for children requiring language support. Three decades earlier, the Massachusetts state legislature, recognizing the needs of the growing immigrant child population, had approved the first state-mandated transitional bilingual education program in the United States (Commonwealth of Massachusetts, 1971). In approving the referendum, Massachusetts followed California and Arizona in replacing a wide-ranging set of bilingual programs with Structured English Immersion (SEI), an instructional model that has as its main purpose the expedited learning of English.

In the 2002–2003 academic year, the year Question 2 was approved by Massachusetts voters, 141,408 Massachusetts public school students were designated NSOLs, or Native Speakers of a Language Other than English. These students represented 14.4% of all Massachusetts public school students (Massachusetts Department of Education [MDE], 2003c). Of these, 51,622 students, or 5.2% of all students, were designated of Limited English Proficiency (LEP). (The Massachusetts Department of Education uses the term Limited English Proficient [LEP] to define a child whose native language is not English and who is not currently able to perform ordinary class work in English [MDE, 2004]. LEPs are also referred to as English language learners or English learners. Here, we use the Department of Education's definition of LEPs and use English learners [ELs] to refer to students enrolled in programs for English learners.) In the Boston Public Schools, a system with an enrollment of close to 63,777 in 2003, nearly one-fourth (23.1%) were children of Limited English Proficiency, representing 47 different countries. The largest language groups among these children were those who spoke Spanish (56.7%), Haitian Creole (10.6%), Chinese dialects (8.3%), Cape Verdean Creole (7.1%), and Vietnamese (6.9%).

There is some evidence that implementation of the referendum has varied substantially across the state (DeJong, Gort, & Cobb, 2005; Rennie Center for Education Research & Policy, 2007); however, despite the scope of the policy change and the number of children affected, 5 years after the implementation of the Structured English Immersion instructional model began in Massachusetts, there is scant information about its impact on ELs. The same is true for Boston, the district with the largest share (29%) of Massachusetts public school children requiring English language support in their schooling. The experience and outcomes of ELs in Boston following the implementation of the policies mandated by Question 2 are yet to be understood.

This chapter thus focuses on the implementation of Question 2 and its effects on the academic outcomes and educational engagement of English learners in Boston. We compare the results from the EL student population along key indicators with all students in general education and with Native Speakers of a Language Other than English (NSOLs) in general education. We present data across 4 years: academic year 2003, the year Question 2 was passed, and the 3 years following (2004–2007), when the referendum was first implemented in Boston. We show that in this time period, the number of students identified as Limited English Proficient declined and that LEP enrollments in English learner programs declined while enrollments of ELs in special education increased. We show also that dropout rates increased and that, while there was some improvement in the standardized test scores for ELs, gaps between ELs and other subpopulations increased.

POLICY CONTEXT AND BACKGROUND

Question 2 entailed major changes in both perspective and practice. The prioritization of immersion programs that rely on the rapid acquisition of English without native language development and support ran counter to more than 30 years of experience in the Boston school district. It also favored one side of what is a heated debate on the value of Structured English Immersion versus other approaches for the education of ELs.

August, Goldenberg, and Rueda (Chapter 9, this volume) show that these new policies run counter to recent research on the education of immigrant children. While affirming the importance of English language acquisition, most recent research on positive models of immigrant adaptation points to the importance of children retaining the ability to function in their original culture even as they adapt to a new one (Portes & Rumbaut, 2001). Similarly, longitudinal studies of immigrant children show that language learning entails a complex combination of contextual and individual factors. English language proficiency, according to the work of Suárez-Orozco, Suárez-Orozco, and Todorova (2008), relies on the overall quality of the programs for language learners and their integration into a healthy school environment, as well as the resources children bring in terms of prior schooling and parental language proficiency. Allowing enough time for a second language to develop before forcing arbitrary performance standards is a critical factor in the success of children (Suárez-Orozco & Suárez-Orozco, 2001; Suárez-Orozco et al., 2008).

Aside from the conceptual changes, restrictive language policies also represent a shift in the practices of districts and schools. Below, we briefly review the implementation of restrictive language policies, as they provide an appropriate framework for the analysis of the experience of Boston.

THE IMPLEMENTATION OF RESTRICTIVE LANGUAGE POLICIES IN CALIFORNIA AND ARIZONA

Issues related to the implementation of English-only policies in California and Arizona are addressed in Chapters 3, 4, 8, and 11 of this volume; we describe here those issues that are pertinent to the understanding of the experience of Massachusetts.

Approach to Policy Implementation as a Factor in Outcomes

The policy changes in California and Arizona are marked by a lack of specificity about what the law allows and by a lack of clear operational definitions of instructional approaches. Districts and schools have been left to interpret the law and develop practice essentially on their own and thus differ widely in their implementation and in the types of programs offered to ELs. Gándara and colleagues (2000) found that how districts addressed parental waiver provisions of the law in California, which are the rights provided by law for parents to waive participation in Structured English Immersion (SEI) programs, was a critical factor in programs available for ELs at the district level. Districts that had strong bilingual education programs and, after Proposition 227's passage, actively supported parents' right to request waivers were, in most cases, able to substantially retain their native-language programs. However, those districts with a lukewarm or negative attitude toward bilingual education tended to be much less committed to enforcing parental waiver rights. In these districts, language programs declined and SEI programs proliferated.

Wright and Pu (2005) argue that outcomes for children were also affected by attitudes toward implementation. In the case of Arizona's Proposition 203, during the first 2 years of implementation parents were allowed to waive participation in SEI, resulting in the availability of a wide variety of offerings for children. In 2003, a stricter enforcement of the waiver provisions began, narrowing the school districts' options. Wright and Pu argue that improvement in test scores between 2002 and 2003 was due to greater flexibility for schools in offering English as a Second Language (ESL) and bilingual education, while the decline of scores in 2004 corresponded to a period of forced closure for most bilingual programs and mandates for English-only instruction for ELs.

Professional Capacity of Teachers

Research points to the need for specific training and ongoing support for teachers implementing SEI (Gándara, Maxwell-Jolly, & Driscoll, 2005; Parrish et al., 2006; Wright & Choi, 2006). Yet both California and Arizona evaluations of SEI implementation have found inadequate professional development to support SEI instruction. In California, for example, Gándara and colleagues (2005) found that English learners "are more likely than any other children to be taught by teachers with an emergency credential" (p. 3) and that schools with higher concentrations of ELs also have higher concentrations of teachers who are not fully credentialed (Gándara et al., 2005; Parrish et al., 2006).

Outcomes of the Policy Change

The student outcomes in both states have remained unchanged from before the restrictive language initiatives (see Chapters 3 and 4, this volume), and there is no evidence that the speed of English acquisition has accelerated with SEI instruction (Parrish et al., 2006; Wright & Pu, 2005). The change in policy in California and Arizona has not had a substantial impact on academic outcomes; perhaps more importantly, the outcomes of ELs in these states remain exceptionally low (Crawford, 2004).

THE MASSACHUSETTS STUDY

This study is based on the analysis of student-level administrative database provided by the Boston Public Schools (BPS), which includes demographic data, enrollment in formation, and testing outcomes on the Massachusetts Comprehensive Assessment System (MCAS) for each BPS student enrolled in academic years 2003 through 2006. As can be seen in the tables throughout this chapter, we compare the outcomes for students in EL programs with those of all students in general education programs and with those of NSOL students in general education programs. This latter comparison between similar students offers a way to assess the impact of the EL programs.

We examine the differences between these groups along dimensions of enrollment, engagement, and academic outcome variables, including attendance rate, out-of-school suspension rate, grade-level retention rate, annual dropout rate, and MCAS English language arts (ELA) and math pass rates. In addition to the quantitative data, researchers collected and analyzed documentary data pertinent to the implementation of Question 2 and interviewed personnel from the Massachusetts Department of Elementary and Secondary Education (one staff person) and the Boston Public Schools (nine staff persons) to understand the context of the implementation. The BPS staff members, who were promised anonymity, came from district leadership, management positions, and the staff in the former Bilingual Education Office. Interviews were conducted during the summer and fall of 2008; they focused on the identification and assessment of LEP students; the enrollment in programs for ELs; teacher training; and the guidance received by the state, district, and schools regarding the implementation of SEI.

THE IMPLEMENTATION OF QUESTION 2 IN MASSACHUSETTS

The Massachusetts English-only law, Chapter 386 of the Acts of 2002 (commonly referred to as Question 2), requires that all books and instructional materials be written in English and that subject matter be taught in that language, although teachers may use a minimal amount of the child's native language when necessary. In order to minimize the use of native languages, the law encourages schools to place children of different languages but of similar English fluency together. As in California and Arizona, the law restricted the time that children could stay in the program to 1 year, after which children would cease to be "English learners" and would be placed into general education classrooms.

Accountability

Chapter 386 mandates that districts identify students who are of limited English proficiency every year and that students in grades 2 through 12 be tested yearly to assess their English proficiency and progress in academic areas. Massachusetts meets national requirements for testing English proficiency with its Massachusetts English Proficiency Assessment (MEPA). One part of the test assesses proficiency in reading and writing at grade spans 3–4, 5–6, 7–8, and 9–12, while another part assesses EL students' proficiency in listening and speaking in grades K–12 (MDE, 2008b). The requirements for subject-matter testing are met through the Massachusetts Comprehensive Assessment System, which was established as part of the Massachusetts Educational Reform Act of 1993. At the time of the observations for this study, MCAS tested English learners in reading (grade 3), English language arts (grades 4, 7, and 10), math (grades 4, 8, and 10), and science (grades 5 and 8) (MDE, 2008a). English learners who have been in U.S. schools for less than 1 year are exempt from the ELA test, and Spanish-speaking ELs who have been in U.S. schools for less than 3 years may take a math test in Spanish in grade 10 (MDE, 2003–2006). Students must pass grade 10 math and ELA exams in order to graduate from high school; the high-stakes requirement began with the tenth-grade testing in 2001 and became a graduation requirement for the class of 2003, the year before the implementation of Question 2 began.

Waivers

As is true in both California and Arizona, Massachusetts allows parents or guardians to request a waiver of enrollment in an SEI program. If the waiver is granted, the child can attend a bilingual education program (which must be offered when more than 20 children who speak the same native language at the same grade level in a school receive a waiver) (Commonwealth of Massachusetts, 2002). Similar to the waiver policy in the other states, parents in Massachusetts can request a waiver if the student already knows English or is at least 10 years old and the school principal and teachers believe it is in his or her best interest, or if the student has special physical or psychological needs. The law requires that the parent request the waiver in person and be provided information about all the programmatic options available. A parent must request a waiver annually. Waiver requests for children over 10 years of age can be approved by the principal, but for children under 10, the requirements are stricter: The student must be in an SEI program for 30 days, the teacher and the principal must make a case for why the child should be placed in a different type of program, and the waiver must be approved by the superintendent of the district.

Assessments of the Implementation of Chapter 386

Massachusetts has not yet fielded a comprehensive evaluation of Chapter 386 and its impact on English learners. Initial research shows that models of implementation have varied substantially across districts and that those districts approaching the process with the most flexibility and with the strongest commitment to teacher development appear to exhibit the most substantial achievement gains (de Jong et al., 2005; Rennie Center for Education Research & Policy, 2007). As was the case in California, some districts have developed a wide array of programs in response to Question 2. Some have continued to cluster their students by language group, while others mix students of different language groups. Some districts have interpreted the law's requirements flexibly and creatively and have thereby developed an array of programs for their students.

A district's approach to the waiver provisions is an indicator of its ability to retain programmatic flexibility. Some Massachusetts districts encourage parental waivers, but others do not. Districts that have encouraged parental waivers have been able to retain their bilingual education programs while offering SEI as an alternative. By using the waiver provisions, districts currently implement two-way bilingual programs, English as a Second Language, transitional bilingual education, world language, and general and modified bilingual education programs in addition to Structured English Immersion (for descriptions of some of these programs, see Morales & Aldana, Chapter 10, this volume). Other districts have not facilitated the waiver process or made it difficult for parents to obtain waivers by not informing parents of their rights or by creating alternative procedures for bypassing enrollment in programs for English learners. In these districts, nearly all the students requiring support in language acquisition are enrolled in SEI programs. Boston is one such district, for reasons that will be shown in a later section of this chapter.

Professional Development for Teachers

The training of teachers in Structured English Immersion practices has also varied among Massachusetts districts. At first, the state was focused on the qualifications of existing transitional bilingual education teachers, particularly their command of English (MDE, 2003a, 2003b). In June 2004, after a year of implementation had passed, the Department of Education provided guidance as to the types of skills necessary for SEI instruction and began to develop training for teachers. The training involved both the teaching of English and sheltered academic content instruction. Teachers of English required licensing at the appropriate grade level. The skill areas for teachers in sheltered content instruction included the following: Category 1: Second Language Learning and Teaching; Category 2: Sheltering Content Instruction; Category 3: Assessing Speaking; and Category 4: Listening, Reading and Writing in the Sheltered Content Classroom (Rennie Center for Education Research & Policy, 2007). Districts were instructed to develop 75 hours of professional development covering the four categories. In 2007, the Rennie Center for Education Policy & Research (2007) reported that only 35% of the estimated number of teachers requiring content training had received it and that 64.2% of the state's EL training needs had been met.

Student Outcomes

So far, there have been no analyses of the outcomes of students under SEI across Massachusetts or in individual districts. The only report of outcomes of English language acquisition (Rennie Center for Education Research & Policy, 2007) found that, after 1 year in Massachusetts schools, only in grades 3 and 4 did the proportion of ELs transitioning out of the program by becoming English proficient rise above 22 percent.

IMPLEMENTING QUESTION 2 IN THE BOSTON PUBLIC SCHOOLS

Boston, the site of the struggle that led to the first state-mandated transitional bilingual education (TBE) in the nation in 1971, voted overwhelmingly against Question 2. Its citizens had reason to be concerned about the change in perspective and in practice, not only for historical reasons, but also because the district enrolled the largest number of EL students in the state. When Question 2 passed, BPS was a typical urban district, with 75% of its students poor and of color; within these groups existed great racial/ethnic diversity and a growing complement of immigrant students (see Table 5.1). In Boston, 42.6% of enrollment consisted of children whose first language was not English.

The implementation of TBE in Boston had a checkered history marked by official inattention and a struggle for accountability waged primarily by parents. It was a process marked by great successes, such as the deployment of TBE in more than nine languages, the involvement of 80 schools in the program, the development of excellent two-way bilingual programs, and the implementation of literacy programs for students who come to the district with little or no schooling in their home country. The district offered four models of bilingual instruction:

Table 5.1. Demographics, Boston Public Schools, 2003.

Characteristic	Percent
Gender (male)	51.4
Poverty (free or reduced-price lunch)	74.9
Race/ethnicity	
Asian/Pacific Islander	8.7
Black	47.1
Latino	29.6
White	14.2
Native language not English	42.6
Limited English Proficiency	23.1

Note: Total enrollment = 63,777 students.

(1) transitional bilingual education (at all levels and in nine languages); (2) two-way bilingual programs in Spanish/English; (3) multilingual education at each grade level, where ELs from different language backgrounds are grouped together and receive content-based instruction from a trained ESL or bilingual education teacher; and (4) native-language literacy programs, which are 2-year intensive literacy programs designed for students 9–21 years of age who come to the United States with limited or no schooling.

However, there were also concerns about TBE in Boston, focusing especially on the number of years some students remained in the program, which in some cases reached 6 years, according to the 1999 report by the Bilingual Education Task Force (Boston Public Schools [BPS], 1999). Contributing factors included barriers such as the lack of available space in general education classrooms once students were ready to transition, the timeliness of language proficiency evaluations, and parental resistance to the transition. There were also concerns about the professional qualifications of bilingual education teachers, particularly their command of English; the lack of a uniform curriculum; the lightness of the monitoring, support, and supervision of the programs; and the isolation of bilingual students from others. A lack of understanding of the needs of children learning a new language pervaded the district, resulting in a resistance to the requirements of educating English learners and a resentment of what was seen as "favoring" ELs over other students in BPS. Without appropriate funding, knowledge, and leadership, these concerns and conflicts went unresolved in the politicized and racialized environment of the Boston Public Schools.

Boston thus began the implementation of Structured English Immersion with limited state guidance and support, with contested perspectives on the existing TBE program, with a recently dismantled parental participation structure, and with a teaching corps largely unfamiliar with bilingual education and the instructional requirements of SEI. Many issues marked the implementation of Question 2 in Boston; here we focus on those that shed light on the academic outcomes observed over a 4-year period. These issues include the planning for the implementation of Question 2, the identification and assessment of students, and the changes in programs for ELs after Question 2.

Planning the Change

The Office of Language Learning and Support Services (OLLSS) stood at the center of the planning and implementation of Question 2 in Boston's schools. When Question 2 passed, OLLSS moved forward on the planning under the principle that the transition would be "orderly and disciplined" (BPS, n.d.). BPS tested all students in the spring of 2003 and defined the programs it would support under the new law (multilingual ESL, two-way dual language, SEI, and native-language literacy). Planning also called for students in TBE to be assigned to SEI and general education according to the level they had attained in TBE; most stage 3 and all stage 4 and 5 students (4,366) exited to general education, and all stage 1 and 2 students (5,442) were assigned to SEI programs (BPS, 2006). The planning also stipulated that transitional bilingual education teachers and the students still in EL programs would remain in the existing language-specific TBE sites to ensure a smoother transition for students, and teaching resources would be in place for schools' implementation of SEI instruction and communication with students' families.

For the district staff, there was much confusion about the changes Question 2 entailed. For some, Question 2 meant that bilingual programs would be disbanded and that special instruction for ELs would disappear. But even for more informed staff, there was little clarity about what SEI was and what it meant for both TBE and general education teachers, about the difference between language and content instruction, and about the role of native language in instruction. Interviews reflect that the district, aside from providing a broad framework, did not provide strong leadership in the transition process.

Identification and Assessment of Students

One of the most salient findings of this study of English learners in Boston is a sharp change in the pattern of identification of students as Limited English Proficient and in their enrollment in programs for ELs. Table 5.2 presents these figures for each of the years of observation. First, we note the steady decline in enrollments in BPS, amounting to a 7.2% drop over the 4-year period. However, there was a much steeper decline (from 23.1% of student enrollment to 16.9%) in the proportion of students designated as LEP.

Interviews suggest that underidentification of English learners took place both because of misassessment of students at the Family Resource Centers (FRCs) and because parents withheld information on language use. The FRCs assumed responsibility for the assessment for all incoming EL students when the Multilingual Communication and Placement Center was discontinued in 2001. Education advocates have consistently raised questions about the training of the assessors in the FRCs (Citizens' Commission on Academic Success for Boston's Children, 2006). Interviews for this study suggest that often FRCs' assessments of English proficiency were based on listening and speaking tests, not the complete battery of testing, which includes reading and writing assessments. This emphasis would tend to underidentify students not capable of classroom work in English. Parents were also a source of misidentification. Because of the confusion during the initial deployment of the programs, parents overreported the use of English in the home in order to avoid having their children designated as LEPs and placed in SEI programs.

Table 5.2. Identification of LEP students and enrollment in selected programs as share of total enrollment, Boston Public Schools, 2003–2006.

Student Group	2003 (%)	2004 (%)	2005 (%)	2006 (%)
Identification as LEP	23.1	16.3	14.2	16.9
Enrolled in EL program	15.5	9.8	9.3	14.9
Transitional bilingual education	93			
English as a Second Language	4.6			
Structured English Immersion		86.8	92.5	95.4
Two-way bilingual	2.4	4.6	4.3	3.2
Other bilingual		8.6	3.1	1.4
Total enrollment	$(N = 63,777)$	$(N = 61,652)$	$(N = 59,608)$	$(N = 59,211)$

Note: Enrollment numbers do not match official figures because of exclusions.

Changes in Enrollment in Programs for English Learners

As the implementation of Question 2 progressed, two trends were revealed: (1) a decline in the enrollments in programs for ELs and (2) an increased concentration of enrollments in the district's "default" program for ELs, that is, Structured English Immersion. Enrollments in programs for ELs declined in the 2 years following the implementation of Question 2 and recovered in the last year (see Table 5.2). The initial decline is explained by the placement into general education of 4,366 students who were formerly in transitional bilingual education (BPS, 2006). The next year, 2005, would see further declines. By 2006, the continued influx of EL students into BPS and the streamlining of the assessment process had increased the enrollments in programs for ELs, but they had not yet reached the enrollments pre–Question 2. By 2006, enrollments in programs for ELs lagged 10.7% behind those in 2003.

The transition between transitional bilingual education and Structured English Immersion has also meant redefinition of programs, as shown in Table 5.2. In 2003, students were distributed among TBE, ESL and two-way bilingual programs; TBE, the "default" program, contained 93.4% of students identified as LEP in programs for ELs. In addition, language support services (such as small-group instruction, mentoring, or counseling) were provided to transitioning students in general education (about 2,500 students). Between 2003 and 2006, TBE programs were replaced by SEI programs as the "default" program for ELs. Over time, SEI displaced both two-way immersion programs and other bilingual programs, representing 95.4% of the enrollments in programs for ELs.

The narrowing of programmatic options for EL students in Boston arises from the district's reluctance to encourage parental waivers of Structured English Immersion. Although waiver provisions were part of the district's orientation to the new law, and policies for waivers for children under 10 were put in place in the first year, Family Resource Centers and schools were not effective in providing parents with information about their right to request waivers or about the procedure for pursuing them (Citizens' Commission on Academic Success for Boston's Children, 2006).

Boston's "opting-out" process was often confused with the waivers permitted under Question 2. Parental opting out was permitted in Boston under the 1971 Chapter 71A Bilingual Education Law and required only the parent's signature on a form opting out of all language services for his or her child and absolving BPS of any responsibility to provide them. Unlike the waiver process, which only "waives" students from SEI and does not disqualify them for services or exempt them from testing or monitoring, opting out meant that students would not receive any language services. Boston has retained the practice of opting out and does not provide services to these students (Massachusetts Department of Elementary and Secondary Education, 2008; Tregar, 2008), although by both federal and state law, their rights to these services continue whether they are enrolled in EL programs or in programs in general education.

Professional Development for Teachers

Those charged with the implementation of Question 2 in Boston were keenly aware that the successful transition from transitional bilingual education to Structured English Immersion depended largely on the capacity of all teachers to adapt their instruction to the new demands of having ELs in their classrooms. A significant amount of the district's—and OLLSS's—energy went to the training of teachers, but educators were faced with institutional barriers that prevented the development of quality instruction to ELs. The contract with the Boston Teachers Union gives the district 20 hours for training, with the content negotiated as part of the contract. Neither the district nor the union ever placed SEI training for general education teachers on the agenda for negotiation. Because of the magnitude of the expenditure, the leadership of BPS has also not been willing to pay for teacher training independent of the contract. Some principals have paid to have their teachers trained, and some have trained all their teachers. BPS provided training for individual teachers who completed it on their own time.

In 2006, in a presentation to the Boston City Council, the deputy superintendent for teaching and learning and the director of OLLSS reported that only about 20% of Boston teachers had received the training hours that, according to the Department of Education and the district, made them qualified to teach English learners (BPS, 2006; MDE, 2003a).

THE IMPACT OF THE IMPLEMENTATION OF QUESTION 2
ON STUDENT ENGAGEMENT AND ACADEMIC ACHIEVEMENT

In assessing the effect of the implementation of Question 2 on student engagement and academic achievement, we compared the outcomes of students in programs for English learners with the outcomes of: (1) students in general education programs and (2) Native Speakers of a Language Other than English (NSOLs) in general education. The first was a comparison with students who were able to function in an English-only classroom, 71.5% of whom were native English speakers. The second comparison involved NSOLs, who were in general education English-only classrooms. These included former students of programs for ELs, students who had opted out of EL programs, and native speakers of other languages who came to BPS already proficient in English. This group was more similar to ELs than the overall population of students in general education because most shared an experience as first- or second-generation immigrants who started their life immersed in a language other than English. They differed from English learners in that, at the time of the comparison, one group was able to function in an English-only classroom while the other required an EL program.

Impact on Student Engagement

Table 5.3 presents the rates for attendance, out-of-school suspensions, and grade-level retentions for the overall BPS population and subgroups. Median attendance rates were relatively stable for all groups, although there was some fluctuation among ELs and among NSOLs. In these two groups, attendance declined slightly in this period. Overall, students in programs for ELs had the highest attendance rates of all groups. Out-of-school suspension rates were relatively steady among all groups during this period, declining slightly in all cases except NSOLs in general education. Students in programs for ELs had lower rates of out-of-school suspensions than both students in general education programs and NSOLs. The rates of suspension among students in general education were more than double those of students in programs for English learners. The grade-level retention rate is the proportion of students in a given schoolyear who were not promoted to the next grade at the end of the year. In this period, grade-level retention rates were stable for all groups except for students in programs for ELs, among whom this rate increased from 8.6% to 13.1%. Students in programs for ELs had the highest grade-level retention rates of all groups.

During this period, the annual dropout rate for students in Boston Public Schools both increased and reached into the lower grades. Table 5.4 presents the middle school and high school dropout rates for the overall BPS population and the subgroups being compared. Focusing first on the middle school dropout rate, we observe a pattern of higher rates in 2005 and a partial recovery in 2006. The magnitude

Table 5.3. Attendance, out-of-school suspensions, and retention, Boston Public Schools, 2003–2006.

Student Group	2003 (%)	2004(%)	2005(%)	2006(%)
Attendance				
All BPS	95.0	95.0	95.0	95.0
All general education programs	95.0	95.0	95.0	94.4
NSOL in general education	96.0	96.0	96.1	95.3
Programs for ELs	96.2	96.1	95.8	95.6
Out-of-school suspensions				
All BPS	7.6	7.1	6.7	6.6
All general education programs	8.3	7.6	7.0	7.2
NSOL in general education	5.0	5.5	5.4	5.9
Programs for ELs	3.7	3.5	3.4	3.4
Grade-level retention				
All BPS	—	8.4	8.6	8.8
All general education programs	—	8.1	8.4	8.3
NSOL in general education	—	7.1	7.8	7.4
Programs for ELs	—	8.6	10.2	13.1

of the increase is similar across all groups. Although the magnitude is slightly higher among students in programs for ELs, the difference is small, suggesting that factors other than those affecting English learners most directly may be salient.

With respect to the high school dropout rate, the pattern for all groups is one of a slight decline in 2004 followed by two years of increasing rates. The increase between 2004 and 2006 was largest among students in programs for ELs. Rates for English learners were lower than those of both comparison groups in the year prior to Question 2; however, in the 3 years after Question 2, ELs had the highest annual high school dropout rates. The differences across the 4 years between ELs and both comparison groups are statistically significant.

Further analysis of the grade at dropout (see Table 5.5) reveals a divergent pattern for students in EL programs compared with students in general education programs after the implementation of Question 2: Students in EL programs dropped out later than students in general education programs. The students in EL programs were more likely to drop out in late high school (grade 10 or 11) and less likely to drop out in middle school than their counterparts in regular education programs. Moreover, the percentage of EL program students to drop out in late high school was sizable and was higher than the percentage of EL program students who dropped out in early high school (grade 9 or 10) in two of the study

Table 5.4. Annual Dropout Rates, Boston Public Schools, 2003–2006.

Student Group	2003 (%)	2004 (%)	2005 (%)	2006 (%)
Middle School				
All BPS	1.1	0.4	4.0	2.6
All general education programs	1.1	0.4	4.0[a]	2.6
NSOL in general education	0.8	0.5	3.7	2.5
Programs for ELs	0.8	0.3	2.7	2.6
High School				
All BPS	7.7	5.3	8.2	10.9
All general education programs	8.4[b]	5.2	8.1	10.7
NSOL in general education	7.4	4.2[c]	6.8[c]	8.9[c]
Programs for ELs	6.3	6.1	9.1	12.0

Note: For this analysis enrolled students who did not attend any days were not excluded.

[a] The difference in the dropout rates of EL and general education students whose native language is other than English was found to be statistically significant (*t*-test; $p = .046$).

[b] The difference in the dropout rates of EL students and students in general education was found to be statistically significant (*t*-test; $p = .000$).

[c] The differences in the dropout rates of ELs and NSOLs in general education were found to be statistically significant (*t*-test; $p = .0001$ in 2004 and 2005 and $p = .000$ in 2006).

years; this pattern is atypical, as most dropping out occurs in early high school (Stearns & Glennie, 2006).

Although the initial implementation of the high-stakes component of MCAS preceded the changes of Question 2, the first class affected by high-stakes testing graduated the summer before the transition between transitional bilingual education and Structured English Immersion in Boston. According to interviews, the envi-

Table 5.5. Grade at dropout, Boston Public Schools, 2003–2006.

Student Group	2003 (%)	2004 (%)	2005 (%)	2006 (%)
Students in general education				
Dropout in middle school	10.3	5.9	26.7	14.1
Dropout in early high school	54.1	51.8	42.5	45.6
Dropout in late high school	35.6	42.3	30.8	40.2
Students in EL programs				
Dropout in middle school	7.9	3.0	12.5	9.4
Dropout in early high school	57.1	26.9	45.6	44.1
Dropout in late high school	35.0	70.1	41.9	46.4

ronment of high-pressure accountability affected the choice of high schools to house SEI programs (and, in some cases, the treatment of ELs) because of concerns about how large concentrations of English learners would affect the academic outcomes for the school. Another explanation for the increased dropout rates is the lack of adequate training of teachers. In a recent study of Latino students in BPS, one-third of whom are ELs, Uriarte, Chen, and Kala (2008) found that the qualification of teachers was one of the most critical factors in lowering the Latino dropout rate in district high schools.

Impact on Academic Achievement

In assessing the effect of the implementation of Question 2 on the academic achievement of ELs, we present the pass rates in grades 4, 8, and 10 for ELs and the same two comparison groups (see Table 5.6). For each grade level, we present the gap in pass rates between the groups being compared.

Grade 4 ELA and Math Pass Rates. Although there has been some variability in English language arts (ELA) pass rates, the overall changes across time are very slight; less than one percentile point separates pass rates in 2003 from those in 2006 for all groups. ELA pass rates are lower for ELs than for both comparison groups in the years measured. Math pass rates have tended to increase for all groups from 2003 to 2006. All groups except English learners made improvements of more than 10 percentage points; while ELs showed improvement, it was less than half that of other groups. The math pass rates for students in programs for ELs were significantly lower than those of both comparison groups.

Grade 8 Math Pass Rates. Although more modest than in grade 4, eighth-grade math pass rates on the MCAS showed improvement across all groups as well. In this case also, the increase for students in programs for ELs was the smallest. As with the grade 4 results, the differences between students in EL programs and the other groups were both large and statistically significant.

Grade 10 ELA and Math Pass Rates. Between 2003 and 2006, all groups increased their pass rates in both ELA and math except for students in programs for ELs, whose pass rates dropped. In ELA both comparison groups showed improvements of more than 10 points, while the rates for ELs dropped 2.9 points in this period. In math, comparison groups improved their pass rates by more than 8 points in the period, while the rates of students in programs for ELs dropped by almost 24 points.

Gaps in MCAS Pass Rates. Although both the ELA and math pass rates tended to increase across the years observed, the pass rates for students in general education programs were substantially higher. A gap in pass rates between all students in programs for ELs and students in general education, as well as NSOLs in gen-

Table 5.6. MCAS pass rates, Boston Public Schools, 2003–2006.

Student Group	2003 (%)	2004 (%)	2005 (%)	2006 (%)
Grade 4 ELA				
All BPS	73.3	77.5	74.1	73.2
All general education programs	77.5	79.3	76.3	77.8
NSOL in general education	86.1	82.1	79.5	86.4
Programs for ELs	56.8	57.1	—	56.9
Grade 4 math				
All BPS	63.2	70.1	68.5	73.7
All general education programs	65.0	71.3	70.0	76.6
NSOL in general education	74.8	77.2	76.5	84.4
Programs for ELs	57.3	57.6	—	63.0
Grade 8 math				
All BPS	48.1	54.0	51.6	53.4
All general education programs	50.9	55.1	53.2	55.8
NSOL in general education	62.3	62.6	54.2	65.6
Programs for ELs	33.1	31.7	—	33.4
Grade 10 ELA				
All BPS	66.8	65.9	67.8	77.4
All general education programs	72.7	72.3	73.3	85.2
NSOL in general education	74.7	69.8	71.9	88.4
Programs for ELs	45.1	26.2	34.8	43.2
Grade 10 math				
All BPS	65.8	68.7	61.0	67.8
All general education programs	63.5	69.5	62.6	71.7
NSOL in general education	67.5	71.1	67.0	76.1
Programs for ELs	69.2	63.3	46.8	45.5

Notes: Fourth- and eighth-grade MCAS pass rates in 2005 for students in EL programs are not reliable because of low enrollments and restrictions in reporting scores for small groups of students in school or grade. All differences between the pass rates of students in programs for ELs and students in general education are statistically significant (χ^2 test; $p < .000$). All differences between the pass rates of students in programs for ELs and NSOLs are statistically significant (χ^2 test; $p < .000$).

eral education, persists. Moreover, these gaps have widened over the course of the study period, particularly among tenth graders. (See Table 5.7.)

For fourth-grade students in programs for ELs, as compared to all students in general education as well as NSOLs in general education, the increase in the English language arts achievement gap was very slight, while that observed in math was substantial in the 3 years observed. However, between these groups, the achievement gap in ELA was larger than that observed in math. The gap in eighth-grade math pass rates increased during this period, in relation both to all general education students and to NSOLs in general education.

Table 5.7. Gaps in MCAS pass rates, Boston Public Schools, 2003–2006.

	Percentile Points			
Student Group	*2003*	*2004*	*2005*	*2006*
Grade 4 ELA				
All general education/EL programs	20.7	22.2	—	20.9
NSOL in general education/EL	29.3	25.0	—	29.5
Grade 4 math				
All general education/EL programs	7.7	13.7	—	13.6
NSOL in general education/EL	17.5	19.6	—	21.4
Grade 8 math				
All general education/EL programs	17.8	23.4	—	22.4
NSOL in general education/EL	29.2	30.9	—	33.4
Grade 10 ELA				
All general education/EL programs	27.6	46.1	38.5	42.0
NSOL in general education/EL	29.6	43.6	37.1	45.2
Grade 10 math				
All general education/EL programs	−5.7	6.2	15.8	26.2
NSOL in general education/EL	−1.7	7.8	20.2	30.6

Note: Fourth- and eighth-grade MCAS pass rates in 2005 for students in EL programs are not reliable because of low enrollments and restrictions in reporting scores for small groups of students in school or grade.

The pass-rate gap was most pronounced among tenth-grade students. At this grade level, the gaps in pass rates in ELA between ELs and students in general education increased substantially in the period, from 27.6 points in 2003 to 42 points in 2006. The achievement gap in math between these two groups changed dramatically, reversing from one favoring ELs by 5.7 points to one favoring students in general education by 26.2 points.

Similarly, the gaps in pass rates in tenth-grade ELA between ELs and NSOLs in general education increased from 29.6 points in 2003 to 45.2 points in 2006. The achievement gap in math between these two groups reversed from one favoring English learners by 1.7 points to one favoring NSOLs in general education by 30.6 points.

CONCLUSIONS

Implementation of Question 2, a referendum that challenged both the perspective and the practice of bilingual education in Massachusetts through its emphasis on English-only instruction, began in September 2003, less than a year after state voters approved it. We found that following the implementation of Question 2, there were substantial decreases in the identification of students who, because of limited

English proficiency, required programs for ELs. Interviews with staff of the Boston Public Schools suggested that these decreases were due in great measure to institutional factors, notably the misassessments at the Family Resource Centers. As a result, enrollments in programs for English learners also declined over the 4-year period.

English learners in BPS also experienced a narrowing of available services, with an increasing concentration of offerings in the "default" Structured English Immersion program. Boston has not pursued the process of parental waivers of participation in SEI programs as a way to expand program offerings for EL students, and LEPs who are not enrolled in programs for ELs do not receive any language support services. The latter is a violation of both state and federal law.

The rise in the dropout rate in Boston has been touted as a crisis, and data in this report support the Parthenon Group's (2007) finding that it is driven in part by the rise in the dropout rate among late-entrant English learners. Our study's assessment of engagement and academic outcomes showed that, although dropout rates increased across BPS subgroups considered here between 2003 and 2006, the magnitude of the increase among ELs was significantly larger than that among students in general education and among NSOLs in general education. Larger dropout rates among ELs than among the other groups are now the norm.

Proponents of Question 2 promised more rapid acquisition of English for ELs in Massachusetts and, with that, a rise in academic achievement and a narrowing of the achievement gap. The results have been quite different. The rise in academic achievement experienced by most subgroups in BPS largely bypassed ELs. Most often, pass rates declined for ELs in ELA and math, and the improvements in pass rates, when found, were smaller than those for other groups. The achievement gaps in both math and ELA, but especially in math, widened between ELs and both students in general education and NSOLs in general education programs.

The state of Massachusetts has a responsibility to monitor the outcomes of this sweeping policy change and to track the performance of EL students in the state. It should embark on such a study immediately. If the findings about EL outcomes at the state level are as consistently negative as those documented for Boston students in this study, the state has the responsibility to either radically improve the implementation of Structured English Immersion or change state policy. Although voters forced this change, it is up to policymakers and state government to execute the voters' mandate in a way that mitigates harm to students. Although our findings reveal that this did not happen in Boston, 6 years after Question 2 passed, educators and policymakers must use the data now available to address the needs of this growing group of the commonwealth's students.

NOTE

The authors thank The Barr Foundation, The Schott Foundation for Education, and The Boston Foundation for the funding to conduct this research and to the William Monroe Trotter Institute for the Study of Black Culture and the Institute for Asian American Studies, both at the University of Massachusetts–Boston, for their financial support, which made possible the early stages of this project. We also thank Tatjana Meschede for statistical analysis; Lusa Lo for her work in conducting interviews; Dan French and Jorge Capetillo for their feedback; and Jim O'Brien for editing the manuscript. Finally, we thank the staffs of the Massachusetts Department of Primary and Secondary Education and the Boston Public Schools for participating in our study; their perspective filled the gaps left by the quantitative data.

REFERENCES

Boston Public Schools (BPS). (n.d.). *Question 2: English language learning in public schools, phase 1, 2003–2004.* Unpublished Powerpoint presentation.

Boston Public Schools (BPS). (1999). *The Bilingual Education Task Force, report to the Boston School Committee.* Boston: Author.

Boston Public Schools (BPS). (2006, May 9). *The status of English language learners in the Boston Public Schools.* Presentation to the Boston City Council, Boston.

Citizens' Commission on Academic Success for Boston's Children. (2006). *Transforming the Boston Public Schools: Roadmap for the new superintendent.* Boston: Massachusetts Advocates for Children.

Commonwealth of Massachusetts. (1971). Massachusetts General Laws Chapter 71A, Transitional Bilingual Education (1971).

Commonwealth of Massachusetts. (2002). Chapter 386 of the Acts of 2002. An Act relative to the teaching of English in Public Schools. Retrieved February 7, 2007, from http://www.mass.gov/legis/laws/seslaw02/sl020386.htm

Crawford, J. (2004). *No Child Left Behind: Misguided approach to school accountability for English language learners.* Presentation at a forum sponsored by the Center for Education Policy. Retrieved November 8, 2008, from http://users.rcn.com/crawj/langpol/Crawford_NCLB_Misguided_Approach_for_ELLs.pdf

de Jong, E., Gort, M., & Cobb, C. (2005). Bilingual education within the context of English-only policies: Three districts' responses to Question 2 in Massachusetts. *Educational Policy, 19*(4), 595–620.

Gándara, P., Maxwell-Jolly, J., & Driscoll, A. (2005). *Listening to teachers of English language learners: A survey of California teachers' challenges, experiences, and professional development needs.* Santa Cruz, CA: Center for the Future of Teaching and Learning.

Gándara, P., Maxwell-Jolly, J., García, E., Asato, J., Gutiérrez, K., Stritikus, T., & Curry, J. (2000). *The initial impact of Proposition 227 on the instruction of English language learners.* Davis: University of California, Linguistic Minority Research Institute.

Massachusetts Department of Education (MDE). (2003a). *English language learners. English language proficiency requirements for teachers under Question 2: English language education in public schools.* Retrieved February 7, 2007, from http://www.doe.mass.edu/ell/proficiencyreq.html?section=attach_b

Massachusetts Department of Education (MDE). (2003b). *Questions and answers regarding *Chapter 71a: English language education in public schools.* Retrieved February 7, 2007, from http://www.doe.mass.edu/ell/chapter71A_faq.pdf

Massachusetts Department of Education (MDE). (2003c). *2002–2003 selected populations report.* Retrieved February 7, 2007, from http://profiles.doe.mass.edu/state_report/ selectedpopulations.aspx?mode=&year=2003&orderBy=&filterBy

Massachusetts Department of Education (MDE). (2003–2006). *MCAS report.* Retrieved February 7, 2007, from http://profiles.doe.mass.edu/state_report/ mcas.aspx?year= 2003

Massachusetts Department of Education (MDE). (2004). *English language learners: Designation of LEP students: School year 2003–04.* Retrieved October 13, 2008, from www.doe.mass.edu/ell/news04/0325lep.html

Massachusetts Department of Education (MDE). (2008a). *MEPA: Massachusetts English Proficiency Assessment.* Retrieved February 7, 2007, from http://www.doe.mass.edu/ mcas/mepa/

Massachusetts Department of Education (MDE). (2008b). *Massachusetts Comprehensive Assessment System: Overview.* Retrieved February 7, 2007, from http://www.doe .mass.edu/mcas/overview.html?faq=9

Massachusetts Department of Elementary and Secondary Education. (2008). *Boston Public Schools: Coordinated program review: Report of findings.* Unpublished document.

Parrish, T., Linquanti, R., Merickel, A., Quick, H., Laird, J., & Esra, P. (2006). *Effects of the implementation of Proposition 227 on the education of English Learners, K–12.* Palo Alto, CA: American Institutes for Research.

Parthenon Group. (2007). *Strategic planning to serve off-track youth: Data review and strategic implications.* Boston, MA: Boston Public Schools, The Parthenon Group, Jobs for the Future, and The Bill and Melinda Gates Foundation.

Portes, A., & Rumbaut, R. (2001). *Legacies: The story of the immigrant second generation.* Berkeley and Los Angeles: University of California Press.

Rennie Center for Education Research & Policy. (2007). *Seeking effective policies and practices for English language learners.* Cambridge, MA: Author. Retrieved November 21, 2008, from www.renniecenter.org/research_docs/ELLReport-final.pdf

Stearns, E., & Glennie, E. J. (2006). When and why dropouts leave high school. *Youth & Society, 38*(1), 29–57.

Suárez-Orozco, C., & Suárez-Orozco, M. (2001). *Children of immigration.* Cambridge, MA: Harvard University Press.

Suárez-Orozco, C., Suárez Orozco, M., & Todorova, I. (2008). *Learning a new land: Immigrant students in American society.* Cambridge, MA: Harvard University Press.

Tregar, B. (2008). *Services to LEP Students: New legal requirements and past/current practice.* Boston: Boston Public Schools. Unpublished document.

Uriarte, M., Chen, J., & Kala, M. (2008). *Where we go to school: Latino students and the public schools of Boston.* Boston: Mauricio Gastón Institute, University of Massachusetts–Boston.

Wright, W. E., & Choi, D. (2006). The impact of language and high-stakes testing policies on elementary school English language learners in Arizona. *Education Policy Analysis Archives, 14*(13). Retrieved October 10, 2008, from http://epaa.asu.edu/epaa /v14n13/

Wright, W. E., & Pu, C. (2005). *Academic achievement of English language learners in post Proposition 203 Arizona.* Tempe: Arizona State University, Education Policy Studies Laboratory, Language Policy Research Unit.

CHAPTER 6

State Language Policies, School Language Practices, and the English Learner Achievement Gap

Russell W. Rumberger and Loan Tran

ALTHOUGH SOME linguistic minority (LM) students arrive at school already proficient in English, most do not. These students—referred to as English learners (ELs) or Limited English Proficient (LEP) students—must not only achieve English proficiency but also learn the same academic content as English-only students. There is a substantial achievement gap between EL students and non-EL, or English-only (EO), students beginning at the first moment they arrive at kindergarten (Gándara & Rumberger, 2009). In the National Assessment of Educational Progress (NAEP), for example, only 7% of EL students scored at or above proficient in the 2005 grade 4 reading test, compared with 32% of EO students (Perie, Grigg, & Donahue, 2005). In grade 8 reading, only 4% of EL students scored above proficient, compared to 30% of EO students. The achievement gap is similarly large in math. Only 11% of EL students score at or above proficient in grade 4, compared to 38% for EO students. In grade 8, only 6% of EL students scored at or above proficient, compared with 30% of EO students.

Both federal and state governments have been involved in addressing the educational needs of English learners through litigation, legislation, and programs. These actions have sought to define the rights of linguistic minority students and have established different educational goals for them at different times. Among those goals are (1) access to the core curriculum, (2) English language proficiency, (3) native-language proficiency, (4) closing of the achievement gap, and (5) cultural competence. These goals and ways to meet them have changed substantially over the last 30 or 40 years at both the federal and state levels. One of the most significant changes came about through ballot initiatives in three states—California, Arizona, and Massachusetts—that substantially curtailed the use of native-language instruction for EL students. Yet these initiatives represent only one of the many ways that states have attempted to address the educational needs of their English learner students.

This chapter examines whether differences in state policies and school practices in educating English learners are related to differences in the size of the EL achievement gap across states and across schools. This chapter first provides a brief overview of state policies regarding the education of EL students (a brief history of federal policies is presented in Chapter 2, this volume) and some descriptive data on the size of the EL achievement gap and instructional practices for EL students across states. It then examines the size of the achievement gap across states using the 2005 NAEP data. Finally, it examines whether differences in the achievement gap across states and across schools are related to policies and practices for educating EL students or other factors, such as student composition, school structure, and school resources. The chapter draws on material from a larger study that examined both state and district variability in the EL achievement gap (Rumberger & Tran, 2008).

THE STATES' ROLE IN EDUCATING LINGUISTIC MINORITY STUDENTS

The history of state legislation regarding the education of linguistic minority students is varied, in part, because many states have had relatively few linguistic minorities until quite recently. According to a recent tabulation by García (2005), 12 states mandate special services for LM students, 12 states permit special services, 1 state prohibits them, and 26 states have no legislation that directly addresses the education of these students. States that have had sizable populations of LM for some time, such as Texas and California, have a longer history of state legislative activity in these areas (although Massachusetts was actually the first state to pass a bilingual education law in 1971). California, for example, passed a state-level comprehensive bilingual education bill, the Chacon-Moscone Bilingual-Bicultural Act, in 1976. Texas passed its first bilingual education bill in 1981.

By and large, most state legislation has focused on the educational goal to "as effectively and efficiently as possible . . . develop in each child fluency in English" (California Education Code, 1976, Section 52161). In the three restrictive-language-policy states—California, Arizona, and Massachusetts—state policy regarding the education of LM students has been dictated by recent ballot initiatives. These initiatives restrict the educational goals for LM students to learning English, and they dictate a single educational program to achieve it: Structured English Immersion (SEI). Access to native-language instruction is severely restricted, requiring a complex process of parental waivers. But in 17 other states, instruction in a language other than English is allowed or required, and 15 states mandate a cultural component (García, 2005).

ASSESSING THE ENGLISH LEARNER ACHIEVEMENT GAP

This chapter presents selected findings from a larger research study that assessed the achievement gap between EL students and EO students across the 50 states and the factors that contribute to it. We addressed the following questions in our study:

1. What is the average achievement gap in math and reading at grades 4 and 8 between EL and EO students in the United States?
2. How much of the variability in the achievement gap is attributable to students and their families, schools, and states?
3. How much of the school-level and state-level variability in the achievement gap can be accounted for by resources and other school inputs versus school practices, including inputs and practices specifically targeted for English learners?

The data come from the 2005 NAEP, a national study of student achievement conducted in all 50 states and the District of Columbia. The study analyzes data from four NAEP assessments: grade 4 reading, grade 4 math, grade 8 reading, and grade 8 math. The data include background information collected from student, teacher, and principal questionnaires (U.S. Department of Education, National Center for Education Statistics, 2008). Teachers identified EL or LEP students and provided information about their English proficiency, instructional program, and whether the student was capable of participating in the NAEP assessment, either with or without accommodations (available only for EL students who had received English instruction for less than 3 years).

The NAEP data were augmented with state-level data from other data sources. Together, the data were used to create a series of variables to measure four characteristics of schools and of states that may impact student achievement: student composition, school structure, school resources, and school policies and practices. The data were analyzed using multilevel modeling techniques. A complete description of the variables and analytic techniques is provided in the larger report (Rumberger & Tran, 2008).

THE SIZE OF THE EL ACHIEVEMENT GAP
NATIONALLY AND AMONG STATES

How large is the achievement gap between English learners and English-only students? One way to address this question is by comparing mean test scores on the NAEP. One difficulty, however, is that some EL students were excluded from taking the NAEP, as described above, and the rate of exclusion varied among schools and states. Nationally, 14% of the identified EL students were excluded from testing in grade 4 reading, 8% were excluded from testing in grade 4 math, and between 10% and 13% were excluded from grade 8 reading and math. Both the percent of students identified as EL and the percent of identified EL students excluded varied widely among states. For example, in California, 33% of all students were identified as EL in the grade 4 reading assessment and only 7% of these were excluded from testing, while in Texas, 16% of the students were identified as EL and 23% of these were excluded from testing.

Differences in the rate of exclusion could affect the reported NAEP scores if the lowest-achieving EL students were more likely to be excluded. Schools and states that excluded more students may show higher EL achievement levels for the EL students who were tested. When using NAEP data to review EL test scores and the EL achievement gap, it is useful to bear this in mind. In the statistical analysis, we examined whether the rate of exclusion affected differences in the EL achievement gap among schools and states.

In order to make comparisons between tests and between years, it is necessary to use a common metric. One such metric is known as an effect size (*ES*). An effect size simply represents the difference in test scores as a fraction of a standard deviation (*SD*). Although there are no absolute standards for judging the magnitude of effect sizes, an *ES* of at least .2 *SD* is generally considered a small effect, an *ES* of at least .5 *SD* is generally considered a medium effect, and an *ES* of at least .8 *SD* is generally considered a large effect (Cohen, 1988). It is useful to compare the size of achievement gaps with interventions designed to reduce them. To illustrate, a review of 232 evaluation studies of the effects of 29 different comprehensive school reform models on student test scores found an average *ES* of .12, although interventions that had been implemented for 8 years or longer had an average *ES* of .50 (Borman, Hewes, Overman, & Brown, 2003).

Table 6.1 shows achievement gaps between English learners and English-only students on the reading and math tests in grades 4 and 8 based on data extracted from the NAEP website. Nationally, the achievement gap in grade 4 reading was 0.92 *SD*, and the achievement gap in grade 4 math was 0.79 *SD*. Both gaps are considered large by the standards reviewed above, although the gap in reading is larger, which of course should not be surprising given that English learners are so designated because they lack proficiency in English. The data also show that the gaps vary widely among states. The first three states listed are those with restrictive language policies, where very few students received native-language instruction (see Rumberger & Tran, 2008, Table 5). The other three states serve large populations of English learners, with two of them (New Mexico and Texas) providing native-language instruction to above-average proportions of EL students, and the other one (Nevada) providing essentially no native-language instruction.

At grade 4, in both reading and math, the states with restrictive language policies and Nevada have achievement gaps that are at least the size of the national

Table 6.1. EL achievement gap in NAEP reading and math scores, grade 4, 2005, selected states.

	English Learners (%)		Scale Score			
	Identified	Tested	All	English-Only	English Learner	Achievement Gap
Reading						
National	11	9	217	220	187	0.92
Arizona	20	18	207	214	175	1.08
California	33	31	207	217	183	0.94
Massachusetts	6	5	231	233	198	0.97
Nevada	16	14	207	212	176	1.00
New Mexico	27	19	207	213	182	0.86
Texas	16	10	219	222	196	0.72
Math						
National	10	10	237	239	216	0.79
Arizona	20	19	230	235	208	0.93
California	33	31	230	238	214	0.83
Massachusetts	7	6	247	249	246	0.79
Nevada	17	16	230	234	209	0.86
New Mexico	25	25	224	229	208	0.72
Texas	15	14	242	245	226	0.66

Note: Achievement gap = [scale score (English-only) – scale score (English learner)] / standard deviation (all).

Source: Data compiled from the National Center for Education Statistics, 2008.

average and, in all but one case, larger than the national average. The two states with the highest proportion of students in native-language instruction have gaps that are smaller than the national average in both reading and math. It is interesting to note that just because a state has a high overall mean achievement level or high achievement levels for both EO and EL students, it does not mean that it has a small achievement gap between both groups of students. In Massachusetts, for example, both EO and EL students score well above the national mean, yet the achievement gap in Massachusetts is slightly above the national mean. In contrast, both EO and EL students score below the national mean in California, yet the achievement gap is about the same as in Massachusetts. As we show below, factors that improve overall student performance may not reduce the achievement gap; conversely, factors that reduce the achievement gap may not improve overall student performance.

The reading and math achievement gaps in grade 8 are larger than in grade 4 (see Table 6.2) and very large in their own right (1.11 *SD* in reading and 1.00 *SD* in

Table 6.2. EL achievement gap in NAEP reading and math scores, grade 8, 2005, selected states.

	English Learners (%)			Scale Scores		
	Identified	Tested	All	English-Only	English Learner	Achievement Gap
Reading						
National	6	5	260	263	224	1.11
Arizona	13	11	255	259	225	0.97
California	22	20	250	258	222	1.03
Massachusetts	3	2	274	275	222	1.51
Nevada	11	9	253	257	221	1.03
New Mexico	16	12	251	255	224	0.89
Texas	8	6	258	261	216	1.29
Math						
National	6	6	278	280	244	1.00
Arizona	14	12	274	279	245	0.94
California	21	20	269	275	241	0.94
Massachusetts	3	21	292	293	242	1.42
Nevada	9	8	270	273	236	1.03
New Mexico	17	15	263	268	239	0.81
Texas	8	6	281	284	242	1.17

Note: Achievement gap = [scale score (English-only) – scale score (English learner)] / standard deviation (all).

Source: Data compiled from the National Center for Education Statistics, 2008.

math). One reason is that some EL students are reclassified as Fluent English Proficient by eighth grade, so the students who remain classified as ELs may have started school at a lower level of English proficiency than other ELs. In addition, some EL students first enter U.S. schools in the upper elementary or early secondary grades, so they may have more catching up to do than more long-term ELs.

These achievement gaps also vary widely among states. Massachusetts, in particular, has an extremely large EL achievement gap even though both its EO and EL students score substantially above the national average. Texas's achievement gaps in both reading and math at grade 8 are also very large, and the state does not normally provide bilingual instruction at the secondary level. It is important to note that in the long-running lawsuit *United States v. Texas* the court found in 2008 that the state's monitoring system allowed weak outcomes for English as a Second Language (ESL) programs in secondary schools to be masked by successful outcomes for bilingual programs in elementary schools and ordered the state to come up with a plan to fix the problem by January 2009. Differences among states in grade 8 EL achievement gaps can also reflect differences between states in the rate of reclassification as students progress through the schooling system. For example, between grades 4 and 8, the percentage of ELs identified in Texas decreased by half, from 15% to 8% (see Table 6.1). In contrast, the percentage of ELs identified in California decreased by about one-third, from 33% in grade 4 to 21% in grade 8. These differences in redesignation rates may reflect more effective instruction at the lower grades, a higher bar to becoming redesignated, or both.

INSTRUCTIONAL PROGRAMS FOR EL STUDENTS

One strategy for helping to close the EL achievement gap is providing an instructional program designed to improve student learning. Teachers of EL students in the NAEP survey were asked to indicate whether the student received (1) no specially designed instruction for LEP students, (2) specially designed instruction in English (e.g., ESL, simplified English), or (3) native-language instruction.

Nationally, the data show that only about half of all EL students received some form of specialized instruction in 2005. In grade 4 reading, 58% received specially designed instruction (SDI) in English and another 5% received native-language instruction (see Rumberger & Tran, 2008, Table 5). In grade 4 math, 44% received SDI and 5% received native-language instruction. In grade 8 reading, 57% received SDI and less than 1% received native-language instruction. And in grade 8 math, only 36% received SDI and 2% received native-language instruction.

The provision of specially designed instruction for EL students varies widely among states. Some states, even with sizable EL populations like Nevada, provide relatively little SDI for EL students. Other states, such as New Jersey, Georgia, and Rhode Island, provide SDI to a majority of their EL students. The provision of native-language instruction varies even more widely. Many states provide no native-language instruction, while Texas and New Jersey provide native-language instruction to more than one-fifth of their EL students in grade 4 reading. The provision of SDI and native-language instruction is even more sparse in grade 8, especially in math. Yet some states, such as New Jersey and Rhode Island, provide native-language instruction to a sizable number of their EL students.

VARIABILITY IN THE EL ACHIEVEMENT GAP
AMONG STATES AND SCHOOLS

The remainder of our study examined the variability in the EL achievement gap among schools and states as well as the extent to which this variability can be explained by differences in state policies and school practices.

First, we determined that about three-quarters of the variability in student achievement is related to differences among students, 15% to 20% of the variability is related to differences among the schools they attend, and between 2% and 5% of the variability is related to differences in the states in which they live (see Rumberger & Tran, 2008, Figure 1). These proportions are very similar to those reported in other studies using large databases to disaggregate student achievement (Rumberger & Palardy, 2004). For example, in the largest study of student achievement ever undertaken, Coleman (1990) found that schools accounted for 5% to 38% of the total variation in student test scores among different grade levels, ethnic groups, and regions of the country.

Next, we determined the proportion of variability in the mean achievement of schools and the mean school achievement gap between EL and EO students that is related to differences among states, rather than among schools within states. We found that states account for 15% to 20% of the variability in mean achievement. Interestingly, states account for a larger proportion of the variability in the mean school EL achievement gap, ranging from 37% to 39%, except in the case of grade 8 math, where the number is only 3% (and may not be accurate, as the reliability of the estimate was low). This finding suggests that states have more influence over the EL achievement gap than they do over average school achievement.

STATE PREDICTORS OF MEAN ACHIEVEMENT AND THE EL ACHIEVEMENT GAP

Next, we identified four types of state-level factors that predicted differences in the mean school achievement and EL achievement gap between states: (1) student composition factors that described the demographic characteristics of students, (2) structural variables that described the structural features of schools, such as location and size, (3) school resource variables that described the characteristics of teachers, and (4) policy and practice variables that described various aspects of state policy regarding standards and accountability, the teaching profession, school finance, and various school practices. A list of all the significant predictors is provided in the larger report (see Rumberger & Tran, 2008, Table 7). Here we focus on predictors of the mean EL achievement gap across states in reading and math in grades 4 and 8.

Only two factors predict differences in the mean EL achievement gap in grade 4 reading across states: (1) the mean reading proficiency of EL students and (2) state policies with respect to standards. Not surprisingly, states varied in the level of English proficiency of their EL students. States with higher mean levels of EL English proficiency in reading had narrower achievement gaps in reading between EL and EO students. (Because EL students have lower achievement than EO students, the EL achievement gap is expressed as a negative number.) One state policy variable also predicted the EL achievement gap in grade 4 reading: the level of state standards as determined by the Editorial Projects in Education Research Center (EPERC) report *Quality Counts* (2008). The standards variable is a composite measure that assessed the rigor of standards in all academic subjects, as well as whether the state provides supplementary resources, including materials provided for particular student populations, such as EL students. According to the EPERC, 35 states provide such resources.

We determined that three factors predict differences in the EL achievement gap in grade 4 math across states, and, interestingly, two concern reading. First, states with EL students at higher levels of English reading proficiency had narrower achievement gaps in math, suggesting that reading proficiency plays an important role in EL performance on the math assessment. Second, the number of pages of reading that students did in and out of school each day was negatively related to the EL achievement gap, suggesting that states that pay too much attention to reading may be sacrificing math performance, at least for EL students. Third, states with higher proportions of Black students had narrower EL achievement gaps.

Five factors predict differences in the EL achievement gap in grade 8 reading across states. First, states with higher proportions of Hispanic students had larger EL achievement gaps. Second, states with higher percentages of students on free and reduced lunch had narrower EL achievement gaps. Third, states with EL students at higher levels of English reading proficiency had smaller EL achievement gaps. Fourth, states with a higher proportion of students receiving specialized designed instruction had lower achievement gaps.

Finally, we created a measure to test whether the effect of receiving specially designed instruction in English varied by the reading proficiency of EL students. This measure addresses the question of whether the effects of specially designed instruction in English are equally beneficial for all EL students or whether it is more effective with less proficient students than with more proficient students. The results suggest a varying effect. The higher the English proficiency of the EL students in the state, the wider the achievement gap associated with an increased proportion of students receiving specialized instruction. Conversely, the lower the English proficiency of the EL students in the state, the smaller the achievement gap associated with an increased proportion of students receiving specialized instruction. This finding suggests that specialized instruction helps to narrow the EL achievement gap when EL students have low English proficiency in reading, but it widens the achievement gap when EL students have high English proficiency, perhaps because such instruction may be inappropriate for more proficient students and may replace more rigorous coursework.

Only two factors were significant predictors of the EL achievement gap in grade 8 math: (1) states with larger average school enrollment had larger achievement gaps, and (2) states with more equitable school finance systems had smaller EL achievement gaps in grade 8 math.

In addition to determining the individual predictors, it is also useful to assess how much of the between-state variability in mean school achievement and mean school EL achievement gaps was explained by the four types of factors. The results (see Figure 6.1) revealed that student composition factors account for two-thirds of the variability in mean school achievement in grade 4 reading, with other factors being less important, although state policy variables account for 13% of the variability. In contrast, student composition variables explain a relatively much smaller proportion of the variability in the EL achievement gap in reading (33%), while state policy and school practice variables explain about 12% of the variability. Grade 4 math shows an opposite pattern—student composition factors play a less important role in explaining mean math achievement (45% versus 68% in reading), while policy and practice variables play a relatively more important role (20% versus 13% in reading). In contrast, student composition factors play a more important role in explaining between-state differences in the EL achievement gap in math (55% versus 33% in reading), with policy and practice factors playing a similar role (12%). Grade 8 reading and math show similar patterns to those of grade 4 reading and math.

Several conclusions can be drawn from these findings. First, states have relatively more influence on the EL achievement gap in reading than they do in overall reading achievement, whereas they have relatively more influence on overall math achievement than they do on the EL achievement gap in math. Second, a wide variety of factors predict between-state differences in student achievement, ranging from student composition to state policies. Third, for the most part, different factors predict between-state differences in mean achievement than predict between-state differences in the mean EL achievement gap. Fourth, in some cases, similar factors predict student achievement across the four outcomes; in other cases, different factors predict student achievement across the four outcomes. Fifth, most of the effects are very small (effect sizes less than .10), except for the student composition factors (which have effect sizes in the .20 range). This finding suggests that individual state-level predictors exert a relatively small effect on student achievement and the EL achievement gap. Collectively, however, the impact of state-level variables can be quite sizable.

SCHOOL PREDICTORS OF MEAN ACHIEVEMENT AND THE EL ACHIEVEMENT GAP

Finally, our research identified four types of school-level factors that predicted differences in the mean school achievement and EL achievement gap between schools: (1) student composition factors that described the demographic characteristics of students, (2) structural factors that described the structural features of schools, (3) school resource factors that described the characteristics of teachers,

Figure 6.1. Proportion of state-level variance explained by type of statistical model.

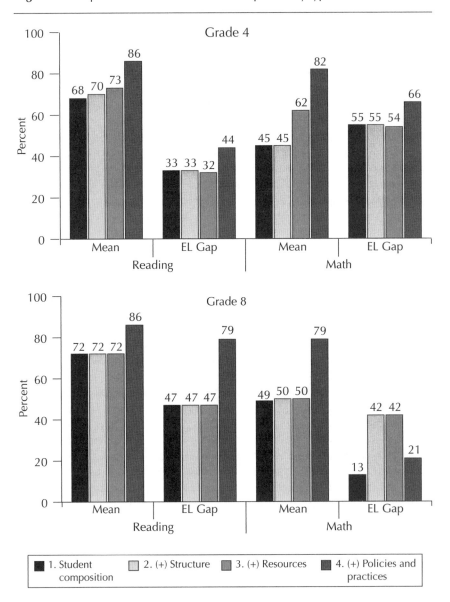

and (4) practice factors that described various aspects of school climate and instructional practices.

Six school-level factors predict differences in the mean EL achievement gap in grade 4 reading across schools. First, schools with higher proportions of students on free and reduced lunch and, second, schools with higher proportions of Black students had smaller EL achievement gaps. This finding should not be surprising, since low numbers of students who are performing at high levels would tend to reduce gaps. Third, schools with higher mean levels of EL English proficiency in reading had narrower achievement gaps in reading between EL and EO students. Fourth, urban schools had slightly smaller EL achievement gaps. Fifth, schools with a higher proportion of EL students excluded from testing had a lower achievement gap. Finally, the lower the English proficiency of the EL students in the school, the smaller the achievement gap associated with an increased proportion of students receiving specialized instruction.

Four school-level factors predict the EL achievement gap in grade 4 math. First, schools with students of higher socioeconomic status (SES) had larger achievement gaps. Second, schools with higher proportions of Black students had narrower EL achievement gaps. Third, schools with EL students at higher levels of English reading proficiency had narrower achievement gaps in math, suggesting that reading proficiency plays an important role in EL students' math achievement. Fourth, the more years of English instruction that students receive, the smaller the achievement gap.

Three school-level factors predict the EL achievement gap in grade 8 reading. First, schools with higher proportions of EL students and, second, schools with higher proportions of Black students had smaller EL achievement gaps. Third, schools with EL students at higher levels of English reading proficiency had lower EL achievement gaps in math.

Finally, five school-level factors predict the EL achievement gap in grade 8 math. First, schools with higher proportions of EL students had lower achievement gaps. Second, schools with higher-SES students had larger achievement gaps. Third, schools with higher proportions of Hispanic students had larger EL achievement gaps, while, fourth, schools with higher proportions of Black students had smaller EL achievement gaps. Fifth, schools with EL students at higher levels of English reading proficiency had lower EL achievement gaps in math ($ES = .27$).

Again, it is useful to assess how much of the between-school variability in mean school achievement and school EL achievement gaps was explained by the four types of factors. Student composition factors account for most of the variability in mean school achievement across all four test areas, ranging from 75% for grade 4 math to 79% for grade 8 math. Student composition factors also account for around half of all the variability among schools in the EL achievement gap across all four test areas, ranging from 41% for grade 8 math to 59% for grade 8 reading. In both mean school achievement and EL achievement, other factors explain relatively little additional variability.

SUMMARY AND CONCLUSIONS

This study examined the achievement gap between English learners and English-only students among schools and states across four achievement areas: reading in grades 4 and 8 and math in grades 4 and 8. Based on the 2005 National Assessment of Educational Progress, the analysis revealed that EL achievement gaps are sizable in all four areas. The gap tends to be larger in reading than in math and larger in grade 8—when at least some EL students have been reclassified as Fluent English Proficient and are no longer included in the EL category—than in grade 4. Based on conventional standards, all of these gaps are considered large and probably understate the true achievement gap between EL and EO students, since between 8% and 14% of all identified EL students were excluded from the NAEP assessments. The rates of exclusion also vary among schools and states, which means that differences in the EL achievement gap for tested students may not represent differences in the achievement gap of all EL students.

The gaps also vary among states. For example, among states with sizable populations of EL students, the EL achievement gap in grade 4 math varies from two-thirds of a standard deviation in Texas to almost 1 standard deviation in Arizona. Although some states have achievement levels that exceed the national averages for both EL and EO students, such states do not necessarily have higher achievement gaps between these two groups of students. Conversely, states with lower achievement levels for both EL and EO students do not necessarily have lower achievement gaps. In other words, EL achievement gaps do not appear to be related to absolute achievement levels of either EO or EL students. Moreover, states with restrictive language policies tended to have larger achievement gaps than those without such policies, especially at grade 4.

The study also found that the extent of specially designed instruction for EL students varied widely among schools and states. Overall, only about half of all EL students nationwide received any form of specially designed instruction to serve their needs, with most students receiving specially designed instruction in English (such as English as a Second Language) and only about 5% or less receiving native-language instruction. In grade 8 math, less than 40% of EL students were receiving specially designed instruction.

We examined differences between states and schools in both overall achievement and in the EL achievement gap. We found that most of the variability in student achievement was related to characteristics of students rather than characteristics of either their schools or their state of residence. Nonetheless, up to one-third of the variability in school mean achievement was related to states, with states accounting for more of the variability in the EL achievement gap than in the variability in overall achievement. This finding suggests that states have more control over the size of the EL achievement gap than over their overall achievement levels and that state policies—such as whether to provide EL students with specialized instruction and, if so, what type—could help reduce the gap.

The analysis identified a range of factors that explained differences in both mean achievement and the EL achievement gap among states and among schools. In general, different factors predicted differences in mean student achievement than predicted differences in the EL achievement gap. In some cases, similar factors—particularly the reading proficiency of EL students—predicted student achievement across the four test outcomes; in other cases, different factors predicted student achievement across the four test outcomes. And most of the effects were very small, with student composition factors somewhat larger. This finding suggests that individual state-level and school-level predictors exert a relatively small effect on student achievement and the EL achievement gap.

Nonetheless, instructional practices, particularly offering specially designed instruction for EL students, helped reduce the achievement gaps among states and schools, at least in some cases. EL instructional practices had a moderate effect on the EL achievement gap in grade 8 reading among states. States where a higher proportion of EL students had specially designed EL instruction in English—particularly EL students with low English reading proficiency—had a lower EL achievement gap. Schools where a higher proportion of EL students with low English reading proficiency had specially designed instruction in English also had a lower EL achievement gap in grade 4 reading.

The small percentage of students receiving native-language instruction limited our ability to detect any effects from this form of specially designed instruction for EL students. But a companion study of the EL achievement gap in 11 large urban districts throughout the United States, some of which had sizable portions of students receiving native-language instruction, found that schools where a higher proportion of students received native-language instruction had much smaller achievement gaps in grade 4 math and somewhat smaller achievement gaps in grade 8 math (Rumberger & Tran, 2008).

Together, the findings from the state-level and district-level analyses support the idea that some form of specially designed instruction—whether in English or in the native language—helps to reduce the EL achievement gap. The fact that only about half of all students receive any form of specially designed instruction and that some states are much more likely to provide it than others means that much more effort needs to be directed to providing appropriate instructional support for EL students. The findings do not answer the long-standing question of whether English or native-language instructional support is consistently superior; rather, they suggest that both forms of support can help reduce the EL achievement gap. Hence, the findings do support the argument that state policies and school practices restricting the use of native-language instruction could limit the ability of states and schools to reduce the EL achievement gap.

Two additional conclusions can be drawn from this study. First, the size of the achievement gap between English learner and English-only students is large, while the impact of variables most under control of schools, districts, and state policy to reduce this gap is very small by comparison. This suggests that attempts to make meaningful reductions in the achievement gap will be difficult at best, especially in the short run, and ultimately will require addressing conditions in families and communities, not just in schools.

Second, the school-related factors that have the most impact on both student achievement and the EL achievement gap are related to student composition of schools. This is consistent with virtually every major study to student achievement beginning with the landmark study by Coleman and colleagues (1966). It suggests that the most effective policy mechanism to improve student achievement and reduce the achievement gap is one of the most challenging to achieve— a more equitable distribution of students among schools. EL students, like ethnic minorities and poor students, are highly segregated in U.S. schools (Orfield & Lee, 2006; Rumberger, Gándara, & Merino, 2006). So the most effective strategy to improve their achievement may involve creating more integrated schools.

REFERENCES

Borman, G. D., Hewes, G. M., Overman, L. T., & Brown, S. (2003). Comprehensive school reform and achievement: A meta-analysis. *Review of Educational Research, 73*, 125–230.

Cohen, J. (1988). *Statistical power analysis for the behavioral sciences* (2nd ed.). Hillsdale, NJ: Erlbaum.

Coleman, J. S. (1990). *Equality and achievement in education.* San Francisco: Westview.

Coleman, J. S., Campbell, E. Q., Hobson, C. J., McPartland, J., Mood, A. M., Weinfeld, F. D., & York, R. L. (1966). *Equality of educational opportunity.* Washington, DC: U.S. Government Printing Office.

Editorial Projects in Education Research Center. (2008). Quality counts 2008. Tapping into teaching: Unlocking the key to student success. *Education Week, 27*(18). Retrieved August 10, 2009, from http://www.edweek.org/ew/toc/2008/01/10/index.html

Gándara, P., & Rumberger, R. W. (2009). Immigration, language, and education: How does language policy structure opportunity? *Teachers College Record, 111*(3), 6–27.

García, E. E. (2005). *Teaching and learning in two languages: Bilingualism and schooling in the United States.* New York: Teachers College Press.

Orfield, G., & Lee, C. (2006). *Racial transformation and the changing nature of segregation.* Cambridge, MA: The Civil Rights Project, Harvard University.

Perie, M., Grigg, W., & Donahue, P. (2005). *The nation's report card: Reading 2005* (NCES 2006-451). U.S. Department of Education, National Center for Education Statistics. Washington, DC: U.S. Government Printing Office.

Rumberger, R. W., Gándara, P., & Merino, B. (2006). Where California's English learners attend school and why it matters. *UC LMRI Newsletter, 15*, 1–2.

Rumberger, R. W., & Palardy, G. J. (2004). Multilevel models for school effectiveness research. In D. Kaplan (Ed.), *Handbook of quantitative methodology for the social sciences* (pp. 235–258). Thousand Oaks, CA: Sage.

Rumberger, R. W., & Tran, L. (2008). *Investigating state, district, and school variability in the English learner achievement gap.* Final report to IES. University of California, Santa Barbara: University of California Linguistic Minority Research Institute.

U.S. Department of Education, National Center for Education Statistics. (2008). *The nation's report card: Background questionnaires.* Retrieved August 10, 2009, from http://nces.ed.gov/nationsreportcard/bgquest.asp

United States v. Texas, 572. F. Supp. 2d 726 (E.D. Texas 2008).

Shifting Landscapes of Professional Practices: English Learner Special Education Placement in English-Only States

Alfredo J. Artiles, Janette K. Klingner, Amanda Sullivan, and Edward G. Fierros

I T HAS BEEN more than 10 years since Proposition 227 was passed in California and almost 10 since Proposition 203 was made law in Arizona. In each state, the numbers of students educated through primary-language instruction have decreased dramatically. Moreover, many other changes have been taking place in the U.S. education reform landscape. In 2001, the No Child Left Behind Act (NCLB) was signed into law, closely followed by Reading First in 2002. The reauthorization of the Individuals with Disabilities Education Improvement Act (IDEA) took effect in 2004. There is emerging evidence that the convergence of this multiplicity of reforms has created unintended negative consequences for low-income, ethnic, and English learner students (Artiles, Sullivan, Waitoller, & Neal, in press; McNeil, Coppola, Radigan, & Vasquez Heilig, 2008; Nichols & Berliner, 2007). These reforms have taken place against a backdrop of increasing numbers of English learners (ELs) in schools throughout the United States.

We are interested in examining what happens to ELs in schools in which language support systems are drastically reduced because these policy changes considerably restrict the educational opportunities available to these learners. To what extent do educational programs and practices shift from a focus on language accommodation for ELs to concerns about ability level in English-only states? Do schools in these states increase EL placement in programs that address the needs of students with disabilities after language support programs are eliminated? Historically, educational systems have created support systems for students considered different due to their language background or ability levels (Minow, 1990). The result was the creation of bilingual and special education. What happens to students who belong to one of these categories of difference when support infrastructures are radically reduced? For instance, do student identities (as indexed by institutional labels such as EL) change? How do the changes in these institutional labels mediate the educational experiences and outcomes of this emerging population? Are the promised outcomes that justified the policy changes obtained?

These are critical questions considering that special education placement of minority students has been debated for 40 years in educational policy and research circles (Donovan & Cross, 2002). These are also timely questions, since research on EL placement in special education is scarce. Building on our past research (Artiles, Aguirre-Muñoz, & Abedi, 1998; Artiles, Rueda, Salazar, & Higareda, 2005; Fierros & Conroy, 2002; Harry & Klingner, 2006), we aimed to determine the patterns of special education placement after the passage of restrictive language policies and to offer some policy recommendations on the aforementioned questions. We are not able to establish a causal relationship between new policies and changes in practice, but we have been able to determine whether there are distinctive patterns of practices occurring alongside these policy changes. This allows us to suggest relationships that should be tested in future research. For this purpose, we briefly discuss research on the impact of restrictive language policies on ELs and related special education issues. In addition, we outline the sources of evidence used for the analyses and present three sets of findings, namely, ELs' special education placement patterns, the association between school poverty level and disability identification risk, and the nature of educational experiences for ELs placed in special education. We conclude with a discussion of our findings and offer recommendations for policy.

EMERGENT RESEARCH ON THE EFFECTS OF RESTRICTIVE LANGUAGE POLICIES

Researchers have conducted numerous studies on the effects of restrictive language policies. After the passage of such policies in California, Arizona, and Massachusetts, several researchers investigated aspects of the new laws that include the policies' impact on teacher practices; academic achievement gaps; the consequences for school climate; and the emotional impact on teachers, parents, students, and administrators (Combs, Evans, Fletcher, Parra, & Jiménez, 2005; Dixon, Green, Yeager, Baker, & Fránquiz, 2000; Gutiérrez, Baquedano-López, & Asato, 2000; Olson, 2007; Parrish, Pérez, Merickel, & Linquanti, 2006; Stritikus & García, 2005). These findings are reviewed in other chapters in this volume;

thus, we discuss only the few studies that examined issues related to restrictive language policies, ELs, and special education.

Mueller, Singer, and Grace (2004) conducted a qualitative study of the impact of California's Proposition 227 on 15 special education teachers' educational planning, assessments, and classroom practices for students identified as ELs with disabilities. Findings indicated that teachers misinterpreted the new law, administrative support was lacking, and parents were excluded from decisions regarding which language should be used for their children's instruction, contrary to the federal IDEA's planning mandates. Special education teachers made decisions about language of instruction based on their own beliefs and available resources. There were no fluent Spanish speakers among the teachers interviewed. Only two of the teachers had earned California's credential for working with ELs.

A study conducted in California with data from the 1998–1999 academic year suggested certain subgroups of ELs had a greater risk of disability identification, particularly in high school (Artiles et al., 2005). Proposition 227 was approved and early implementation was carried out during this year. The study also reported that ELs placed in bilingual education programs had a *lower* risk of special education placement compared to their peers in English immersion programs. Socioeconomic status (SES) mediated EL placement risk in complex ways. Whereas a higher proportion of low-SES ELs were identified in the learning disabilities (LD) category, a higher proportion of high-SES ELs were identified in the speech and language impairment (SLI) group. We did not find additional studies that examined academic or other outcomes for ELs identified as having disabilities or that investigated changes in the likelihood that ELs would be placed in special education after restrictive language policies were implemented. Thus, we know little about how the new policies have affected ELs with disabilities or ELs who might be considered for special education placement.

INVESTIGATION OF ENGLISH LEARNER DISABILITY
IDENTIFICATION IN CALIFORNIA AND ARIZONA

We addressed two questions in this study:

1. What were the EL special education placement trends before and after language support programs were drastically reduced in California and Arizona?
2. What were the educational experiences of ELs in these states? We examined indicators of the nature of educational experiences such as the level of placement segregation, the impact of school poverty level on disability identification risk, and opportunity to learn (e.g., access to language supports) for ELs.

Under Arizona statute, an EL is defined as "a child who does not speak English or whose native language is not English, and who is not currently able to perform ordinary classroom work in English" (Arizona Statute 15-751). The state of California defines an EL as "a child who does not speak English or whose native language is not English and who is not currently able to perform ordinary classroom work in English, also known as a Limited English Proficiency or LEP child" (California Education Code §305.306).

SETTING THE CONTEXT: EVIDENCE SOURCES AND PROCEDURES

The primary data for our analysis was drawn from the Office of Civil Rights (OCR) Elementary and Secondary School Surveys for the 1998, 2000, 2002, 2004, and 2006 academic years. Unfortunately, OCR does not report opportunity-to-learn data by disability status, so these analyses focus only on ELs.

Data sources included the Elementary/Secondary School Universe Data (U.S. Department of Education, 2008) for 1995–2006 and the Arizona State Department of Education (ADE) for the 1997–2006 academic years. Some of the targeted data were not available for both states (e.g., California Department of Education data on placement segregation).

The analysis focused on placement patterns for English learners and English proficient students across and within the mild or "subjective" disability categories—learning disabled, mental retardation, emotional/behavioral disorders, and (whenever feasible) speech or language impairment. These are the so-called high-incidence categories and comprise about 85% of students identified for special education in the nation (U.S. Department of Education, 2006).

We calculated placement risks for each target group (i.e., ELs, English proficient students) in overall special education enrollment and in each target disability category (Artiles & Rueda, 2002; Donovan & Cross, 2002). We also calculated the risks of the target student groups for various educational outcomes. Technical details about the definitions and calculations of the risk measures (i.e., risk index and relative risk ratio) can be found elsewhere (Artiles et al., 2005; Donovan & Cross, 2002).

We used a comparative measure called the relative risk ratio, which estimates the chance a target group of students (e.g., English learners) has to exhibit a particular outcome (such as placement in special education) compared to another group (e.g., English proficient students). A value of 1 indicates that the target group (i.e., ELs) is equally likely to be identified as the comparison group in the category or placement of interest. Following the research literature (Waitoller, Artiles, & Cheney, in press), we used 1.50 and 0.50 as the cutoff scores to determine over- and underrepresentation, respectively.

EL SPECIAL EDUCATION PLACEMENT TRENDS

Arizona

Table 7.1 displays the Arizona student enrollment demographics for the 1999–2006 academic years. The number of districts reporting EL data has increased over this period. Across all academic years, ELs were consistently less likely to be identified for the aggregated special education placement data. However, Table 7.1 also suggests that although the EL overall enrollment decreased from 2004 to 2005, EL special education enrollment increased. Note that English proficient student enrollment in special education remained unchanged during these years.

Our analysis also suggested that English learners' risk for special education placement increased between 1999 and 2006. However, the risk indicators did not reflect overrepresentation patterns.[1] Nevertheless, we observed different risk patterns when the placement evidence was examined by separate mild disability cate-

Table 7.1. Arizona enrollment, 1999–2006.

Year	Number of Districts Reporting EL Enrollment	Total Enrollment	Special Education Enrollment [a]	EL Enrollment [a]	ELs in Special Education [b]	English Proficient Students in Special Education [c]
1999	127	634,145	56,521 (8.91%)	109,747 (17.30%)	7,792 (7.10%)	48,729 (9.26%)
2000	122	710,732	61,583 (8.66%)	118,261 (16.63%)	8,928 (7.55%)	52,655 (8.89%)
2001	117	723,027	63,558 (8.80%)	130,298 (18.02%)	9,550 (7.33%)	54,008 (9.11%)
2002	160	843,187	75,290 (8.92%)	149,048 (17.67%)	13,359 (8.99%)	61,895 (8.92%)
2003	178	879,703	109,371 (12.44%)	160,853 (18.28%)	16,393 (10.19%)	92,978 (12.93%)
2004	181	897,349	121,203 (13.51%)	150,420 (16.76%)	17,367 (11.55%)	103,836 (13.90%)
2005	198	933,733	128,899 (13.80%)	133,294 (14.28%)	17,422 (13.51%)	111,477 (13.92%)
2006	210	962,629	134,466 (13.97%)	139,351 (14.48%)	18,288 (13.22%)	117,178 (14.23%)

[a] Percentages in parentheses are share of total enrollment.

[b] Percentages in parentheses are share of EL enrollment.

[c] Percentages in parentheses are share of special education enrollment.

Source: Compiled using data from the Arizona Department of Education.

gories. For instance, EL risks for learning disability and mild mental retardation identification were slightly lower before 2002, though risks increased substantially after 2003. The relative risk for ELs identified as LD relative to English proficient students achieved overrepresentation levels after 2005; specifically, ELs were 63% more likely than their counterparts to be identified in the LD category. English learners were not overrepresented in the mental retardation category between 1999 and 2006, though their placement risk approached overrepresentation levels in 2005 and 2006. ELs had lower identification risks in speech and language impairments and emotional/behavioral disorders, with a marked underrepresentation trend in the latter category.

At the district level, analysis of the overall special education identification was somewhat unstable from year to year. Although the overall special education placement risks did not reach overrepresentation levels between 1999 and 2006 (mean risk indices ranged between 0.95 and 1.43), we found that between 16% and 30% of all districts in Arizona had overrepresentation levels during this time period. This is an important insight, since it shows that aggregate risk indicators at the state level are not sensitive to the problematic EL special education placement practices at the district level.

The patterns observed in the evidence for EL overall special education placement were reflected in the learning disability (LD) category. We found that ELs' risk for LD identification fluctuated over time during these years, though the data reflected EL overrepresentation patterns after 2002. The percentage of districts with EL overrepresentation levels was substantial. In 1999, about one-fourth of all Arizona districts showed EL overrepresentation in the LD category. By 2006, this figure had doubled to about 50% of the state's districts showing overrepresentation levels.

Different EL placement risk patterns were found in the other high-incidence categories. EL risks for speech and language impairments (SLI) and mental retardation (MR) identification tended to be about the same or lower than those of their English proficient peers. At the same time, however, between 17% and 26% of the districts had EL overrepresentation in the MR category, and between 9% and 24% of districts exhibited EL overrepresentation in SLI.

English learners' risk for an emotional/behavioral disorder (E/BD) diagnosis was the lowest of all of the categories, reflecting substantial underrepresentation patterns compared to their English proficient counterparts during these years. It should be noted that, despite the absence of EL overrepresentation patterns at the state level, between 3% and 9% of the state's districts reached EL overrepresentation levels in the E/BD category.

California

The special education placement data from California indicate that the overall school enrollment increased from 3.8 million to 4.7 million students between 1998 and 2006 (see Table 7.2). The proportion of students identified in special education, however, remained relatively stable at around 10% of the total enrollment. Enrollment of ELs decreased slightly in 2000 from 26% to 24%; nevertheless, this enrollment was at about 27% between 2002 and 2006. It is interesting that the special education enrollment rate for English proficient learners is inversely related to the EL enrollment in these programs. More specifically, while English proficient student special education enrollment decreased from 11% in 1998 to 9% in 2006, EL special education enrollment almost doubled from 6% in 1998 to 11% in 2006 (see Table 7.2).

EL placement rates in high-incidence disability categories reflects a complex configuration. ELs had a lower special education placement risk than English proficient learners between 1998 and 2002. This pattern changed in 2004 when both groups of students had the same probability of being placed in these programs. The same pattern was observed in 2006.

English learners had either an equal or lower chance of being diagnosed with the MR label in 1998, 2000, and 2006. In 2002 and 2004, ELs were 59% and 30% more likely, respectively, to be placed in this category. ELs were less likely to be diagnosed as having LD in 1998 and 2000. After 2002, however, English learners were more likely to be identified as LD, though the risk index never reached overrepresentation levels. We found that ELs' risk level in 2006 approached a significant level of overrepresentation (34% more likely than their English profi-

Table 7.2. California enrollment, 1998–2006.

Year	Total Enrollment	Special Education Enrollment [a]	EL Enrollment [a]	ELs in Special Education [b]	English Proficient Students in Special Education [c]
1998	3,871,640	372,669 (9.63%)	1,001,612 (25.87%)	55,271 (5.52%)	317,398 (11.06%)
2000	5,936,245	592,539 (9.98%)	1,425,263 (24.01%)	108,597 (7.62%)	483,942 (10.73%)
2002	4,361,219	433,902 (9.95%)	1,165,579 (26.73%)	99,627 (8.55%)	334,275 (10.46%)
2004	4,741,071	465,684 (9.82%)	1,288,729 (27.18%)	132,752 (10.30%)	332,932 (9.64%)
2006	4,770,609	463,271 (9.71%)	1,301,515 (27.28%)	138,924 (10.67%)	324,347 (9.35%)

[a] Percentages in parentheses are share of total enrollment.

[b] Percentages in parentheses are share of EL enrollment.

[c] Percentages in parentheses are share of special education enrollment.

Source: Compiled using data from the U.S. Department of Education Office of Civil Rights.

cient peers). Although the risk indicators for E/BD placement reflected an upward trend, these data were at a significant underrepresentation level across all years.

Poverty and Placement Risk

School poverty level is important in assessing the risk that ELs have for placement in special education. Drawing from 2004 placement evidence, we observed that ELs were underrepresented in all high-incidence disability categories in Arizona's high-poverty schools (see Table 7.3). In contrast, ELs in low-poverty schools had a higher placement risk in overall special education placement (27% more likely, corresponding to a relative risk ratio of 1.27) and in the LD category (24% more likely). It is also important to note that EL placement risk *increased* as school poverty level *decreased* across the three disability categories. Although overrepresentation was observed only in the MR category in low-poverty schools

Table 7.3. State relative risk ratio by school poverty level and proportion of districts (LEAs) with EL overrepresentation, 2004.

	High Poverty		Low Poverty	
	State RRR	*LEAs with RRR > 1.5*	*State RRR*	*LEAs with RRR > 1.5*
Arizona				
All disabilities	0.52	13%	1.27	12%
Learning disability	0.77	17%	1.24	20%
Mental retardation	0.51	13%	1.51	24%
Emotional disorder	0.14	2%	0.24	7%
California				
All disabilities	0.73	7%	1.34	27%
Learning disability	1.30	26%	0.93	20%
Mental retardation	1.52	12%	1.14	9%
Emotional disorder	0.31	6%	0.22	3%

Notes: The relative risk ratio (RRR) is the number of students in a particular group (e.g., ELs in special education) as a proportion of all students in a designated group (e.g., special education). A ratio of 1 indicates equal representation, less than 1 is underrepresentation, and more than 1 is overrepresentation. Poverty levels were calculated by ranking districts by the percentage of students receiving free or reduced-price lunch. "High Poverty" refers to the upper third of all districts, while "Low Poverty" refers to the lower third.

Sources: Data compiled from the U.S. Department of Education Office of Civil Rights and the 2005 U.S. Department of Education, National Center for Education Statistics, Common Core of Data Public School Universe.

at the state level (51% more likely than English proficient students), a considerable proportion of low-poverty districts in Arizona had overrepresentation risk ratios (i.e., 20% to 24% of districts), most notably in the LD and MR categories.

California, however, showed a rather different pattern. EL overrepresentation was observed at the state level only in high-poverty schools in the MR category (52% more likely). In addition, the EL overall special education placement risk at the state level was higher in low-poverty schools. Nevertheless, English learners had a greater risk for identification in each high-incidence disability category in high-poverty schools. The analysis at the district level indicated that 20% to 26% of local education agencies had EL overrepresentation in the LD category.

In summary, our findings suggest that EL placement trends, similar to those for racial minority students, must be conducted at multiple levels to obtain a comprehensive understanding of the differences in placement risks. For instance, the special education placement risks at the state level often did not reflect the presence of disproportionate EL representation in special education at the district level. Descriptive enrollment figures for both states, however, indicated that increasing numbers of ELs were being placed in special education. In Arizona, English learner overrepresentation was recently observed in the LD category, whereas in California, MR overrepresentation was identified at some point in time. E/BD underrepresentation was consistent over time across the two states. District placement data in Arizona suggested that a considerable proportion of local educational agencies (LEAs) had EL overrepresentation. Finally, school poverty level matters, since it had complex associations (both positive and negative) with EL placement risk in these two states. Of course, it is important to keep in mind that *both* underrepresentation and overrepresentation can constitute serious inequities. In the case of the former, students may not be receiving critically important services; in the case of the latter, they may be unfairly labeled and inappropriately assigned to classes and programs that are more harmful than helpful to their academic growth.

EDUCATIONAL EXPERIENCES OF ELS
WITH HIGH-INCIDENCE DISABILITIES

The second goal of this study was to examine the educational experiences of ELs in terms of opportunity to learn. The educational performance of a particular group of students is often examined in the research literature without taking into account whether certain key factors might have shaped or mediated their performance. This is an important consideration since most low-income, ethnic minority, and linguistic minority students attend schools with students who have similar demographic profiles (Orfield & Lee, 2005). These schools tend to be underfunded, staffed by less qualified teachers, and characterized by less demanding curricula

(Anyon, 2005). There are very few studies, however, on how these structural conditions might affect ELs and ELs with special needs. Thus, we examined various indicators of opportunity to learn for ELs, including school suspensions, expulsions, placement in programs for gifted students, and segregation level of special education placements.

Table 7.4 presents the proportion of ELs who qualified for *but did not receive* language supports in these states between 2000 and 2004. Arizona reported a stable proportion across this time period (about 10%), whereas California's percentage increased from 10% to 14%. Sometimes students do not receive services because parents request that they be exempted, and other times schools simply do not offer appropriate services for these students. Moreover, although we found an upward trend for EL school suspensions over time in the two states, the overall pattern suggests that ELs had a lower risk of being suspended from school than their English proficient peers. With regard to school expulsions, the two states had disparate patterns. Arizona showed an unstable trend from one year to the next. In fact, ELs were almost twice as likely as their non-EL counterparts to be expelled from school in Arizona in 2000 (as evidenced by a relative risk ratio of 1.98, see Table 7.5) but had a lower expulsion risk in 2002 and 2006. The California data, in contrast, show lower expulsion risks for English learners, though there was a clear upward trend. Placement in gifted and talented programs can have a significantly positive impact on a student's educational career, providing access to many more opportunities. Unfortunately, ELs were consistently less likely to be placed in these programs over time in both states.

Federal policy stipulates that students with disabilities receive services in the least restrictive environment (LRE), which is determined on a case-by-case basis. The LRE offers a continuum of options that range from most integrated (e.g., general education classroom) to least integrated (e.g., residential facility). The majority (greater than 90%) of students with disabilities in the nation are educated in regular school buildings, and the vast majority of students with high-incidence disabilities are placed in general education classrooms. Students with E/BD are an exception, since national placement data indicate these students tend to be placed in more segregated programs. An important question, therefore, is whether ELs

Table 7.4. Percentage of ELs who qualified for but did not receive language supports, 2000–2004.

	2000	*2002*	*2004*
Arizona	9	10	9
California	10	10	14

Source: Data compiled from the U.S. Department of Education Office of Civil Rights.

Table 7.5. Relative risk of opportunities to learn for ELs compared to English proficient learners, 1998–2006.

	Suspension	*Expulsion*	*Gifted/Talented*
Arizona			
1998	0.57	0.81	0.13
2000	0.66	1.98	0.16
2002	0.80	0.46	0.16
2004	0.64	1.03	0.11
2006	0.86	0.26	0.11
California			
1998	0.58	0.00	0.14
2000	0.57	0.34	0.14
2002	0.62	0.38	0.13
2004	0.70	0.53	0.17
2006	0.71	0.57	0.11

Note: Numbers in the table represent relative risk ratios. This is the number of students in a particular group (e.g., ELs in special education) as a proportion of all students in a designated group (e.g., special education). A ratio of 1 indicates equal representation, less than 1 is underrepresentation, and more than 1 is overrepresentation.

Source: Data compiled from the U.S. Department of Education Office of Civil Rights.

are placed in more segregated special education programs than their English proficient peers *with the same disabilities.*

Only data from Arizona were available to address this question. In Arizona, students with disabilities receive services in public schools in (1) the general education classroom, (2) a resource room (removed from the general education classroom between 21% and 60% of the schoolday), or (3) a special education classroom (removed from the general education classroom over 60% of the schoolday).

Three trends are apparent in the Arizona data. First, ELs' chances to receive services in general education classrooms oscillated between having an equal chance to being underrepresented in general education classrooms between 1999 and 2006. Second, after 2002, ELs had a greater risk than their English proficient peers of receiving special education services in resource programs that removed them from the general education classroom for a significant portion of the school day. Third, ELs were consistently underrepresented in the most segregated placement options, which include separate school and residential facilities or hospitals.[2] This third finding merits further study, as such programs can represent a significant investment on the part of the state, one that is disproportionately not made for EL students.

In summary, the evidence on the educational experiences of ELs in Arizona and California reflects an ambiguous picture. ELs had fewer chances of being suspended, though the data suggest an upward trajectory. EL expulsion data, on the other hand, varied across states. Arizona had substantial shifts that included lower and greater risk patterns. Meanwhile, access to gifted-and-talented programs remained elusive. Finally, ELs tended to be overrepresented in programs that kept them outside of the general education classroom between 20% and 60% of the schoolday.

IMPLICATIONS OF THE FINDINGS

Proponents of restrictive language policies in California and Arizona promised that ELs would transition rapidly and efficiently to using English as well as increase their academic achievement. Embedded in these promises was the assumption that this group of students would be placed in general education classrooms and have the same opportunities to learn as their English-speaking peers. Our study examined some potential consequences of these promises. More specifically, we investigated whether ELs were increasingly placed in special education at a time when general education was given greater responsibility to educate these learners. Our findings raise concerns about the invisibility of EL disproportionality in special education, the complex role poverty seems to be playing in these placement patterns, and the opportunities to learn that are available to ELs.

Challenging the Invisibility of the Problem:
The Need for Multilevel Analysis

Examinations of disproportionate representation have generally been conducted at national and state levels rather than district levels and without examining patterns for population subgroups. Some analyses have focused on the risk of special education placement as a whole without looking at risk ratios for specific disability categories. Yet disproportionality patterns do not always show up at aggregate levels. In fact, the relative risk ratios in both states do not reflect disproportionate representation levels. Nevertheless, increasing numbers of ELs have been placed in special education since restrictive language policies were passed in California and Arizona. The placement analysis by disability category suggests that ELs tend to be overrepresented in LD in California and in MR in Arizona.

An important implication of our results points to the need to look below the surface of broad indicators. Although disproportionality levels were not problematic at the state level, we found a sizable proportion of school districts in Arizona in which ELs were overrepresented in the high-incidence categories. The case of LDs was the most acute in Arizona, since over half of the districts in the state had EL overrepresentation in 2005 and 2006. California had a similar pattern in the LD category, though the proportion of districts was lower. Are there differences in the ways these language policies are being implemented in the districts that showed overrepresentation levels? Or do they result from mainstream teachers being unable to adequately address these students' needs? Furthermore, the role of school poverty level was puzzling in explaining EL overrepresentation, considering the disparate patterns in these states. ELs in both states had a greater risk ratio in high-poverty schools when the data were examined across all disabilities. This pattern was observed again in Arizona's high-incidence categories. However, the California data in these categories showed the opposite pattern—that is, *lower* risk ratios in low-poverty schools. How are low- and high-poverty districts implementing these restrictive language policies in Arizona and California to produce distinct placement risk levels for ELs? What roles are parents, administrators, and district officials playing in these puzzling trends? These are important issues to examine in future research that could offer guidance for policymakers and education officials in making more cost-effective use of resources by targeting the districts and schools in which problems are identified.

California has a long history of litigation regarding testing bias with minority students, particularly in the MR category. It is possible this history mediated placement trends in California. Arizona, however, does not share this legacy. The anti-immigrant climate and policies have been polarizing in recent years in this state, and it is not clear whether placement trends are associated with the broader sociopolitical context.

Our findings suggest that important changes are occurring in the educational experiences of ELs at a time when restrictive language policies are being implemented in these states. For instance, the EL special education enrollment doubled in California, as did the EL enrollment in LD in Arizona. Are the general education systems in these states increasingly relying on special education as a way of coping with the unrealistic requirements of these restrictive language policies or the lack of preparation of teachers to meet these students' needs? It is urgent to examine these issues more closely in future studies.

Beyond Disability Placement Patterns:
Tracking Opportunity to Learn

Disproportionate representation has been studied historically through the analysis of placement patterns in special education programs or disability categories. Antecedents to these practices, such as opportunity-to-learn gaps, have been neglected. Although our analysis was constrained by the limited availability of relevant evidence, our findings suggest some worrisome trends. The trend in Arizona to remove ELs from their general education classrooms for special education services at increasingly greater rates than their English proficient peers is cause for concern. This finding is especially problematic when one considers that few special education teachers have received adequate preparation in working with ELs and are ill equipped to provide the linguistic support they need (Baca & Cervantes, 2004). In fact, Zehler and her colleagues (2003) found that most ELs in special education tend to be educated in English immersion models by teachers with little training in serving EL students. Disproportionate representation has long been a concern but takes on added importance for ELs who are placed in programs staffed by teachers who are not fully qualified to address their needs. In addition, a substantial proportion of ELs lost access to language supports in both states, and this trend is increasing in California. Restricted access to programs that can significantly advance a student's career (e.g., gifted-and-talented programs) is also a reason for concern. The question arises as to whether EL placement patterns are shaped to some extent by these opportunity gaps. It is highly unlikely that the vast achievement gaps between EL and non-EL students will be narrowed when opportunities to learn for this population are increasingly curtailed.

POLICY RECOMMENDATIONS

First, *monitor the extent to which particularly vulnerable groups are affected by restrictive language policies.* Currently, only aggregated scores for all English learners are tracked, but we have identified disproportionality at the school and district level. Policymakers and practitioners need this information to make more informed decisions regarding ELs' education and to protect students from inappropriate identification, which can have long-term negative consequences.

Second, *improve information infrastructures to gauge policy impact.* For example, we did not find databases that included specific information about ELs' language proficiency levels and disability status, and existing data sets do not provide sufficient information about the local practices that affect the opportunities to learn provided to ELs or that lead to their placement in special education. Greater articulation is needed across institutions that specialize in language minority students, students with special needs, and educational equity in order to develop a comprehensive system of data collection that will allow researchers and policymakers to answer these urgent questions.

Finally, we have used relative risk ratios to analyze disproportionality of special education placement because we argue that simply looking at placement data can obscure inequities among groups. However, *there is a need to refine guidelines to measure and track the problem.* There is no agreement in the field about what level of disproportionality constitutes a problem. Until we reach consensus on the nature and severity of reduced opportunities to learn, disproportionate placement in special education, and disproportionate restrictiveness of services, it is unlikely we will make significant progress in addressing these concerns.

NOTES

This is a revised version of a paper presented at the Restrictive Language Policies UCLA Roundtable, April 11, 2008. The first author acknowledges the support of the Center for Advanced Study in the Behavioral Sciences at Stanford University and the National Center for Culturally Responsive Educational Systems (NCCRESt) under grant #H326E020003 awarded by the U.S. Department of Education, Office of Special Education Programs. Endorsement of the U.S. Department of Education of the ideas expressed in this special issue should not be inferred.

1. Tables showing actual risk ratio data can be found at The Civil Rights Project website (www.civilrightsproject.ucla.edu).

2. Tables showing actual incidence levels can be found at The Civil Rights Project website (www.civilrightsproject.ucla.edu).

REFERENCES

Anyon, J. (2005). *Radical possibilities: Public policy, urban education, and a new social movement.* New York: Routledge.

Artiles, A. J., Aguirre-Muñoz, Z., & Abedi, J. (1998). Predicting placement in learning disabilities programs: Do predictors vary by ethnic group? *Exceptional Children, 64*, 543–559.

Artiles, A. J., & Rueda, R. (2002). General guidelines for monitoring minority over-representation in special education. *CASE Newsletter, 43*(5), 5–6.

Artiles, A. J., Rueda, R., Salazar, J. J., & Higareda, I. (2005). Within-group diversity in minority disproportionate representation: English language learners in urban school districts. *Exceptional Children, 71*, 283–300.

Artiles, A. J., Sullivan, A., Waitoller, F., & Neal, R. (in press). Latinos in special education: Equity issues at the intersection of language, culture, and ability differences. In E. Murillo (Ed.), *Handbook of Latinos in education.* Mahwah, NJ: Erlbaum.

Baca, L., & Cervantes, H. (2004). *The bilingual special education interface.* Columbus, OH: Merrill.

Combs, M. C., Evans, C., Fletcher, T., Parra, E., & Jiménez, A. (2005). Bilingualism for the children: Implementing a dual-language program in an English-only state. *Educational Policy, 19*, 701–728.

Dixon, C., Green, J., Yeager, B., Baker, D., & Fránquiz, M. (2000). "I used to know that": What happens when reform gets through the classroom door. *Bilingual Research Journal, 24*(1), 1–14.

Donovan, M. S., & Cross, C. T. (Eds.). (2002). *Minority students in special and gifted education.* Washington, DC: National Academies Press.

Fierros, E., & Conroy, J. (2002). Double jeopardy: An exploration of restrictiveness and race in special education. In D. Losen & G. Orfield (Eds.), *Racial inequity in special education* (pp. 39–70). Cambridge, MA: Harvard University Press.

Gutiérrez, K. D., Baquedano-López, P., & Asato, J. (2000). "English for the children":

The new literacy of the old world order, language policy and educational reform. *Bilingual Research Journal, 24*(1&2), 87–112.

Harry, B., & Klingner, J. (2006). *Why are so many minority students in special education? Understanding race & disability in schools.* New York: Teachers College Press.

Individuals with Disabilities Education Improvement Act of 2004. Public Law 108-446. Washington, DC: United States Congress.

McNeil, L. M., Coppola, E., Radigan, J., & Vasquez Heilig, J. (2008). Avoidable losses: High-stakes accountability and the dropout crisis. *Education Policy Analysis Archives, 16*(3). Retrieved February 2, 2009, from http://epaa.asu.edu/epaa/v16n3/

Minow, M. (1990). *Making all the difference: Inclusion, exclusion, and American law.* Ithaca, NY: Cornell University Press.

Mueller, T. G., Singer, G. H. S., & Grace, E. J. (2004). The Individuals with Disabilities Education Act and California's Proposition 227: Implications for English language learners with special needs. *Bilingual Research Journal, 28*(2), 231–251.

Nichols, S. L., & Berliner, D. C. (2007). *Collateral damage: How high-stakes testing corrupts America's schools.* Cambridge, MA: Harvard Education Press.

Olson, K. (2007). Lost opportunities to learn: The effects of education policy on primary language instruction for English learners. *Linguistics and Education, 18,* 121–141.

Orfield, G., & Lee, C. (2005). Segregation 50 years after *Brown*: A metropolitan challenge. In L. Weis & M. Fine (Eds.), *Beyond silenced voices* (pp. 3–20). Albany: State University of New York Press.

Parrish, T. B., Pérez, M., Merickel, A., & Linquanti, R. (2006). *Effects of the implementation of Proposition 227 on the education of English language learners, K–12. Findings from a 5-year evaluation: Final report.* San Francisco: American Institutes of Research/WestEd.

Stritikus, T. T., & García, E. (2005). Revisiting the bilingual debate from the perspectives of parents: Policy, practice, and matches or mismatches. *Educational Policy, 19*(5), 729–744.

U.S. Department of Education. (2006). *26th Annual Report to Congress on the Implementation of the Individuals with Disabilities Education Act.* Washington, DC: Author.

U.S. Department of Education. (2008). *Common core data.* Washington, DC: U.S. Department of Education, National Center for Education Statistics.

Waitoller, F., Artiles, A. J., & Cheney, D. (in press). The miner's canary: A review of overrepresentation research and explanations. *Journal of Special Education.*

Zehler, A. M., Fleischman, H. L., Hopstock, P. J., Stephenson, T. G., Pendzick, M. L., & Sapru, S. (2003). *Descriptive study of services to LEP students and LEP students with disabilities: Policy report—Summary of findings related to LEP and SPED-LEP student.* Washington, DC: Development Associates.

Undermining Teacher Competencies:
Another Look at the Impact
of Restrictive Language Policies

Ester J. de Jong, M. Beatriz Arias, and María Teresa Sánchez

IN RAPID PROGRESSION, voters passed legislation to dismantle bilingual education in California (Proposition 227), Arizona (Proposition 203), and Massachusetts (Question 2), dramatically affecting instructional practices for English learners
(ELs). To date, research that examines the impact of these policies has focused
primarily on programmatic changes within schools and districts or on changes in
student academic achievement and English language proficiency, thus overshad-
owing other educational areas that may be affected.

This chapter shifts the current research focus by examining the impact of
restrictive language policies on teachers and teacher educators. After a brief discussion of how *impact* has become defined in the aftermath of the three propositions, the chapter incorporates data from Arizona and Massachusetts to show that
both the preparation of teachers and their daily practices have been affected by
these policies. We do not intend to present parallel cases. Rather, we use each case
to separately present one particular area of impact that warrants closer attention,
namely, the limits that have been set on the development of teacher expertise, illustrated by the Arizona case, and the use of bilingual expertise for providing access
to optimal learning environments, demonstrated by the Massachusetts case. We
conclude with policy recommendations for teacher preparation and professional
development.

RESTRICTIVE LANGUAGE POLICIES AND "SCOPE OF IMPACT"

The majority of studies on the impact of restrictive language policies have focused on programmatic issues (i.e., instructional-model choices made as a result of these policies) (Combs, Evans, Fletcher, Parra, & Jiménez, 2005; de Jong, Gort, & Cobb, 2005; García & Curry-Rodriguez, 2000) or changes in English language development and academic achievement as measured by program exit rates or standardized achievement test scores (e.g., Grissom, 2004; Hill, 2004; Mahoney, Thompson, & MacSwan, 2004; Parrish, Perez, Merickel, & Linquanti, 2006; Thompson, DiCerbo, Mahoney, & MacSwan, 2002; Wright & Choi, 2006). Other areas that are affected by the three propositions, such as teachers and communities, have largely remained invisible. These areas appear to fall outside of the policies' prevailing definition of the problem (lack of language proficiency on the part of ELs) and the solution (Structured English Immersion programs) and have not been an integral part of the analysis of the policies' impact.

Policy impact is a multidimensional and distributed event (e.g., Gándara, Rumberger, Maxwell-Jolly, & Callahan, 2003; Sloan, 2006). Policy changes can have an effect at many different levels (e.g., state, district, school, and classroom) (Ricento & Hornberger, 1996). Individuals negotiate and implement policies differently depending on their state or district context, the professional communities they are a part of, and even their personal experiences (de Jong, 2008; Stritikus, 2003; Varghese & Stritikus, 2005). Given the multifaceted nature of policy processes, we argue that the impact of restrictive language policies needs to be considered beyond the current program-model and language-outcome discussion.

Research shows that state educational policies can frame the socialization of new teachers, especially when these policies prescribe instructional practice (Achinstein, Ogawa, & Speiglman, 2004), and that state policies that specify instructional practices can have an especially potent impact on teacher practice (Ogawa, Sandholtz, Martinez-Flores, & Scribner, 2003). Similarly, studies of educational reform have emphasized the central role of teachers in policy implementation and negotiation at the local level (Cohen & Ball, 1990; Ricento & Hornberger, 1996). However, significantly fewer studies have included teachers' or other stakeholders' views on the impact of policies on classroom practices (although see de Jong, 2008; Sánchez, 2006; Stritikus, 2003; and "Highlighting Success in Bilingual Education," 2002). Ultimately, teachers are the core of policy implementation because as they "interpret and modify received policies, they are, in fact, primary language policymakers" (Evans & Hornberger, 2005, p. 99). Since teachers' knowledge and skill base will affect their decisions about curriculum and instructional approaches, it is worth considering how restrictive language policies have affected both the development of teacher expertise as well as its application in the classroom.

THE CASE STUDIES

The Arizona case examines the impact of a restrictive language policy on teacher preparation through, first, a content analysis of the course requirements for the Structured English Immersion (SEI) endorsement, the Bilingual Education (BLE) endorsement, and the English as a Second Language (ESL) endorsement and, second, through an analysis of survey data collected from 71 undergraduates (pre-service teachers) enrolled in a teacher preparation program, 18 novice teachers (first- or second-year teachers), and 15 experienced teachers (4 or more years of teaching). The survey examined the participants' perspectives on their ability to teach ELs and how their SEI coursework helped them work effectively with ELs.

In the Massachusetts case study, the focus is on practicing teachers' views on the impact of a restrictive language policy on their practice. Data were collected through semistructured interviews with 41 teachers working in three large or medium-sized school districts in the second or third year of Question 2 implementation (for details, see de Jong, 2008; Sánchez, 2006).

RESTRICTIVE LANGUAGE POLICY AND TEACHER PREPARATION: ARIZONA'S PROP 203

Arizona's teaching force parallels the demographic profile of current teachers and teachers entering the education field nationally: female, White, and English monolingual (Zumwalt & Craig, 2005). According to the National Center for Education Statistics in 2006, there were approximately 52,000 public or charter Arizona schoolteachers in that year (Sable & Garofano, 2007). The most recent teacher ethnicity data (Molnar & Allen, 2005) indicates that 85% of Arizona teachers are White, with the other 15% distributed among Hispanic (10%), Native American (2%), African American (2%) and Pacific Islander or Asian (2%) (percentages total over 100 due to rounding).

This teacher demographic composition is in stark contrast with student demographics. Arizona's public school enrollment in 2006 was 47% White, 39% Hispanic, 6% Native American, 5% African American, and 2.5% Pacific Islander or Asian (rounded) (Sable & Garofano, 2007). Fourteen percent of Arizona's enrollment was EL students (Arizona Department of Education [ADE], 2007). ELs are represented at every school level and in every Arizona county, and the probability is very high that teachers will encounter ELs in their teaching career. Clearly, teachers with little exposure to or experience with ELs need preparation in the best practices used to instruct these students. Yet the Arizona Department of Education reported that over 42% of current teachers of EL students do not hold the required endorsements. The foregoing facts have raised two concerns regarding teacher preparation and supply in Arizona, namely, the mismatch between student and teacher ethnicity and the clear need for more teachers prepared to teach ELs.

Research on teacher preparation for ELs finds that in order to be successful, in addition to the broad skills and competencies necessary for all teachers, teachers of ELs must be able to (1) draw on established principles of second-language learning (Harper & de Jong, 2004), (2) understand the variations among the language and educational backgrounds and experiences of EL students (Lucas & Grinberg, 2008), (3) have an awareness of the sociopolitical dimensions of language use and language education (Lucas & Grinberg, 2008), and (4) understand English learners and their families, especially the impact of language and culture on communities living in poverty (Merino, 2007). In addition, teachers in preparation need time to practice recently learned strategies with ELs. It is not enough to just inform teachers of the recommended competencies that are beneficial to use with English learners; teacher educators need to provide opportunities for prospective teachers to learn about teaching ELs in authentic learning environments with these students. Opportunities to practice balancing instructional time in the classroom, noting the need for more time to teach ELs due to their academic and language variability, are essential. Finally, research on teacher preparation also emphasizes that most teachers report that they have not received this type of preparation (Gándara, Maxwell-Jolly, & Driscoll, 2005).

Our analysis of Arizona's teacher preparation shows that post–Proposition 203, teacher preparation for ELs has been significantly reduced both quantitatively and qualitatively. The content of this curriculum is not reflective of the competencies identified in the research. The new, universally mandated teacher endorsement restricts access to a broad range of competencies necessary to adequately instruct ELs and focuses on teaching ELs merely as an instructional strategy under SEI.

REQUIREMENTS FOR HIGHLY QUALIFIED
TEACHERS AFTER PROPOSITION 203

Most teachers in Arizona are prepared through the accredited college "pipeline," with the three state-supported universities accounting for the largest segment of teacher preparation. Approximately 3,000 teachers are newly certified every year, and over 2,200 of these graduate from state universities (Morrison Institute for Public Policy, 2003). Prior to 2006, specialist ESL and BLE teachers were required to obtain an ESL or BLE endorsement, either at the undergraduate (27 credits) or graduate (24 credits) level. There were no requirements for general education teacher candidates to complete coursework related specifically to instructing ELs.

In the wake of Proposition 203, policy changes were made affecting the preparation of all teachers in the state. In an effort to prepare instructional personnel for the anticipated mainstreaming of English learners into English-only classrooms, new guidelines for the preparation of teachers of ELs post–Proposition 203 were issued in 2006 by Board Rule (R7-2-613), and a new SEI endorsement was mandated for every teacher, supervisor, principal, career and technical educator, and superintendent in Arizona. The rule also established the criteria and content required to obtain the mandated endorsement. With respect to teacher training, ADE mandated the addition of 6 credit hours to the teacher preparation curriculum, requiring an SEI endorsement for all pre-service teachers after 2006. Under the rule, all teacher candidates must have an SEI endorsement in order to receive their teaching certification and begin working in schools. Teacher preparation programs are currently embedding the required SEI courses into their existing programs to ensure that when pre-service teachers graduate, they have the requisite hours mandated to obtain their SEI endorsement (ADE, 2007).

Table 8.1 presents the total hours and credits required for the SEI endorsement as well as for the ESL/BLE endorsements. While the ADE requires that all teachers complete SEI endorsement courses, it left intact the ESL/BLE endorsements at the undergraduate and graduate level. This meant that some teachers-in-preparation can still opt to participate in programs leading to state-approved ESL/BLE endorsements, even though very few dual-language or bilingual programs remain. The first column identifies the components and hours required for the SEI endorsement. A total of 6 credit hours or 90 total seat hours is required for the SEI endorsement. In contrast, the components and credit hours required for the ESL/BLE endorsements far exceed those required for SEI, at 27 and 24 credit hours at the undergraduate and graduate levels, respectively.

Clearly, the SEI endorsement is not as comprehensive or in-depth as the ESL/BLE endorsement. One impact of Proposition 203 on teacher preparation is the watering down of the curricular requirements to become a highly qualified teacher for ELs. Whereas the ESL/BLE endorsements require 360 to 405 total hours of preparation, it is assumed that the next generation of teachers of ELs, who now must complete only an SEI endorsement to be deemed qualified to work with these students, need only 90 hours of specialized coursework. While candidates and practicing teachers still have the option of obtaining the full ESL/BLE endorsement, there is little incentive to do so, as both teachers with ESL/BLE and teachers with SEI endorsements are considered equally qualified to teach ELs.

In fact, although most studies of the impact of restrictive language policies find that principals are still anxious to have bilingual teachers on their staffs to mediate the instructional environment, communicate with parents and community, and assess the understanding of EL students, such policies tend to reduce the numbers of bilingual teachers available in the schools, thus creating more chal-

Table 8.1. A comparison of Arizona's Structured English Immersion (SEI) and Bilingual/English as a Second Language (BLE/ESL).

SEI Endorsement	BLE/ESL Endorsement (undergraduate)	BLE/ESL Endorsement (graduate)
SEI foundations 4 hours	Foundations of instruction for ELs 3 credits (45 hours)	Foundations of instruction for ELs 3 credits (45 hours)
		Linguistics/sociolinguistics 3 credits (45 hours)
SEI strategies 49 hours	Language arts methods in BLE/ESL settings 3 credits (45 hours)	BLE or ESL methods 3 credits (45 hours)
	SEI for linguistically diverse students 3 credits (45 hours)	ESL in BLE settings (for BLE only)/Teaching reading and writing to ELs (for ESL only) 3 credits (45 hours)
	Teaching content: Math, science, and social studies methods in BLE/ESL settings 9 credits (135 hours)	
Assessment & data analysis/proficiency standards 9 hours & 4 hours		Assessment 3 credits (45 hours)
Parent/home/school 3 hours	School community/family culture/parental involvement 3 credits (45 hours)	School community/family culture/parental involvement 3 credits (45 hours)
Flexible assignment 21 hours	Practicum	Practicum: 2 years in BLE/ESL classroom
	Second-language proficiency for BLE/second language study for ESL 6 credits (90 hours)	Second-language proficiency for BLE/second language study for ESL 6 credits (90 hours)
Total: 90 hours (6 credits)	Total: 405 hours (27 credits)	Total: 360 hours (24 credits)

lenges for the schools that serve these students. Data from the ADE Teacher Certification Unit in 2009 show a fairly dramatic decline (16%) of bilingual teachers in the state's classrooms since the introduction of the SEI endorsement requirement in 2006. With a large increase in the number of EL students, this decline places more pressure on the existing bilingual teachers, who are looked to for assistance from their monolingual colleagues. This finding was also evident in California (see, e.g., Maxwell-Jolly, 2000). Thus, as teachers and schools have to meet the needs of increasing numbers of students, they have fewer and fewer resources to address these challenges.

DEPTH AND BREADTH OF TEACHER PREPARATION

Not only are fewer hours allocated to preparing teachers to be highly qualified to teach ELs, but the content of that preparation is also strictly defined by the Arizona Department of Education. Unlike other teacher preparation courses, developed by university faculty, the SEI endorsement courses must meet content criteria established by the ADE and the course syllabi must be submitted to and approved by the ADE. The ADE identified six SEI objectives in its curricular framework: (1) EL standards, (2) data analysis and application, (3) formal and informal assessments, (4) SEI foundations, (5) SEI strategies, and (6) parent/home/school scaffolding. Each objective is allocated a specific minimal number of hours, and every syllabus submitted to the ADE for approval must reflect this time allocation. Thus, the Arizona Department of Education has usurped the authority of faculty to determine what and how to teach in the preparation of teachers for English learners. This requirement is especially notable in that there was no demonstration that the ADE had skills that were superior to those of university faculty in this area.

As Table 8.1 shows, over half of the SEI curriculum is allocated to a review of English-only strategies to be used with ELs. Only a minimal amount of the endorsement focuses on theoretical foundations, reflection on how acquisition of a second language (L2) differs from acquisition of native language (L1), or understanding of the sociopsychological aspects of second-language learning. In contrast, for the ESL/BLE endorsement, teachers-in-preparation are instructed in SEI for linguistically diverse students (see Table 8.1) as well as in foundations of instruction for ELs, methods in each of the content areas (literacy, math, science, and social students), and social foundations in the parental and community aspects of instructing ELs. At the undergraduate level, the entire ESL/BLE endorsement entails at least 21 credit hours in the above-mentioned areas, which includes a classroom practicum. At the graduate level, the ESL/BLE endorsement requires at least 18 credit hours in the foundations of EL instruction, ESL/BLE strategies, linguistics, assessment, and school/community issues in EL settings. Additionally, at the graduate level, a practicum of at least 2 years in an ESL/BLE classroom in addition to proficiency in a second language or 6 credit hours of language courses are required for the ESL/BLE endorsement.

Data from the survey administered to novice and experienced teachers supported the finding that teachers participating only in SEI preparation were limited in their understanding of the role of the first language in the classroom. Most of the novice teachers indicated that they had limited knowledge of how to integrate students' primary language in the classroom. Novice teachers also indicated limited knowledge of how language proficiency interacts with learning. These findings support our concern that a narrow teacher preparation curriculum such as that required by SEI results in a narrowing of teacher understanding in critical areas for ELs, such as language proficiency and the role of primary language.

Notwithstanding the type of program students are in, English-only or bilingual, teachers must understand how to address the needs of students who are functioning primarily in their first language. Understanding of how second-language learning occurs is a critical aspect of meeting the students' needs.

The SEI endorsement is consistent with the state's English-only philosophy, paying limited attention to knowledge of alternative second-language learning methods and to sociocultural components of second-language acquisition that have been considered essential to the ESL/BLE endorsement. The depth of the coursework is thus limited and deprives teachers-in-preparation of a comprehensive awareness of other successful instructional approaches. The SEI endorsement is also dominated by a strategies-based approach to instruction of ELs. As Table 8.1 illustrates, the majority of hours are spent on strategy development. While these strategies are certainly an important part of teachers' toolkit, they are nonetheless only tools, and a skilled craftsperson uses his or her broader knowledge to determine when and how to use them. Relying so heavily on strategy instruction is akin to teaching a carpenter to saw but not providing the knowledge necessary to determine when to use a saw and when to use an awl.

A complicating factor in the preparation of teachers of ELs in Arizona has been the imposition of the 4-hour English language development instructional block, as required by Arizona Revised Statutes 15-756.01 (see Chapter 2 of this volume for an overview and Chapter 9 of this volume for a critique of the policy). The curriculum required in the 4-hour block, emphasizing structures of the English language, grammar, and vocabulary, does not match the curriculum required for the SEI endorsement; there is no training related to the English Language Development (ELD) block in the SEI curriculum. Thus, even if teachers are "prepared" to teach ELs with an SEI endorsement, they have not been prepared to work with ELs in a segregated 4-hour instructional block. The confounding effects of the ELD requirement have yet to be explored.

RESTRICTIVE LANGUAGE POLICY AND TEACHER COMPETENCY: MASSACHUSETTS'S QUESTION 2

In Arizona, the impact of the restrictive language policy on how teachers of ELs are expected to be prepared has become a highly visible and contested area. In Massachusetts, the state's restrictive language policy placed severe restrictions on the expertise of practicing teachers. Massachusetts was the first state in the nation to mandate transitional bilingual education (TBE) programs to meet the needs of ELs in 1971. Almost 40 years later, it became the third state to pass a law restricting the use of primary-language instruction for ELs.

The amended law (General Laws of Massachusetts, Chapter 71A, 2003), most often referred to as Question 2, is similar in language and proposed policies to

Propositions 227 and 203; however, two-way immersion (TWI) programs are unaffected by the law (Vaishnav, 2003). The waiver process to implement bilingual programs other than TWI in Massachusetts is also stricter, particularly for ELs under the age of 10. For these ELs, districts must provide a 250-word written rationale for placing the child in a bilingual program, which cannot be related to the child's English proficiency, and parents must annually renew their child's enrollment in a bilingual program. Additionally, prior to enrollment in a bilingual classroom, ELs must be temporarily placed in an English-only classroom for at least 30 days, thus losing instructional time when the student is then moved to another instructional setting.

Like Propositions 227 and 203, Question 2 emphasizes SEI instruction. The law states that "teachers may use a minimal amount of the child's native language when necessary" but that all instructional materials to teach content or literacy must be in English (Chapter 71A: Section 2). Moreover, as in the other states, the law recommends, though does not mandate, that districts place students from different language backgrounds together in the same classroom (Chapter 71A: Section 4). (See Chapter 5, this volume, for an extensive overview of implementation of Question 2 in Massachusetts.) The latter would discourage the use of languages other than English by students and teachers and increase reliance on English as a lingua franca among different non-English speakers. The recommendation to group students across languages by English proficiency privileges English language development over content learning. In fact, SEI is described as a "language acquisition approach" through English-medium instruction. Additionally, the wider the age span in a multilingual classroom, the more challenging it is for teachers to adhere to grade-level curriculum expectations.

Question 2 took effect in schoolyear 2003–2004. Prior to Question 2, 60% of the state's ELs were in TBE, 25% were receiving ESL services, and 15% were in mainstream classrooms without any support ("Bilingual by the Numbers," 2002). After the passage of Question 2, 69.3% were enrolled in SEI programs, 2.3% were enrolled in TWI programs, and 4.7% were enrolled in other types of bilingual education programs. Of the 23.8% of ELs enrolled in mainstream classrooms, 15.8% were in school districts that did not offer any program for ELs, while 8% were enrolled in mainstream classes because the parents had opted out of an EL program (Massachusetts Department of Education, 2004).

The English-only provisions laid out in Question 2 created both ideological (insistence on monolingual practices) and structural (organization of the SEI classroom) requirements that made it difficult for teachers to use strategies to effectively scaffold learning for their ELs (see also Gort, de Jong, & Cobb, 2008). Our investigation of the experiences of 41 SEI teachers in three districts, most of whom were former bilingual education teachers, yielded the finding that most felt ineffective at providing access to high-quality literacy and content instruction for beginning ELs under the new English-only regime. Teachers also struggled to negotiate multiple proficiency levels within their classrooms.

Lost Learning Opportunities for Beginning ELs

Decisions about when to use students' primary language, how much to use it, and for what purposes proved challenging for several of the SEI teachers we interviewed. The ambiguity of the law resulted in the implementation of widely varying practices by teachers. Several teachers we interviewed mentioned that they believed they could only use the students' primary language orally. Others mentioned that they allowed students to read and/or write in their primary language in the classroom, although these teachers often emphasized that they did not teach students to read in the primary language, presumably due to the strict language of the policy mandate. One teacher told us that if her students felt like reading in Spanish, "I allowed them. If this goes against Question 2, I don't know. But I have the books in the library. But I'm not teaching them in Spanish." Many teachers second-guessed themselves after the passage of Question 2 when it came to using students' primary language in their instruction, even though they may have been prepared in their training to do so. Similar to the Massachusetts case, researchers studying teachers' response to the passage of California's Proposition 227 also encountered differences in teachers' interpretations of the use of students' native language (Alamillo & Viramontes, 2000; Paredes, 2000; Stritikus & García, 2000).

Comparing the use of the primary language in their former bilingual classrooms to their current SEI placements, SEI teachers reported a noticeable difference in quality of instruction for literacy development. One teacher reported that her students often asked her to reread a book in Spanish "because they see that the book is interesting but they don't understand it in English." On the few occasions that one SEI kindergarten teacher used Spanish, she saw that her students' responses were different when she read a book in Spanish from when she read it in English. When she read the English version of "The Gingerbread Man," students were quiet and asked some vocabulary questions. When she read it in Spanish, students were excited and participated more; they asked questions about the story and shared experiences. After that episode, the teacher was very concerned that she could not use more Spanish in her class: "I then realized—Wow! Am I restricting their imagination and their mental development when I read them the stories in English?"

The teachers particularly commented on the impact of the limited use of students' primary language for newcomers with limited primary-language literacy skills and beginning ELs. Most SEI teachers felt that SEI with use of the primary language was more appropriate for the intermediate and advanced ELs, particularly those with strong primary-language literacy skills. Although their attitudes toward implementing SEI for these students were more positive, SEI teachers expressed concerns about the affective consequences for these students, such as self-concept, attitudes toward school, and identity. They were also concerned about their inability to cover the same amount of content as a mainstream classroom teacher (see also de Jong, 2008; Sánchez, 2006).

However, SEI classrooms do not serve only intermediate/advanced students. They also enroll newcomers with little or no English whose schooling has been interrupted and newcomers who were literate in their primary language but who have some or no English proficiency. SEI teachers expressed strong reservations regarding their ability to meet these students' literacy and content needs without systematically using the students' primary language. The SEI teachers found teaching English letter–sound correspondence and vocabulary to beginning-level ELs very difficult, stressful, and frustrating: "When I show [Spanish-speaking students] a picture of a 'shoe' and their mind is thinking 'zapato' and I'm saying, 'this is a /sh/,' they are—'What are you talking about?' . . . I found that ridiculous." One teacher who used to teach in the Haitian-Creole/English TBE program also felt this disparity with the SEI program when working with students with low-level literacy skills:

> I truly believe, based on what I [have] observed [that] if the teacher has the option of using both languages . . . Haitian children would advance much faster. Because you see it! You see that they are not able to keep up a lot of the times with the English. . . . You see that they need that native-language support.

These examples illustrate how restricting teachers from using their bilingual competence as well as their knowledge of bilingualism and the role of primary language in literacy, concept, and social development created less than an optimal learning environment for ELs, particularly those at the beginning levels of English acquisition and those with limited primary-language literacy skills. Teachers felt largely prohibited from creating more bilingual environments in their SEI classrooms because the law defines SEI as an English-only approach to teaching ELs. The need to constantly negotiate the use of students' primary language according to what the law prescribed rather than based on students' needs, or the reality of their level of language competence, placed significant stress on the teachers and thus impacted their practices.

The law clearly sets explicit limits on the use of the primary language, even though there is room for negotiation and interpretation due to the phrases "minimal amount" and "when necessary." The SEI teachers in this study constantly weighed their decision to use the students' primary language against the restrictive language of the law. Even when their pedagogical expertise and direct experience told them that the use of the primary language would be more effective, their choice was mediated through the monolingual framework of the law. There was clear tension between the teachers' pedagogical understandings about the way the primary language can be used purposefully and strategically to support English language development (and as underpinned by research—see Brisk, 2006; Gersten & Baker, 2000; Lucas & Katz, 1994) and the explicit limits on primary-language use in the SEI context as set by the law.

Negotiating Multiple Proficiency Levels

In combination with the restrictions of the use of primary language, the SEI teachers also felt less efficacious due to the organization of EL programs. Teachers had to negotiate a wide range of proficiency levels and primary-language literacy levels and, given the law's mandate, had to accomplish this without capitalizing on primary-language resources.

The law's 30-day requirement that all ELs first be placed in an English-only environment (with more fluent students) directly affected beginning ELs' access to opportunities for learning appropriate to their grade level. Bilingual program teachers who were forced to spend the first 30 days teaching in English indicated that they could provide merely low-level, basic English skills instruction and therefore were falling behind from the first day of school. SEI teachers who received beginning ELs temporarily in their classroom agreed that valuable instructional time that could have been spent providing access to the grade-level content was now reduced to a waiting period "because really nothing is happening for that month, although we try the best we can when we can. . . . It's a waste of time." Many teachers felt frustrated at being put in a situation that prevented them from being effective teachers without any ability to alter it.

Even without the 30-day rule, the SEI teachers faced a wide range of proficiency levels among students in their classrooms due to grouping policies within the SEI model. Each of the districts attempted to group students by grade level, resulting in classrooms with multiple English proficiency levels. Under these conditions, combined with lack of primary-language access, teachers experienced several challenges.

First, teachers mentioned that maintaining grade-level expectations for all students, including access to an appropriate level of texts, was extraordinarily challenging, if not impossible. This learning environment particularly disadvantaged ELs at beginning stages of English language acquisition and those with limited primary-language literacy. For instance, when one SEI kindergarten teacher visited her colleagues' mainstream kindergarten classrooms, she observed a big difference in the level of learning that was occurring in those classrooms when compared with her own classroom. She noticed that in kindergarten mainstream classrooms, "the students are getting more enriched because the stories are more deep, more interesting. The [SEI curriculum] stories are simpler; they are for vocabulary development. The mainstream ones are for students to think."

Second, teachers recounted that student participation and access to the content were negatively affected. The SEI teacher mentioned above also found that in mainstream classrooms there were fewer interruptions while the teachers were reading aloud and that mainstream children asked questions about the storyline rather than solely about vocabulary. In her SEI classroom, the opposite happened, as SEI students constantly interrupted her because they did not understand the vocabulary. With so many interruptions, the students lost the storyline.

Finally, teachers had to constantly negotiate ways to cover the grade-level curriculum when students had different English proficiency levels, while using minimum amounts of native-language instruction. They felt that their ability to create effective grade-level linguistic and content learning was undermined. Teachers were uncomfortable because they felt that they were lowering the students' academic expectations. Their experiences highlight the danger that SEI may in fact transform into a low-level track for ELs within schools. Research on school tracking has shown the pervasive consequences of school practices and programs that stimulate the lowering of academic expectations, particularly in students from minority groups and of lower socioeconomic status (Oakes, 2005). Given that research to date has shown that, far from being a 1-year program, SEI programs enroll ELs for multiple years (Grissom, 2004), this finding raises concern regarding long-term achievement patterns for ELs.

DISCUSSION

The impact of restrictive language policies is not limited to changes in delivery models or standardized test scores. We have used the contexts of Arizona and Massachusetts to illustrate the importance of also considering how teacher education and practicing classroom teachers are affected by restrictive language policies. Almost insidiously, the policies do not specifically address teacher qualifications beyond the requirements that teachers must be fluent in English. Yet, in response to the implementation of the new laws and the subsequent increased placement of many ELs in mainstream classrooms (and further reinforced by stringent accountability for ELs under federal law), teacher preparation and the role of bilingual expertise for ELs have been affected.

The Next Generation of Teachers of English Learners

While perhaps seen as a "secondary" effect that cannot be measured by standardized tests of student achievement, the impact of these policies on teachers and their expertise has significant implications for the current and next generation of students taught by bilingual and monolingual teachers. As our data show, the current system not only fails to prepare future teachers adequately but also limits practicing teachers in their ability to provide effective learning environments for their students.

The Arizona case shows the importance of paying attention to the first area of impact, (pre-service) teacher preparation. Teacher preparation programs affect not only the skills that teachers develop but also the lenses that future teachers will use to educate ELs. In Arizona, teachers of ELs are required to complete only 90 hours of a prescribed curriculum that emphasizes "strategies" over the theoretical foundations that are necessary to inform their teaching practice. As a result, the teaching of ELs requires that teachers reduce the tools in their toolkit and focus on form rather than function—strategies rather than deeper understanding of what students are experiencing as second-language learners. Little attention is given to the fact that teachers must also engage in changes in curriculum content, sequencing, and assessment practices, as well as understand which strategies for native speakers are inappropriate for ELs and which need specific adaptations in order to be effective with ELs. Yet studies of effective classrooms have illustrated that all these aspects of teaching must be included when considering optimal learning environments for ELs (e.g., García, 2005; Gersten & Geva, 2003; Téllez & Waxman, 2006). Moreover, studies exploring the skill and knowledge base of teachers of ELs stress the importance of understanding the nature of academic language proficiency as well as the role of language and culture in schooling, which are foundational concepts that need to inform pedagogical choices (de Jong & Harper, 2005; Walqui, 2008). This superficial treatment of EL teacher preparation ignores the expertise base that has been identified in the field as necessary for teachers of ELs (see also Lucas & Grinberg, 2008; Téllez & Waxman, 2006; Wong Fillmore & Snow, 2002).

Teachers completing their credential under the current policy in Arizona will also lack a holistic perspective of the English learners they will be teaching. The absence of issues of bilingual development, of an understanding of the role of primary language in effective instruction for ELs, and of its role in communication with parents and the community may prevent future teachers from knowing how to incorporate and build on students' prior knowledge. The importance of understanding linguistic interactions between the primary language and English and the impact of these interactions on second-language acquisition and instruction has been shown not only for bilingual but also for English-dominant or English-only classrooms (Brisk, 2006; Cummins, 2005; Gersten & Baker, 2000; Lucas & Katz, 1994).

Additional Consequences of Restrictive Language Policies

Some might argue that the SEI endorsement is at least a first step toward preparing teachers of ELs. While mainstream teachers do receive somewhat more preparation than before, we argue that, without further requirements for professional development, the minimal approach and mismatch with current research on high-quality EL teacher preparation in Arizona shortchange EL students. A survey of 5,300 educators in California in the wake of the passage of Proposition 227 found that the majority of those who had the state's minimal required preparation (similar to that of Arizona) considered themselves inadequately prepared to meet these students' needs (Gándara et al., 2005). In the case of Arizona, moreover, the current policy creates an uninformed lens through which pre-service teachers are coming to view ELs, their communities, and the strategies for instructing them. The perspective thus created has consistently been associated with schools and classrooms that lead to low achievement for minority students (García, 2005).

Practicing teachers are also negatively affected by restrictive state policies. The bilingual expertise of SEI teachers in Massachusetts was essentially discounted under the implementation of Question 2. The dominance of English in multilevel proficiency SEI classrooms undermined their ability to create learning environments they knew to be effective for literacy and content development for ELs. The SEI teachers were limited in terms of both using their language proficiency in the students' native language and applying their knowledge base about bilingualism and second-language acquisition to their instruction. Importantly, these restrictions on teachers' decision making came with significant consequences for their ELs, especially beginning ELs and those students with limited primary-language literacy skills. Due to the restrictions set on bilingual practices, the SEI classroom did not provide these students with access to quality instruction that met grade-level expectations.

Restrictive language policies were intended to accelerate English acquisition for ELs. Many studies have already shown that the 1-year SEI requirement has failed (e.g., Grissom, 2004; Parrish et al., 2006). The Massachusetts experience documented the impact of restrictive language policies on the quality of instruction—or, more accurately stated, the lack thereof. Practicing teachers felt that their ability to meet the needs of the most at-risk EL population (beginning ELs, ELs with limited literacy in their primary language, ELs with interrupted schooling) was greatly undermined by the law's restrictions on whether and how to use the native language. They were unable to provide effective literacy instruction in English and had to water down their expectations for subject-matter teaching. The practicing teachers' experiences illustrate the potential negative consequences for EL achievement, particularly for beginning-level ELs, when teachers are unable to use their knowledge and competence to strategically use the primary language in their classrooms.

The expertise needed to effectively teach ELs is both devalued and diminished in Arizona and Massachusetts as a result of restrictive English-only policies. The impact on practicing and future teachers and hence on the quality of instruction provided for ELs is and will be significant. Our concern is for the future teachers of ELs, who, as a result of restrictive state policies, may be subjected to a biased curriculum and may be unaware of best practices for their students. In Arizona, teachers-in-preparation are not given the opportunity to develop a framework for how to better serve the needs of ELs. We are also concerned about the impact on practicing teachers, teachers who see their efficacy diminish as a result of restrictive language policies. Clearly in our Massachusetts study, teachers experienced tensions between what they knew to be pedagogically sound and what they were required to do. Unfortunately, the evidence suggests that teachers who feel ineffective become demoralized and are more likely to leave the field or give up on trying to improve their skills (Darling-Hammond, 2003; National Commission on Teaching and America's Future, 2003).

POLICY RECOMMENDATIONS

Based on the research and experiences in Arizona and Massachusetts, we make the following specific policy recommendations related to the three restrictive language policies. First, the federal government should spearhead a research effort to determine the effectiveness of different prototypes for preparing pre-service teachers of ELs and help the states to define the meaning of "highly qualified teacher" for EL students.

Second, states need to develop comprehensive policies for preparing teachers of ELs that ensure a broad knowledge and skill base for mainstream teachers while maintaining the necessary specialized expertise base for specialist teachers, such as ESL and bilingual teachers.

Third, teacher preparation programs need to ensure that their graduates understand the language policy context in which they are or will be working and that these graduates are able to advocate for effective practices for ELs regardless of the program in which they teach.

Fourth, states with restrictive language policies should be required to monitor their effect on the teacher corps—tracking teachers' satisfaction, sense of efficacy, and rate of leaving teaching.

Finally, districts should establish clear policies about how the native language of students can and should be used to support effective instruction, even within an SEI classroom.

REFERENCES

Achinstein, B., Ogawa, R., & Speiglman, A. (2004). Are we creating separate and unequal tracks of teachers? The effects of state policy, local conditions, and teacher characteristics on new teacher socialization. *American Educational Research Journal, 41*(3), 557–603.

Allamillo, L., & Viramontes, C. (2000). Reflections from the classroom: Teacher perspectives on the implementation of Proposition 227. *Bilingual Research Journal, 24*(1&2), 155–167.

Arizona Revised Statutes, Title 15, Article 3.1, §15-751-17.755 (2000).

Arizona Department of Education (ADE). (2007). Curricular framework for (SEI) endorsement. Retrieved March 9, 2009, from http://www.ade.state.az.us/oelas

Arizona Office of the Auditor General. (2007). *Baseline study of Arizona's English language learner programs and data: Fiscal year 2007.* Phoenix, AZ: Author.

Arizona State Board of Education Rules, R7-2-613.J. (2006).

Bilingual by the numbers. (2002, November 3). *Boston Globe,* p. A34.

Brisk, M. E. (2006). *Bilingual education: From compensatory to quality schooling* (2nd ed.). Mahwah, NJ: Erlbaum.

Cohen, D. K., & Ball, D. L. (1990). Relations between policy and practice: A commentary. *Educational Evaluation and Policy Analysis, 12*(3), 331–338.

Combs, M. C., Evans, C., Fletcher, T., Parra, E., & Jiménez, A. (2005). Bilingualism for the children: Implementing a dual-language program in an English-only state. *Educational Policy, 19*(5), 701–728.

Cummins, J. (2005). A proposal for action: Strategies for recognizing heritage language competence as a learning resource within the mainstream classroom. *Modern Language Journal, 89,* 585–592.

Darling-Hammond, L. (2003). Keeping good teachers: Why it matters, what leaders can do. *Educational Leadership, 60*(8), 6–13.

de Jong, E. J. (2008). Contextualizing policy appropriation: Teachers' perspectives, local responses, and English-only ballot initiatives. *Urban Review, 40*(4), 350–370.

de Jong, E. J., Gort, M., & Cobb, C. D. (2005). Bilingual education within the context of English-only policies: Three districts responses to Question 2 in Massachusetts. *Educational Policy, 19*(4), 595–620.

de Jong, E. J., & Harper, C. A. (2005). Preparing mainstream teachers for English language learners. *Teacher Education Quarterly, 32*(2), 101–124.

Evans, B., & Hornberger, N. H. (2005). No Child Left Behind: Repealing and unpeeling federal language education policy in the United States. *Language Policy, 4,* 87–106.

Gándara, P., Maxwell-Jolly, J., & Driscoll, A. (2005). *Listening to teachers of English language learners: A survey of California teachers' challenges, experiences, and professional development needs.* Santa Cruz, CA: The Center for the Future of Teaching and Learning.

Gándara, P., Rumberger, R., Maxwell-Jolly, J., & Callahan, R. (2003). English learners in California schools: Unequal resources, unequal outcomes. *Educational Policy Analysis Archives, 11*(36). Retrieved September 26, 2006, from http://epaa.asu.edu/epaa/v11n36/

García, E. (2005). *Teaching and learning in two languages: Bilingualism and schooling in the United States.* New York: Teachers College Press.

García, E. E., & Curry-Rodriguez, J. E. (2000). The education of Limited English Proficient students in California schools: An assessment of the influence of Proposition 227 in selected districts and schools. *Bilingual Research Journal, 24*(1&2), 15–36.

General Laws of Massachusetts, Chapter 71A. (2003). Transitional Bilingual Education. Retrieved April 5, 2004, from http://www.state.ma.us/legis/laws/mgl/71A-1htm

Gersten, R., & Baker, S. (2000). What we know about effective instructional practices for English-language learners. *Exceptional Children, 6*(4), 454–470.

Gersten, R., & Geva, E. (2003). Teaching reading to early language learners. *Educational Leadership, 60*(8), 44–49.

Gort, M., de Jong, E. J., & Cobb, C. D. (2008). Seeing through a bilingual lens: Structural and ideological contexts of structured English immersion in three Massachusetts districts. *Journal of Educational Research and Policy Studies, 8*(2), 41–67.

Grissom, J. B. (2004). Reclassification of English learners. *Education Policy Analysis Archives, 12*(36). Retrieved August 2, 2004, from http://epaa.asu.edu/epaa/v12n36

Harper, C. A., & de Jong, E. J. (2004). Misconceptions about teaching ELLs. *Journal of Adolescent and Adult Literacy, 48*(2), 152–162.

Highlighting success in bilingual education [Special issue]. (2002). *Bilingual Research Journal, 26*(1).

Hill, E. G. (2004). *A look at the progress of English language learners.* Sacramento, CA: Legislative Analysts' Office.

Lucas, T., & Grinberg, J. (2008). Responding to the linguistic reality of mainstream teachers: Preparing all teachers to teach English language learners. In M. Cochran-Smith, S. Feiman-Nemser, D. J. McIntyre, & K. E. Demers (Eds.), *Handbook of research on teacher education: Enduring questions in changing contexts* (3rd ed.; pp. 606–636). New York: Routledge.

Lucas, T., & Katz, A. (1994). Reframing the debate: The roles of native languages in English-only programs for language minority students. *TESOL Quarterly, 28*(3), 537–561.

Mahoney, K., Thompson, M., & MacSwan, J. (2004). *The condition of English Language Learners in Arizona: 2004.* Tempe: Arizona State University, Education Policy Studies Laboratory.

Massachusetts Department of Education. (2004). *Limited English Proficient students and program types.* Retrieved December 8, 2004, from http://www.doe.mass.edu/ell/statistics/dptype.pdf

Maxwell-Jolly, J. (2000). Factors influencing implementation of mandated policy change: Proposition 227 in seven northern California school districts. *Bilingual Research Journal, 24*(1&2), 37–56.

Merino, B. (2007). Identifying critical competencies for teachers of English learners. *UCLMRI Newsletter, 16*(4), 1–8.

Molnar, A., & Allen, D. (2005). *Arizona education by the numbers 2005.* Retrieved March 9, 2009, from http://epsl.asu.edu/aepi/Report/EPSL-0509-/08-AEPI.pdf

Morrison Institute for Public Policy. (2003). *Is there a teacher shortage? Demand and supply in Arizona.* Tempe: Morrison Institute for Public Policy, School of Public Affairs, College of Public Programs, Arizona State University.

National Commission on Teaching and America's Future. (2003). *No dream denied: A pledge to America's children.* Washington, DC: Author.

Oakes, J. (2005). *Keeping track: How schools structure inequality* (2nd ed.). New Haven, CT: Yale University Press.

Ogawa, R. T., Sandholtz, J. H., Martinez-Flores, M., & Scribner, S. (2003). The substantive and symbolic consequences of a district's standards based curriculum. *American Educational Research Journal, 40,* 147–176.

Paredes, S. M. (2000). How Proposition 227 influences the language dynamics of a first- and second-grade mathematics lesson. *Bilingual Research Journal, 24*(1&2), 179–198.

Parrish, T. B., Perez, M., Merickel, A., & Linquanti, R. (2006). *Effects of the implementation of Proposition 227 on the education of English language learners, K–12. Findings from a five-year evaluation: Final report.* San Francisco: American Institutes of Research/WestEd.

Ricento, T. K., & Hornberger, N. H. (1996). Unpeeling the onion: Language planning and policy and the ELT professional. *TESOL Quarterly, 30*(3), 401–427.

Sable, J., & Garofano, A. (2007). *Public elementary and secondary school student enrollment, high school completions, and staff from the Common Core of Data: School year 2005–2006.* Washington, DC: National Center for Education Statistics.

Sánchez, M. T. (2006). *Teacher's experiences implementing English-only educational legislation.* Unpublished doctoral dissertation, Lynch School of Education, Boston College, Boston.

Sloan, K. (2006). Teacher identity and agency in school worlds: Beyond the all good/all bad discourse on accountability-explicit curriculum policies. *Curriculum Inquiry, 36*(2), 119–152.

Stritikus, T. (2003). The interrelationship of beliefs, context, and learning: The case of a teacher reacting to language policy. *Journal of Language, Identity, and Education, 2*(1), 29–52.

Stritikus, T., & García, E. E. (2000). Education of Limited English Proficient students in California schools: An assessment of the influence of Proposition 227 on selected teachers and classrooms. *Bilingual Research Journal, 24*(1&2), 1–11.

Téllez, K., & Waxman, H. (2006). *Preparing quality educators for English language learners: Research, policies, and practices.* Mahwah, NJ: Erlbaum.

Thompson, M. S., DiCerbo, K., Mahoney, K. S., & MacSwan, J. (2002). ¿Éxito en California? A validity critique of language program evaluations and analysis of English learner test scores. *Education Policy Analysis Archives, 10*(7). Retrieved August 2, 2004, from http://epaa.asu.edu/epaa/v10n7

Vaishnav, A. (2003, July 16). Romney hits softening of bilingual law, says override by legislators was "arrogance." *Boston Globe*, p. A1.

Varghese, M. M., & Stritikus, T. T. (2005). "Nadie me dijo: (Nobody told me)." Language policy negotiation and implications for teacher education. *Journal of Teacher Education, 56*(1), 73–87.

Walqui, A. (2008). The development of teacher expertise to work with adolescent English learners: A model and a few priorities. In L. S. Verplaetse & N. Migliacci (Eds.), *Inclusive pedagogy for English language learners: A handbook of research informed practices* (pp. 103–126). Mahwah, NJ: Erlbaum.

Wong Fillmore, L., & Snow, C. E. (2002). What teachers need to know about language. In C. T. Adger, C. E. Snow, & D. Christian (Eds.), *What teachers need to know about language* (pp. 7–53). Washington, DC: Center for Applied Linguistics.

Wright, W. E., & Choi, D. (2006). The impact of language and high-stakes testing policies on elementary school English language learners in Arizona. *Education Policy Analysis Archives, 14*(13). Retrieved March 9, 2009, from http://epaa.asu.edu/epaa/v14n13/

Zumwalt, K., & Craig, E. (2005). Teacher's characteristics: Research on the demographic profile. In M. Cochran-Smith & K. Zeichner (Eds.), *Studying teacher education: The report of the AERA panel on research and teacher education* (pp. 111–156). Mahwah, NJ: Erlbaum.

PART III

Is There Evidence for Superior Alternatives to Restrictive Language Policies?

CHAPTER 9

Restrictive State Language Policies:
Are They Scientifically Based?

Diane August, Claude Goldenberg, and Robert Rueda

THE RESULTS OF national testing in 2005 indicate that nearly half (46%) of fourth-grade students in the English learners (EL) category scored below basic in mathematics, with nearly three-quarters (73%) scoring below basic in reading. Middle school achievement in mathematics and reading were also very low, with more than two-thirds (71%) of eighth-grade ELs scoring below basic in both math and an equal percent of these students scoring below basic in reading (Fry, 2007). Therefore, improving educational outcomes for ELs must become a priority for educators in the United States.

In response to concern about the achievement of these students, several states have adopted policies that place restrictions on the language that can be used in their education. In three states—California, Arizona, and Massachusetts—mandates consist of severely limiting or eliminating the use of students' home (non-English) language. In one state, Arizona, state policies go further by prescribing the instructional program that is acceptable. (See Chapter 2, this volume, for a description of these state policies.) This chapter examines the research base for policies that restrict or prohibit the use of the home language for the instruction of English learners as well as policies related to effective language and literacy instruction.

HOW DOES ENGLISH-ONLY INSTRUCTION COMPARE WITH INSTRUCTION IN BOTH ENGLISH AND THE HOME LANGUAGE?

The use of English learners' home language to promote their academic achievement in school—the "bilingual education question"—has of course been the single most controversial issue in the education of ELs. But it is the one about which we have perhaps the most scientifically grounded information.

Evaluations of Bilingual Education Programs Compared with English-Only Programs

Historically, reviews and research on the educational outcomes of students receiving native-language instruction have reached conflicting conclusions. In an early review, Baker and de Kanter (1981) examined more than 300 evaluations of programs designed for second-language learners. To be included in the review, a study had to either employ random assignment of children to treatment conditions or take measures to ensure that children in the comparison groups were equivalent; studies with no control group were rejected. Of the studies initially located, only 28 satisfied the authors' criteria. These studies were qualitatively reviewed and given a global positive or negative score—"yes" they supported bilingual instruction; "no" they did not. There was no attempt to quantify the degree to which study findings yielded positive or negative results. Baker and de Kanter offer the following conclusion from their review: "The case for the effectiveness of transitional bilingual education is so weak that exclusive reliance on this instruction method is clearly not justified" (p. 1).

Rossell and Baker (1996) used the Baker and de Kanter (1981) review, as well as the work of Baker and Pelavin (1984), as the basis for their own review, in which they considered studies that evaluated alternative second-language programs. Of the 300 program evaluations read, they found only 72 that were methodologically acceptable. Their review included only studies of "good quality," which they defined as having random assignment to programs, or statistical control for pretreatment differences between groups when random assignment was not possible, and applying appropriate statistical tests to examine differences between control and treatment groups. Other criteria included outcome measures consisting of standardized test scores in English and similar student samples in both the bilingual and English-only programs. Using the same qualitative approach to analysis, Rossell and Baker concluded that most methodologically adequate studies failed to find transitional bilingual education more effective than programs with English-only instruction: "Thus the research evidence does not support transitional bilingual education as a superior form of instruction for limited English proficient children" (p. 7). It should be noted that the authors of these two studies do not state that English-only instruction is more effective; they merely state that bilingual instruction was not found to be superior and should not be the only approach mandated by law.

While these reviews have been characterized as anti–bilingual education, it is important to note that they found no overall differences between bilingual and English immersion strategies, not that use of the native language was inferior to English-only instruction with respect to academic outcomes.

Slavin and Cheung (2005) conducted a best-evidence synthesis, an approach that uses a systematic literature search, quantification of outcomes and effect sizes, and extensive examination of individual studies that meet inclusion criteria. A total of 17 studies met their inclusion standards. They found that "among 13 studies focusing on elementary reading for Spanish-dominant students, 9 favored bilingual approaches on English reading measures, and 4 found no differences, for a median effect size of +0.45. Weighted by sample size, an effect size of +0.33 was computed, which is significantly different from zero ($p < .05$)" (p. 247). The +0.45 effect size indicates a medium positive effect for bilingual education, approximately equivalent to increasing performance on a standardized test by 20 percentile points. Even after taking into account, or weighting, differences in the sample of students, there was still a significant effect for bilingual approaches. In sum, a bilingual approach was found to yield superior results with respect to English reading outcomes.

Four studies (Francis, Lesaux, & August, 2006; Greene, 1997; Rolstad, Mahoney, & Glass, 2005; Willig, 1985) used meta-analytic techniques[1] in examining the effectiveness of bilingual approaches compared with English-only approaches and therefore took into account the program effects found in each study, even if they were not statistically significant. As Greene (1997) points out, "simply counting positive and negative effect sizes is less precise than a meta-analysis because it does not consider the magnitude or confidence level of effects" (p. 11). In fact, simple vote counting procedures are known to be conservatively biased, and the magnitude of the bias increases as the number of studies increases (Lipsey & Wilson, 2001).

Willig (1985) conducted a meta-analysis of the studies reviewed by Baker and de Kanter (1981), making several changes with regard to inclusion criteria. First, she eliminated five studies conducted outside the United States (three in Canada, one in the Philippines, and one in South Africa) because of significant differences in the students, the programs, and the contexts in those studies. She also excluded one study in which instruction took place outside the classroom. Finally, she excluded one study because it was not a primary study, but a review. Her overall conclusion is quite different from that of Baker and de Kanter: "positive effects for bilingual programs . . . for all major academic areas" (p. 297). However, it should be noted that Willig was asking a fundamentally different question from that explored by Baker and de Kanter. Whereas the latter were interested in determining whether bilingual education should be mandated, Willig considered a more modest question: whether bilingual education works. As she notes, she conducted a series of comparisons. One set of comparisons examined how bilingual programs with and without English as a Second Language (ESL) instruction compared with "submersion programs," or programs in which English learners are placed in all-English classrooms with no special instructional support. A second set of comparisons examined bilingual programs that included ESL support with immersion programs that also included ESL support. For both sets of comparisons, Willig concludes that bilingual education does work better than the English-only programs with which it was compared.

Greene (1997) performed a meta-analysis of the set of studies cited by Rossell and Baker (1996), but the analysis included only 11 of those 72 studies. In addition to the criteria used by Rossell and Baker, Greene looked at studies that measured the effects of bilingual programs after at least 1 academic year. If students were not assigned to treatment and control groups randomly, adequate statistical control for this nonrandom assignment was defined as requiring controls for individual previous test scores, as well as at least some of the individual demographic factors known to influence those scores, such as family income and parental education. In all, Greene rejected studies cited by Rossell and Baker because they were duplicative of other studies in the review (15 studies), could not be located (5 studies), were not evaluations of bilingual programs (3 studies), did not have appropriate control groups (14 studies), measured outcomes after a short period of time (2 studies), and inadequately controlled for differences between students assigned to bilingual and English-only programs (25 studies). This last factor is critically important and often overlooked in the research. In order to maximize limited resources, schools often assign the least fluent English speakers to the bilingual programs, where they can be assured of a teacher who is able to communicate with them (Ramírez, Yuen, Ramey, & Pasta, 1991). Among the studies that met the author's standard of methodological adequacy, including all those using random assignment to conditions, Greene found that the evidence favored programs that made use of native-language instruction (effect size = 0.21).

Rolstad and colleagues (2005) also concluded that learning to read in the home language promotes reading achievement in the second language. The authors reviewed 17 studies conducted since Willig's 1985 meta-analysis. Studies were included if they involved K–12 language minority students not enrolled in special education, provided the necessary statistical information needed for a meta-analysis, and provided sufficient description of the treatment and control groups. Seventeen studies yielding 156 instances of program comparisons on one or more outcome measures were used in the meta-analysis. The authors note the wide variability in program, grade, sample size, and outcome measures. For studies that compared English learners in bilingual instruction to English learners in English-only instruction, findings indicate a positive effect in English outcomes for bilingual education (effect size = 0.23) as well as in native language outcomes (effect size = 0.86). Additionally, the authors found that the developmental bilingual programs were superior to transitional bilingual programs in which students are exited from native-language instruction when they are transitioned into English instruction.

Finally, Francis and colleagues (2006) conducted a meta-analysis with 15 studies that met their methodological criteria. The 15 studies yielded 71 effect sizes across 26 samples of students. The samples included students in both elementary and secondary schools and students possessing a range of abilities. Overall, bilingual education had a positive effect on reading outcomes in English that was small to moderate in size. The results of the one study that was designed to evaluate bilingual instruction for a specific population—Spanish speakers receiving special education services—favored a bilingual approach for these learners. Moreover, children in the bilingual programs studied not only developed facility with English literacy to the same extent as their peers educated in English but also developed literacy skills in their native language; thus, they achieved the advantage of being both bilingual and biliterate.

Differences in conclusions can be attributed in part to differences in the questions asked, the criteria for including studies, and the methods used to synthesize findings. With regard to the research questions asked in the analyses discussed here, for example, the nature of the samples differed depending on the question (e.g., Willig eliminated studies conducted outside the United States, whereas Baker and de Kanter did not). Standards for methodological rigor also differed across the reviews (e.g., Greene eliminated 61 studies that had been included by Rossell and Baker).

Nevertheless, readers should understand how unusual it is to have five quantitative reviews on the same issue conducted by five groups of independent researchers with diverse perspectives. The fact that they all reached essentially the same conclusion is extraordinary. The four meta-analyses (Francis et al., 2006; Greene, 1997; Rolstad et al., 2005; Willig, 1985) and one best-evidence synthesis found differences in favor of native-language instruction, with effect sizes ranging from small to moderate. Of interest is Willig's (1985) conclusion that the better the technical quality of the study—for example, if a study used random assignment as opposed to creating post hoc comparison groups—the larger the effects.

In brief, we can say with confidence that teaching ELs to read in their home language, or in their primary and second languages simultaneously (at different times during the day or week), compared with teaching them to read in their second language only, boosts their reading achievement in the second language. We are less confident about the effect of primary-language instruction in other curricular areas, such as math or social studies. In reading, however, there is general consensus—although not unanimity—in the research literature. However, there are a large number of questions about the role of the primary language in the education of ELs for which we have scant research evidence.

Other Research Related to Bilingual Instruction

There are various theories that can explain the positive outcomes for students instructed in bilingual programs. A likely one is what educational psychologists and cognitive scientists call "transfer." Transfer, one of the most venerable and important concepts in education, means that what a student learns about one thing or in one context contributes to learning about other things and in other contexts. For example, learning basic arithmetic helps with learning more advanced math or being a smarter shopper.

With respect to English learners, a substantial body of research suggests that if students learn something in one language, they can more easily learn it in another language (Cummins, 1979); generally, this holds "across a wide range of ages, across normally developing and disabled readers, across language pairs that are structurally close and distant, and across varying levels of language proficiency" (Dressler & Kamil, 2006, p. 231). Significant cross-language relationships have been noted in both sound–symbol awareness (i.e., identifying letters with their sounds) and word reading (Abu-Rabia, 1997; Chitiri & Willows, 1997; Da Fontoura & Siegel, 1995; Durgunoglu, Nagy, & Hancin-Bhatt, 1993; Gholamain & Geva, 1999) and spelling (Edelsky, 1982; Fashola, Drum, Mayer, & Kang, 1996; Nathenson-Mejía, 1989; Zutell & Allen, 1988). With respect to vocabulary development, studies show that various aspects of vocabulary knowledge appear to transfer across languages, such as cognate recognition in Spanish–English bilinguals (García, 1991, 1998; Hancin-Bhatt & Nagy, 1994; James & Klein, 1994; Jiménez, García, & Pearson, 1996; Nagy, García, Durgunoglu, & Hancin-Bhatt, 1993; Saville-Troike, 1984). Reading comprehension skills in students who are biliterate often correlate significantly across languages (Goldman, Reyes, & Varnhagen, 1984; Nagy, McClure, & Mir, 1997; Reese, Garnier, Gallimore, & Goldenberg, 2000; Royer & Carlo, 1991; Verhoeven, 1994). Similar relationships have been found for reading strategies, again investigated primarily with older students.

Another theory that can help explain the positive outcomes for students instructed in bilingual programs is cognitive load theory (Paas & Kester, 2006; Paas, Renkel, & Sweller, 2003). This theory relates to working memory, or the part of the cognitive system that provides temporary storage and manipulation of information necessary for complex cognitive tasks, such as language comprehension, learning, and reasoning. The theory suggests that learning happens best under conditions that are aligned with human cognitive architecture, including the well-documented finding that short-term memory is limited in the number of elements it can contain simultaneously. For the most part, this theory has been applied to instructional design with adults, although there is some limited work looking at second-language learning. The theory suggests that while some aspects of learning are characterized by intrinsic cognitive load, which is not amenable to instruction, other types of cognitive load (extraneous cognitive load) are generated by the manner in which information is presented to learners and can be modified by instructional conditions. In essence, presenting complex instructional concepts and problems to English learners in an unfamiliar language generates extraneous cognitive load—and thus less efficient learning. While this theory has not yet been widely applied in second-language research, it has major implications for instruction and helps explain some of the findings noted above. In essence, native-language instruction can help reduce cognitive load and make learning more efficient, especially at lower levels of English proficiency.

RESEARCH RELATED TO THE EFFECTS OF BILINGUALISM

There are several areas of research that do not address the effects of bilingual instruction but rather address the effects of *being* bilingual and the *use of* bilingual abilities on various aspects of development and social interaction. While this research does not address the consequences of bilingual instruction per se, it may offer some insight into how bilingualism in general should be regarded in the larger society. This research is in several loosely related domains, including cognitive flexibility, family cohesion, and self-esteem. Each is briefly described below.

Cognitive Flexibility

From a cognitive perspective, children who develop healthy degrees of bilingualism tend to exhibit greater ability to focus on and use language productively (Bialystock, 2001; Diaz & Klinger, 1991; Galambos & Hakuta, 1988; Nagy, Berninger, & Abbott, 2006). Called "metalinguistic awareness," this skill has been associated with improved comprehension outcomes irrespective of language background (Nagy et al., 2006).

Bialystock (2001) noted three types of cognitive flexibility or metalinguistic development—metalinguistic knowledge (knowledge *about* language), metalinguistic ability (the capacity to use knowledge about language as opposed to the capacity to use language), and metalinguistic awareness (attention that is actively focused on the explicit properties of language). Bialystock noted that all linguistic use involves these dimensions to some extent, and thus these should be conceptualized as moving along a continuum rather than representing an either/or state. Nevertheless, the earliest claims for bilingual advantages focused on metalinguistic development (Clark, 1978; Diaz, 1983). Early studies found evidence in support of this claim (Ben-Zeev, 1977; Bialystock, 1988; Cummins, 1978; Ricciardelli, 1992). In spite of a few contradictory findings (Rosenblum & Pinker, 1983), there has been fairly consistent evidence supporting bilingual advantages at the word-awareness level (Yelland, Pollard, & Mercuri, 1993). Similar advantages have been found for syntactic awareness (the ability to judge the grammatical acceptability of a sentence) (Bialystock & Majumder, 1998; Galambos & Goldin-Meadow, 1990; Galambos & Hakuta, 1988) or, in later research, sentences that contain incorrect semantic information, which is a more difficult task (Gathercole, 1997). Bialystock (2001) has noted, along with other researchers, that both the degree of balance of the two languages and the level of proficiency in each language are significant mediators of these positive effects. The implication is that approaches that foster high degrees of bilingualism in two languages would be expected to foster these advantages in comparison to programs that focus on one language only.

Family Cohesion

"Family cohesion" has been defined as "the emotional bonding that family members have toward one another" (Olson, Russell, & Sprenkle, 1984, p. 60), and most definitions include dimensions of affection, support, helpfulness, and caring among family members (Barber & Buehler, 1996). High levels of family cohesion have shown significant correlations with outcomes such as lower rates of substance use, juvenile delinquency, and alcohol use (Coohey, 2001; Gil, Wagner, & Vega, 2000).

There is some indication that increased family cohesion is associated with native-language use at home. Baer and Schmitz (2001) investigated levels of family bonding and self-reported cultural orientation in Mexican adolescents (grades 6, 7, and 8), compared with non-Hispanic White individuals, during the transition from early to mid-adolescence. The relationship between family variables (language use, family structure, parental education, and gender) and family cohesion were examined with a cohort-sequential design. The study found that Mexican American students who were less acculturated and who spoke Spanish to their parents showed a significant increase in family cohesion at mid-adolescence compared to Mexican American students who were more acculturated and spoke English to their parents and to non-Hispanic White students.

Links have also been demonstrated between bilingual development and improved family cohesion and self-esteem. Portes and Hao (2002) hypothesized that balanced bilingualism in the children of immigrants would have positive effects on "family solidarity and personality adjustment, reflecting cultural continuity and mutual understanding across generations, [whereas] limited bilingualism and English monolingualism would have the opposite effects" (p. 893). In testing this hypothesis, the authors surveyed 2,442 immigrant parents in person in their own languages, with questions that sought to determine degrees of family solidarity and family conflict. These variables were then correlated with immigrant children's own language adaptations (e.g., English monolingualism, fluent bilingualism, limited bilingualism, etc.). The results suggested that the degree of bilingualism attained by the children predicted increased family cohesiveness and better achievement, rather than parents' knowledge of English (a self-assessment), which had little to do with promoting their children's self-esteem. The authors define the attainment of bilingual fluency as "*selective* acculturation involving a mix of the old and the new rather than complete acculturation" (p. 906), and it is this linguistic and cultural capital that provides the greatest potential of preserving family ties and cohesiveness.

A second study corroborates these findings. Vom Dorp (2000) surveyed three groups of upper elementary school children: monolingual English speakers, English-instructed Spanish–English bilinguals, and bilingually instructed Spanish–English bilinguals. She found that, controlling for socioeconomic status, ethnicity, gender, and schooling achievement, Spanish–English bilinguals who were bilingually instructed displayed higher global self-concept scores than Spanish–English bilinguals who received English-only instruction. Further, the bilingually instructed group also had higher mean scores on family cohesion ratings than the English-only bilinguals.

Self-Esteem and Identity

At the most basic level, identity refers to "a person's understanding of who they are" (Taylor, 1992, p. 25). There is a robust literature on issues related to language and identity (Benet-Martinez & Haritatos, 2005; Cortese, 2005; Ramirez-Esparza, Gosling, Benet-Martínez, Potter, & Pennebaker, 2006). Recent work suggests that identity is tied to many factors in addition to language, such as age, social status, and gender. Moreover, identities are dynamic and multifaceted, responsive to ever-changing features of interactions based on participants, situation, purpose, and so on (Lanza & Svendsen, 2007).

Studies have suggested that students recognize early on the connection between language use and identity (Olsen, 2000; Suárez-Orozco & Suárez-Orozco, 2000). There is also some evidence that in additive situations, where the home language is valued and utilized in instruction, self-esteem and confidence are positively impacted (Lee, 2008). Lee (2008) investigated the relationship of self-esteem, ethnic identity formation, and "bilingual confidence" among a sample of Chinese students ($n = 110$) in western Canada using survey methods. With grade point average (GPA) controlled, it was found that there was a relationship between ethnic identity and a more global self-esteem, or an individual's general feelings of self-worth. Moreover, language self-efficacy had a significant effect on global, academic, and social self-esteem.

Portes and Zady (2002), using survey data and interviews in Miami and San Diego, examined a variety of factors related to self-esteem with 5,267 second-generation eighth- and ninth-grade students from various groups. Second-generation status for children was defined as having lived in the United States for at least 5 years or being the child of at least one immigrant parent. Half of the sample participants were born outside the United States before age 12. The other half were

U.S. born, and the sample was also evenly distributed by grade and gender. Among other factors in this complex study that were found to predict self-esteem, students who were bilingual were able to bridge the two cultures, and bilingualism was related to higher self-esteem.

Unfortunately, while bilingualism has been linked to positive self-esteem and identity, it can also be associated with negative effects, depending on features of the larger social context. In a study about childhood literacy among Mexican American students, Martinez-Roldán and Malavé (2004) found that students were socialized at home to devalue Spanish as a result of strong negative opinions and beliefs about Mexican immigrants and bilingual education that their parents had heard and internalized in their interaction with the wider community. Martinez-Roldán and Malavé (2004) argued that a main problem some Latino immigrants and their children face is the "process of self-devaluation when they de-emphasize their heritage language and portray their ethnic group in a negative way" (p. 176).

INSTRUCTED SECOND-LANGUAGE ACQUISITION

Supporters of English-only instruction have frequently invoked the time-on-task principle: They argue that students taught in English only learn English faster because they spend more time involved in English. While intuitively appealing, this assertion is not supported by the research (August & Shanahan, 2006). In Arizona, most students are currently provided with 4 hours of "English language development" instruction distinguished from other types of instruction in that the content "emphasizes the English language itself." While materials may reflect content from a variety of disciplines, the materials must "predominantly feature specific language constructions that align with the English language objectives based on the EL proficiency Standards and Discrete Skills Inventory" (Arizona Task Force, 2007, p. 1 FAQs). This section describes what we know about instructed second-language acquisition and whether the research base in this area aligns with the model being implemented in Arizona. (See Chapter 2, this volume, for a description of this model.)

From a research perspective, there are three troubling aspects of the Structured English Immersion program as currently formulated in Arizona. The first is the focus on discrete skills with time allotments dedicated to each skill (e.g., oral English and conversation, conversational English and academic language, grammar, reading, vocabulary, and writing). Current research on effective instructed second-language acquisition highlights the importance of balancing a focus on discrete skills with a focus on meaning (Ellis, 2005). It is important to note, however, that most research on instructed second-language acquisition has been carried out with learners over the age of 14 and includes studies focused on teaching English as a foreign language. Thus, findings presented here might not apply to children younger than 14. Nonetheless, effective instruction might teach pre-selected grammatical structures germane to the learning tasks at hand but also ensure that students understand the meaning of these structures and have opportunities to engage in authentic receptive (listening and reading) and productive (speaking and writing) communication related to the task. In summary, a learning principle that underlies effective instructed second-language acquisition is that while direct teaching of language forms and functions helps second-language learners, they will learn language best if they also engage in activities that require them to "use language in ways that closely resemble how language is used naturally outside the classroom" (Ellis, 2005, pp. 5–6), in essence, in a manner that integrates the various skills and focuses on authentic communication. Likewise, research on effective literacy instruction for second-language learners (August & Shanahan, 2006) calls for developing oral language proficiency in the context of reading and writing. Thus, while engaged in reading and writing, students practice talking about the topic at hand and learning the vocabulary connected with the topic.

The second aspect of Arizona's model that is problematic is grouping English learners by proficiency level instead of integrating them with proficient speakers of the second language. Some grouping of students might not be detrimental. In fact, research on ability grouping suggests that for specific subjects such as reading or math, ability grouping for periods during the day is an effective practice (Slavin, 1987, 1989). Yet Arizona requires a 4-hour block of time for English language development—80% of the schoolday—lasting until students are English proficient. Although some argue that additional time-on-task studying English will speed up the acquisition of English, research does not support this supposition. An important principle of instructed second-language acquisition is that successful second-language learning requires extensive second-language input as well as sufficient opportunity to use the new language. While it is useful to consider the relative contributions of input and output to acquisition, it is also important to acknowledge that both co-occur in oral interaction and that both computational and sociocultural theories of second-language acquisition have viewed social interaction as the matrix in which acquisition takes place (Ellis, 2005). As Hatch (1978) famously put it: "One learns how to do conversation, one learns how to interact verbally, and out of the interaction syntactic structures are developed" (p. 404). Thus, interaction is not just a means of automatizing existing linguistic resources but also of creating new resources. Simply stated, giving students ample opportunities for interaction in English—including input as well as opportunities to talk and write—is essential for second-language (English) acquisition.

Moreover, grouping English learners by proficiency levels ignores the fact that English proficiency is only one dimension of students' ability in school-related tasks. They will have varying levels of content knowledge because of prior schooling or family experiences as well as varying ability with early reading skills because ability in these skills is more related to phonological processing than English proficiency. Grouping students solely on the basis of English proficiency ignores important differences in other skills and abilities, presenting significant instructional challenges for the teacher.

The third problem with the Arizona immersion model is its almost exclusive focus on English language development rather than domain knowledge until students are English proficient. A curriculum that focuses almost exclusively on language proficiency will fail to develop the domain knowledge students need to comprehend the text they are reading. E. D. Hirsch (2006) argues that U.S. students fail at math, science, and reading partly because reading experts have overlooked the most important aspect of literacy—domain knowledge. It is Hirsch's contention that reading comprehension depends on learning factual background knowledge in a broad array of subjects. That approach, which assumes students can apply all-purpose cognitive skills and critical thinking strategies to unfamiliar texts on any subject, deprives students of the substance and intellectual structure they need to read successfully. It can also negatively affect student achievement in each subject area (not just reading). Reading deficits become more pronounced when students must read to learn (Chall, Jacobs, & Baldwin, 1990), and these problems are compounded over time as students lag further and further behind and don't have the knowledge to make sense of ever more challenging texts (Cunningham & Stanovich, 1998).

LENGTH OF TIME REQUIRED FOR ENGLISH LEARNERS TO ACHIEVE GRADE-LEVEL PROFICIENCY IN ENGLISH

Legislation in two states makes assumptions about the time it will take English learners to acquire sufficient proficiency in English to learn in mainstream classrooms. In California, state law now permits English learners to receive sheltered English Immersion[2] or Structured English Immersion for only 1 year; thereafter instruction must take place in mainstream educational settings (unless parents request a waiver). In Massachusetts, students are permitted to remain in English learner programs for 3 years. The laws appear to be silent on the kind of support ELs should receive once they are exited from special programs.

Policies that assume such rapid acquisition of English are extremely unrealistic. With regard to the time required to become English proficient, it is important to make a distinction between language needed to learn complex academic subjects and conversational language that is less cognitively demanding and embedded in context (Collier, 1995; Cummins, 1981; Snow, 1987). For students to cope with the demands of mainstream class work, they need to attain mastery of academic English as well as conversational language. Recent work by Hakuta, Goto-Butler, and Witt (2000) indicates that it can take English learners from 3 to

5 years to acquire oral language proficiency and 4 to 7 years to acquire academic language. Findings are based on large samples of students in four school districts, two in California and two in Canada. In three of the districts the English learners were schooled entirely in English, and in the district that provided a bilingual option, student outcomes in oral language proficiency and in academic language were equivalent. Collier (1987; Collier & Thomas, 1989) examined the development of content-area knowledge in a group of 1,548 middle-class English learners with grade-level skills in their first language attending middle class suburban schools and found that it took this group of students from 4 to 8 years of schooling to reach national norms in all subjects as measured by Science Research Associates (SRA) tests in reading, language arts, social studies, and science. It is notable that these students did eventually reach grade-level norms, a finding that has not been replicated in other U.S. studies. Finally, findings from a 5-year statewide evaluation (Parrish et al., 2006) found that the likelihood of an English learner meeting the linguistic and academic criteria needed to be reclassified to fluent proficient after 10 years in California schools is 40%.

One important issue related to acquiring grade-level proficiency in English literacy is that in the earliest stages of learning to read—when the focus is on sounds, letters, and how to combine these to form words that can be read—English learners are more likely to make progress that is comparable to that of English speakers, providing the instruction is clear, focused, and systematic. In other words, when the oral English language requirements are relatively low—as they are for learning phonological skills (the sounds of the language and how words are made up of smaller constituent sounds), letter–sound combinations, decoding, and word recognition—ELs are more likely to make adequate progress, as judged by the sort of progress we would expect of English speakers. But as content gets more challenging and language demands increase, more and more complex vocabulary and syntax are required, and ELs generally do not make the same kind of progress as their English proficient peers (Shanahan & Beck, 2006). It is in the area of these text-level skills such as reading comprehension and writing that there is a need for accommodations to instructional methods and curriculum developed for monolingual speakers to make the content more accessible and comprehensible to ELs (August & Shanahan, 2006).

CONCLUSIONS AND POLICY RECOMMENDATIONS

First, state policies should not prohibit use of the home language for instruction. The clearest finding to emerge from the research reviewed above is that primary-language instruction—particularly in reading, which is what by far most of the research addresses—promotes reading achievement in English. Five independent quantitative syntheses have all come to this same conclusion. There is thus no legitimate scientific basis for proscribing instruction in the home language. More-over, there is some, albeit more limited, evidence that in an all-English instructional context, the home language can provide useful support in helping students acquire literacy and academic skills in English. Additionally, a number of benefits—cognitive, social, and psychological—accrue to students who are allowed to develop strong competencies in two languages.

Second, English Language Development (ELD) instruction requires attention both to learning the forms of the language and using the language for communication. Despite continued controversy over what constitutes effective ELD instruction, there is a general consensus (at least for older students) that some combination of explicit teaching of language forms (e.g., syntax, morphology, pronunciation, pragmatics) and opportunities for communicative use of the language is required for second-language acquisition. There are no research-based formulas available, but districts and states should formulate ELD policies that provide students with structured, explicit second-language instruction in English balanced with ample experience using English to learn/discuss academic content and accomplish a wide range of communicative tasks.

Third, schools should try to accelerate ELs' English acquisition but not be subject to artificial pressures to exit ELs from the support services they need to access grade-level content and learn grade-level skills. The most current research we have suggests that it can take ELs 5 to 7 or more years to develop English proficiency levels that will allow them to succeed in mainstream English classrooms. This finding suggests that artificially limiting ELs to 1 or 2 years of instructional support due to their language limitations is unrealistic and could serve to disadvantage ELs further. At the same time, more rapid acquisition of English, particularly the academic English required for school success, is likely to improve ELs' academic outcomes. Unfortunately, we do not know from the research to what extent English acquisition can be accelerated through school-based instruction.

Finally, states and the federal government should promote efforts to deepen our understanding of the role of the home language in the acquisition of English academic skills and the best methods for developing English literacy and language proficiency in ELs. Beyond the finding that primary-language reading instruction promotes reading achievement in English (and in the primary language), there are more questions than answers. These include, for example:

- Is primary language instruction more beneficial for some learners than for others?
- What should be the relative emphasis (on a daily, weekly, yearly basis) for promoting knowledge and skills in the primary language and developing these skills in English, and how should instruction be structured to accomplish the program's goals?

- What level of skill in the students' primary language does the teacher need to possess in order to be effective?
- In an English immersion situation, what is the most effective way to use the primary language to support children's learning?
- Is there an optimal amount of time (during the schoolday and as students go up the grades) for ELs to receive instruction in the home language?

For promoting achievement only in English, 1 year in primary-language instruction might (or might not) be any better than 3 years or 6 years. However, 6 years of primary-language instruction might be much more effective than 1 year if the goal is primary-language development in addition to English academic competence—that is, full bilingualism. Many would argue that this ought to be our educational goal for English learners (see, most recently, Gándara & Rumberger, 2006).

There is also a great need for additional research on effective language and literacy instruction for English learners. A recent review (August & Shanahan, 2006) uncovered approximately 36 experimental studies focused on developing literacy in ELs published between 1980 and 2002. The National Reading Panel (National Institute for Child Health and Human Development, 2000) uncovered approximately 450 such studies focused on developing literacy in English monolinguals. There is even less research on effective instructed second-language acquisition (Saunders & Goldenberg, in press).

NOTES

This chapter builds on our previous work—*Developing Literacy in Second-Language Learners*. For more information, see *Developing Literacy in Second-Language Learners*, edited by Diane August and Timothy Shanahan, published in 2006 by Taylor and Francis, New York, NY.

1. A meta-analysis is a statistical technique that allows researchers to combine data from many studies and calculate the average effect of an instructional procedure. It is useful because studies often come to conflicting conclusions. Some find positive effects of a program, other find negative effects of the same type of program, and yet others find no effects. Even among studies that report positive findings, the effects can be small or large. The questions a meta-analysis addresses are these: Taking into account all the relevant studies on a topic, *overall*, is the effect positive, negative, or zero? And if it is overall positive or negative, what is the magnitude of the effect—large, and therefore meaningful; small, and therefore of little consequence; or something in between? Are there additional factors—for example, student characteristics—that influence whether effects are large or small?

2. Sheltered English Immersion is a strategy often used in Structured English Immersion to introduce content instruction.

REFERENCES

Abu-Rabia, S. (1997). Verbal and working-memory skills of bilingual Hebrew–English speaking children. *International Journal of Psycholinguistics, 13*(1), 25–40.

Arizona Task Force. (2007). Structured English Immersion models of the Arizona English Language Learners Task Force. Retrieved September 23, 2008, from https://ade.state.az.us/ELLTaskForce/SEIModels9-15-07.pdf

August, D., & Shanahan, T. (2006). *Developing literacy in second language learners: Report of the National Literacy Panel on Language-Minority Children and Youth.* Mahwah, NJ: Erlbaum.

Baer, J. C., & Schmitz, M. F. (2001). Ethnic differences in trajectories of family cohesion for Mexican American and non-Hispanic White adolescents. *Journal of Youth and Adolescence, 36,* 583–592.

Baker, K., & de Kanter, A. (1981). *Effectiveness of bilingual education: A review of the literature.* Final draft report. Washington, DC: U.S. Department of Education, Office of Technical and Analytic Systems.

Baker, K., & Pelavin, S. (1984, April). *Unique problems and solutions in evaluating bilingual programs.* Paper presented at the annual meeting of the American Educational Research Association, New Orleans, LA.

Barber, B. K., & Buehler, C. (1996). Family cohesion and enmeshment: Different constructs, different effects. *Journal of Marriage and Family, 58,* 443–451.

Benet-Martinez, V., & Haritatos, J. (2005). Bicultural identity integration (BII): Components and psychological antecedents. *Journal of Personality, 73,* 1015–1050.

Ben-Zeev, S. (1977). The influence of bilingualism on cognitive strategy and cognitive development. *Child Development, 48,* 1009–1018.

Bialystock, E. (1988). Levels of bilingualism and levels of linguistic awareness. *Developmental Psychology, 24,* 560–567.

Bialystock, E. (2001). *Bilingualism in development: Language, literacy, and cognition.* New York: Cambridge University Press.

Bialystock, E., & Majumder, S. (1998). The relationship between bilingualism and the development of cognitive processes in problem-solving. *Applied Psycholinguistics, 19,* 69–85.

Chall, J. S., Jacobs, V. A., & Baldwin, L. (1990). *The reading crisis: Why poor children fall behind.* Cambridge, MA: Harvard University Press.

Chitiri, H. F., & Willows, D. M. (1997). Bilingual word recognition in English and Greek. *Applied Psycholinguistics, 18*(2), 139–156.

Clark, E. V. (1978). Awareness of language: Some evidence from what children say and do. In A. Sinclair & W. J. M. Levelt (Eds.), *The child's conceptualization of language* (pp. 17–43). Berlin: Springer-Verlag.

Collier, V. P. (1987). Age and rate of acquisition of second language for academic purposes. *TESOL Quarterly, 21*(4), 617–641.

Collier, V. P. (1995). Acquiring a second language for school. *Directions in Language and Education, 1*(4), 3–13.

Collier, V. P., & Thomas, W. P. (1989). How quickly can immigrants become proficient in English? *Journal of Educational Issues of Language Minority Students, 5,* 26–38.

Coohey, C. (2001). The relationship between familism and child maltreatment in Latino and Anglo families. *Child Maltreatment, 6,* 130–142.

Cortese, G. (2005). *Identity, community, discourse: English in intercultural settings.* New York: Peter Lang.

Cummins, J. (1978). Bilingualism and the development of metalinguistic awareness. *Journal of Cross-Cultural Psychology, 9,* 131–149.

Cummins, J. (1979). Linguistic interdependence and the educational development of bilingual children. *Review of Educational Research, 49*(2), 222–251.

Cummins, J. (1981). The role of primary language development in promoting educational success for language minority students. In *Schooling and language-minority students: An educational framework* (pp. 3–49). Los Angeles: California State Department of Education.

Cunningham, A. E., & Stanovich, K. E. (1998). The impact of print exposure on word recognition. In J. Metsala & L. Ehri (Eds.), *Word recognition in beginning literacy* (pp. 235–262). Mahwah, NJ: Erlbaum.

Da Fontoura, H. A., & Siegel, L. S. (1995). Reading, syntactic, and working memory skills of bilingual Portuguese–English Canadian children. *Reading and Writing, 7*(1), 139–153.

Diaz, R. M. (1983). The impact of bilingualism on cognitive development. In E. W. Gordon (Ed.), *Review of Research in Education* (Vol. 10; pp. 23–54). Washington, DC: American Educational Research Association.

Diaz, R. M., & Klinger, C. (1991). Towards an explanatory model of the interaction between bilingualism and cognitive development. In E. Bialystock (Ed.), *Language processing in bilingual children* (pp. 140–185). New York: Cambridge University Press.

Dressler, C., & Kamil, M. I. (2006). First and second language literacy. In D. August & T. Shanahan (Eds.), *Developing literacy in second language learners: Report of the National Literacy Panel on Language-Minority Children and Youth* (pp. 197–238). Mahwah, NJ: Erlbaum.

Durgunoglu, A. Y., Nagy, W. E., & Hancin-Bhatt, B. J. (1993). Cross-language transfer of phonological awareness. *Journal of Educational Psychology, 85,* 453–465.

Edelsky, C. (1982). Writing in a bilingual program: The relation of L1 and L2 texts. *TESOL Quarterly, 16*(2), 211–228.

Ellis, R. (2005). *Instructed second language acquisition.* New Zealand: Research Division, Ministry of Education.

Fashola, O. S., Drum, P. A., Mayer, R. E., & Kang, S.J. (1996). A cognitive theory of orthographic transitioning: Predictable errors in how Spanish-speaking children spell English words. *American Educational Research Journal, 33*(4), 825–843.

Francis, D. J., Lesaux, N. K., & August, D. (2006). Language of instruction. In D.L. August & T. Shanahan (Eds.), *Developing literacy in a second language: Report of the National Literacy Panel on Language-Minority Children and Youth* (pp. 365–410). Mahwah, NJ: Erlbaum.

Fry, R. (2007). *How far behind in math and reading are English language learners?* Washington, DC: Pew Hispanic Center.

Galambos, S. J., & Goldin-Meadow, S. (1990). The effects of learning two languages on levels of metalinguistic awareness. *Cognition, 34,* 1–56.

Galambos, S. J., & Hakuta, K. (1988). Subject-specific and task-specific characteristics of metalinguistic awareness in bilingual children. *Applied Psycholinguistics, 9*, 141–162.

Gándara, P., & Rumberger, R. W. (2006). *Resource needs for California's English learners.* Santa Barbara: University of California Linguistic Minority Research Institute.

García, G. E. (1991). Factors influencing the English reading test performance of Spanish-speaking Hispanic children. *Reading Research Quarterly, 26*(4), 371–392.

García, G. E. (1998). Mexican-American bilingual students' metacognitive reading strategies: What's transferred, unique, problematic? *National Reading Conference Yearbook, 47*, 253–263.

Gathercole, V. C. M. (1997). The linguistic mass/count distinction as an indicator of referent categorization in monolingual and bilingual children. *Child Development, 68*, 832–842.

Gholamain, M., & Geva, E. (1999). Orthographic and cognitive factors in the concurrent development of basic reading skills in English and Persian. *Language Learning, 49*(2), 183–217.

Gil, A. G., Wagner, E. F., & Vega, W. A. (2000). Acculturation, familism and alcohol use among Latino adolescent males: Longitudinal relations. *Journal of Community Psychology, 28*, 443–458.

Goldman, S. R., Reyes, M., & Varnhagen, C. K. (1984). Understanding fables in first and second languages. *NABE Journal, 8*, 835–866.

Greene, J. P. (1997). A meta-analysis of the Rossell and Baker review of bilingual education research. *Bilingual Research Journal, 21*(2/3), 1–22.

Hakuta, K., Goto-Butler, Y., & Witt, D. (2000). *How long does it take English learners to attain proficiency?* University of California Linguistic Minority Research Institute Policy Report 2000-1. Retrieved May 28, 2008, from http://faculty.ucmerced.edu/khakuta/research/publications/%282000%29—HOW LONG DOES IT TAKE ENGLISH LEARNERS TO ATTAIN PR.pdf

Hancin-Bhatt, B., & Nagy, W. E. (1994). Lexical transfer and second language morphological development. *Applied Psycholinguistics, 15*(3), 289–310.

Hatch, E. M. (1978). *Second language acquisition: A book of readings.* Rowley, MA: Newbury House.

Hirsch, E. D. (2006). The case for bringing content into the language arts block and for a knowledge-rich curriculum core for all children. *American Educator.* Retrieved January 12, 2008, from www.aft.org/pubsreports/american_educator/issues/spring06/hirsch.htm

James, C., & Klein, K. (1994). Foreign language learners' spelling and proof-reading strategies. *Papers and Studies in Contrastive Linguistics, 29*, 31–46.

Jiménez, R. T., García, G. E., & Pearson, D. P. (1996). The reading strategies of bilingual Latina/o students who are successful English readers: Opportunities and obstacles. *Reading Research Quarterly, 31*(1), 90–112.

Lanza, E., & Svendsen, B. A. (2007). Tell me who your friends are and I might be able to tell you what language(s) you speak: Social network analysis, multilingualism, and identity. *International Journal of Bilingualism, 11*(3), 275–300.

Lee, J. W. (2008). The effect of ethnic identity and bilingual confidence on Chinese youth's self-esteem. *Alberta Journal of Educational Research, 54*(1), 83–96.

Lipsey, M. W., & Wilson, D. B. (2001). *Practical meta-analysis.* Thousand Oaks, CA: Sage.

Martinez-Roldán, C. M., & Malavé, G. (2004). Language ideologies mediating literacy and identity in bilingual contexts. *Journal of Early Childhood Literacy*, *4*(2), 155–180.

Nagy, W. E., Berninger, V., & Abbott, D. (2006). Contributions of morphology beyond phonology to literacy outcomes of upper elementary and middle-school students. *Journal of Educational Psychology*, *98*(1), 134–147.

Nagy, W. E., García, G. E., Durgunoglu, A. Y., & Hancin-Bhatt, B. (1993). Spanish–English bilingual students' use of cognates in English reading. *Journal of Reading Behavior*, *25*(3), 241–259.

Nagy, W., McClure, E., & Mir, M. (1997). Linguistic transfer and the use of context by Spanish–English bilinguals. *Applied Psycholinguistics*, *18*(4), 431–452.

Nathenson-Mejía, S. (1989). Writing in a second language: Negotiating meaning through invented spelling. *Language Arts*, *66*(5), 516–526.

National Institute for Child Health and Human Development. (2000). *Report of the National Reading Panel. Teaching children to read: An evidence-based assessment of the scientific research literature on reading and its implications for reading instruction* (NIH Publication No. 00-4769). Washington, DC: U.S. Government Printing Office.

Olsen, L. (2000). Learning English and learning America: Immigrants in the center of a storm. *Theory into Practice*, *39*, 196–202.

Olson, D., Russell, C. S., & Sprenkle, D. H. (1984). Circumplex model of marital and family systems IV: Theoretical update. In D. H. Olson & R. C. Miller (Eds.), *Family studies: Vol. 2. Review yearbook* (pp. 59–74). Beverly Hills, CA: Sage.

Paas, F., & Kester, L. (2006). Emerging topics in cognitive load research: Learner and information characteristics in the design of powerful learning environments. *Applied Cognitive Psychology*, *20*(3), 281–285.

Paas, F., Renkl, A., & Sweller, J. (2003). Cognitive load theory and instructional design: Recent developments. *Educational Psychologist*, *38*(1), 1–4.

Parrish, T. B., Merickel, A., Pérez, M., Linquanti, R., Socias, M., Spain, A., et al. (2006). *Effects of the implementation of Proposition 227 on the education of English learners, K–12: Findings from a five-year evaluation (final report)*. Palo Alto and San Francisco: American Institutes for Research and WestEd.

Portes, A., & Hao, L. (2002). The price of uniformity: Language, family and personality adjustment in the immigrant second generation. *Ethnic and Racial Studies*, *25*(6), 889–912.

Portes, P., & Zady, M. F. (2002). Self-esteem in the adaptation of Spanish-speaking adolescents: The role of immigration, family conflict, and depression. *Hispanic Journal of Behavioral Sciences*, *24*(3), 296–318.

Ramírez, J., Yuen, S., Ramey, D., & Pasta, D. (1991). *Final Report: Longitudinal study of structured English immersion strategy, early exit and late-exit bilingual education programs for language minority children*. (Report No. 300-87-0156; prepared for U.S. Department of Education). San Mateo, CA: Aguirre International.

Ramirez-Esparza, N., Gosling, S., Benet-Martínez, V., Potter, J., & Pennebaker, J. (2006). Do bilinguals have two personalities? A special case of cultural frame-switching. *Journal of Research in Personality*, *40*, 99–120.

Reese, L., Garnier, H., Gallimore, R., & Goldenberg, C. (2000). Longitudinal analysis of the antecedents of emergent Spanish literacy and middle-school English reading achievement of Spanish-speaking students. *American Educational Research Journal*, *37*(3), 633–662.

Ricciardelli, L. A. (1992). Bilingualism and cognitive development in relation to threshold theory. *Journal of Psycholinguistic Research, 21*, 301–316.

Rolstad, K., Mahoney, K., & Glass, G. (2005). The big picture: A meta-analysis of program effectiveness research on English language learners. *Educational Policy, 19*(4), 572–594.

Rosenblum, T., & Pinker, S. T. (1983). Word magic revisited: Monolingual and bilingual children's understanding of the word–object relationship. *Child Development, 54*(3), 773–780.

Rossell, C. H., & Baker, K. (1996). The educational effectiveness of bilingual education. *Research in the Teaching of English, 30*(1), 7–69.

Royer, J. M., & Carlo, M. S. (1991). Assessing the language acquisition progress of Limited English Proficient students: Problems and a new alternative. *Applied Measurement in Education, 4*(2), 85–113.

Saunders, W., & Goldenberg, C. (in press). *Research to guide English language development instruction.* Sacramento: California State Department of Education.

Saville-Troike, M. (1984). What really matters in second language learning for academic achievement? *TESOL Quarterly, 18*(2), 199–219.

Shanahan, T., & Beck, I. L. (2006). Effective literacy teaching for English-language learners. In D. L. August & T. Shanahan (Eds.), *Developing literacy in a second language: Report of the National Literacy Panel on Language-Minority Children and Youth* (pp. 415–488). Mahwah, NJ: Erlbaum.

Slavin, R. (1987). Ability grouping and student achievement in elementary schools: A best-evidence synthesis. *Review of Educational Research, 57*, 293–336.

Slavin, R. (Ed.). (1989). *School and classroom organization.* Hillsdale, NJ: Erlbaum.

Slavin, R. E., & Cheung, A. (2005). A synthesis of research on language of reading instruction for English language learners. *Review of Educational Research, 75*(2), 247–284.

Snow, C. E. (1987). Beyond conversation: Second language learners' acquisition of description and explanation. In J. Lantolf & A. Labarca (Eds.), *Research in second language learning: Focus on the classroom* (pp. 3–16). Norwood, NJ: Ablex.

Suárez-Orozco, M., & Suárez-Orozco, C. (2000). Some conceptual considerations in the interdisciplinary study of immigrant children. In E. T. Trueba & L. I. Bartolome (Eds.), *Immigrant voices: In search of educational equity* (pp. 17–36). Lanham, MD: Rowman & Littlefield.

Taylor, C. (1992). *Multiculturalism and "the politics of recognition."* Princeton, NJ: Princeton University Press.

Verhoeven, L. T. (1994). Transfer in bilingual development: The linguistic interdependence hypothesis revisited. *Language Learning, 44*(3), 381–415.

Vom Dorp, I. E. (2000, p. 262). *Biliteracy, monoliteracy and self-concept in native Spanish-dominant and native English-dominant fifth graders.* Unpublished doctoral dissertation, University of New Mexico, Albuquerque.

Willig, A. C. (1985). A meta-analysis of selected studies on the effectiveness of bilingual education. *Review of Educational Research, 55*, 269–317.

Yelland, G. W., Pollard, J., & Mercuri, A. (1993). The metalinguistic benefits of limited contact with a second language. *Applied Psycholinguistics, 14*, 423–444.

Zutell, J., & Allen, V. (1988). The English spelling strategies of Spanish-speaking bilingual children. *TESOL Quarterly, 22*(2), 333–340.

Learning in Two Languages:
Programs with Political Promise

P. Zitlali Morales and Ursula S. Aldana

R ESTRICTIVE LANGUAGE policies, as they have been promulgated in California, Arizona, and Massachusetts, attempted to either seriously curtail or outright ban the use of an English learner's primary language for purposes of instruction. These laws were designed to stop an instructional practice that was characterized as harmful to students who were learning English. However, in the various state campaigns, there was very little discussion about exactly what instructional practices these were or how they may have varied from classroom to classroom and school to school. In fact, there are many ways in which primary language is used in the instruction of English learners and many goals that such programs pursue. For example, the primary language can be used to aid children in the transition to English-only learning, or it can be a core of instruction, alongside English throughout a student's school career. The primary language may be employed only sporadically by a visiting classroom aide, it can be used by one teacher while others instruct only in English, and it can be woven throughout the instructional day by the bilingual classroom teacher.

Similarly, different programs can have very different goals. Some "bilingual" programs have the goal of transitioning students to English-only as soon as possible, or at the point where students have learned to read; others have a goal of creating biliterate students; and still others' goals are to create students who are completely competent in both languages of instruction. Some programs have the goal of developing full biliteracy for English learners and native English speakers simultaneously. The aim of this chapter is to review the literature on instructional programs in two languages and create a taxonomy of programs, showing their various objectives, structures, known outcomes, additional benefits, and specific challenges. Such a taxonomy can be helpful to policymakers and practitioners in determining which goals align with their priorities and what is known about our ability to achieve those goals within different program types.

WHAT DOES LEARNING IN TWO LANGUAGES LOOK LIKE?

In the United States, bilingual programs mostly serve students who are in the process of learning English as their second or other language. The overwhelming majority of these programs are offered in Spanish (due to the rise of Spanish-speaking groups fueled by immigration to the United States) and English, but over the years various other immigrant groups have lobbied for and established bilingual programs involving Mandarin, Korean, Russian, Vietnamese, and more (García, 2009).

Although most bilingual education programs serve language minority students, they differ in their use of the target language, the length of time students stay in the program, the instruction or pedagogy utilized, and their specific goals. They can also differ in the students they target for inclusion in the program. A variety of models for bilingual education programs exist, yet the most common programs are early-exit (transitional) programs, late-exit (developmental) programs, and dual-immersion (or two-way) programs (see Table 10.1). Many schools also use English as a Second Language (ESL) programs and Structured English Immersion (SEI) as ways to educate English learners; their main goal is to assimilate students as quickly as possible into English. Since ESL and SEI models do not normally include instruction in the primary language and are therefore not bilingual programs, we do not discuss them here.

Early-Exit or Transitional Bilingual Education (TBE)

Early-exit programs, also known as transitional bilingual education (TBE), teach students to read and sometimes teach other academic subjects in their primary language (the minority language), while also explicitly teaching English. Usually by fourth grade, students are placed in mainstream classrooms in English, along with other students who have never been in a bilingual program. The explicit goal of these early-exit programs is to help students become competent learners in English as quickly as possible and without falling too far behind their English-speaking classmates in subject-matter learning. The primary language is used as a bridge to English, but there is no intention to continue building on the primary language.

Table 10.1. Language education programs in the United States today.

Program	Language Used	Components	Duration	Goals	Outcomes and Benefits	Challenges and Limitations
Transitional Bilingual Education (Early Exit)	90–50% of instruction initially in the home language Increasing percentage of English used over time, up to 90%	Initial literacy and some subject matter instruction in the home language ESL and subject matter instruction at students' level of English Teachers certified in bilingual education	1–3 years Students exit when they are proficient in English	Linguistic assimilation English acquisition without falling behind academically	Positive reading outcomes in English May reduce instructional time lost Provide social and psychological transition	Usually only English learners enrolled Students generally do not develop primary language skills beyond a rudimentary level
Developmental Bilingual Education (Late Exit)	90–50% of instruction initially in the home language Gradual decreasing to 50% or less of home language use by grade 4, or a 50/50 from beginning	Initial literacy in home language, and some subject instruction in home language ESL initially and subject matter instruction at students' level of English Teachers certified in bilingual education	5–6 years	Bilingualism and biliteracy Academic achievement in English	Students develop stronger bilingual and biliteracy skills than early-exit programs, as well as the ability to learn in a second language	Usually only English learners are enrolled Without support for primary language after elementary school, students may lose bilingual and biliteracy skills
Two-Way Bilingual Education (Two-way Dual Language, Two-Way Immersion, Dual Immersion, Dual Language)	90:10 model: 90% home language, 10% other language in early grades, moving to 50:50 model: parity of both languages	Emergent bilinguals and native English speakers taught literacy and subjects in both languages Peer tutoring Teachers certified in bilingual education	5–6 years	Bilingualism and biliteracy Academic achievement in English	More positive attitudes toward both languages Intergroup relations are enhanced Best academic outcomes among all models	Balancing numbers of strong English models with minority language speakers

Source: Adapted from Crawford, 2004, p. 42; García, 2009, p. 186.

While biliteracy *may* be achieved, it is not usually an explicit goal of the program. The advantage of such programs is that they can help to build on existing skills and abilities that students have already achieved in their primary language. Furthermore, early-exit programs have been found to reduce the achievement gap in reading between English learners and English speakers more than Structured English Immersion type programs (García, 2009; Thomas & Collier, 2002). The disadvantage of early-exit/TBE programs is that students generally do not develop their primary-language skills beyond a very rudimentary level, and there is no evidence of longer-term cognitive advantages.

Late-Exit or Developmental Bilingual Education

Similar to early-exit programs, late-exit programs (also known as developmental bilingual education) have the goal of eventually transitioning students out of primary-language and into English-only instruction. Unlike early-exit programs, however, late-exit programs intend for students to be strong readers in two languages and to learn vocabulary in core subjects so that they can learn math, science, and other subjects in more than one language. The goal of late-exit programs is often to "maintain" skills in the primary language, yet evidence suggests that students often begin to transition to English on their own, earlier than the program planned, as they are acutely aware of the program's goal to transition to English. Students usually make a full transition to English by fifth or sixth grade, with the intent that they will continue receiving some primary-language instruction through the end of elementary school or even middle school.

Most commonly, however, bilingual programs are not available in middle schools due to the lack of bilingual personnel in the various subject areas. It is often difficult to find teachers who have command of a specific curricular area and also have strong competencies in two languages (García, 2009). Scheduling classes that accommodate students from bilingual and nonbilingual programs is also a challenge at the middle school level and beyond. The advantages of late-exit programs include stronger bilingual and biliteracy skills as well as the ability to learn in a second language. Students eventually lose many of these skills, however, since bilingual instruction is not normally continued beyond the upper elementary grades.

Dual or Two-Way Immersion

Dual-immersion programs enroll both English-dominant and minority language speakers in the same class. Although the goal is to have 50% English-dominant and 50% minority language speakers, the percentages vary depending on the program and the population of students the school serves. The overall objective of these programs is for both groups of students to become bilingual and biliterate.

Since they are maintenance programs, the minority language never ceases to be used for instructional purposes.

Two-way dual-immersion programs are built on the premise that such programs can create equal-status environments. The work of Gordon Allport (1954) and Elizabeth Cohen and Rachel Lotan (1995) underlies the assumptions of the model—that children will learn from one another and learn to like one another if they are exposed to learning situations in which their status is equalized. Thus, instruction for language majority and language minority students must be structured so that both languages have equal importance in the learning environment, and the goals of instruction are to achieve competence in both. In this way, the traditionally socially disadvantaged group gains an equivalent status in the classroom to the socially advantaged group.

One common model of two-way immersion programs is a 90/10 model in which 90% of instruction is in the minority language and 10% is in English at the kindergarten level. The percentage of English instruction increases each year until a 50/50 balance is reached, usually by third grade. Another model is a 50/50 model in which the language of instruction is always 50% English and 50% minority language (Christian, Howard, & Loeb, 2000). Some educators argue, however, that this is not sufficient input of the non-English language, especially for those students who will only experience the second language in the classroom. Either way, both languages are given equal status in instruction, and the minority language–speaking students serve as the model for the English-dominant students.

Interest in dual-immersion programs has increased dramatically in recent years (Howard & Christian, 2002). The Center for Applied Linguistics (CAL) reported 335 dual-language programs in the United States during the 2007–2008 schoolyear (see Figure 10.1). However, this number reflects only the dual-immersion programs that self-reported to CAL, and the actual number of dual-immersion programs is in fact much larger. For instance, Texas reported 263 dual-language programs (Texas Two-Way/Dual Language Consortium, n.d.), and California, notwithstanding Proposition 227, reported 201 such programs in 2006 (California Department of Education, 2006).

Dual-immersion models are a popular and viable alternative to more traditional transitional models of bilingual education programs (Christian et al., 2000). Dual-immersion or two-way models differ from the transitional model in that they specify maintenance of the primary language as a goal, rather than just eventual transition to English. This goal supports bilingualism and biliteracy. In some cases, dual-immersion models are exempt from propositions that restrict bilingual education, such as Question 2 in Massachusetts. In California and Arizona, dual-immersion programs can be established by parent request if sufficient numbers of parents press the school district.

It is an irony, perhaps, that in California Proposition 227 intended to dismantle bilingual education, and yet it may have served to increase the number

Figure 10.1. Dual-language programs in the United States, 1962–2007.

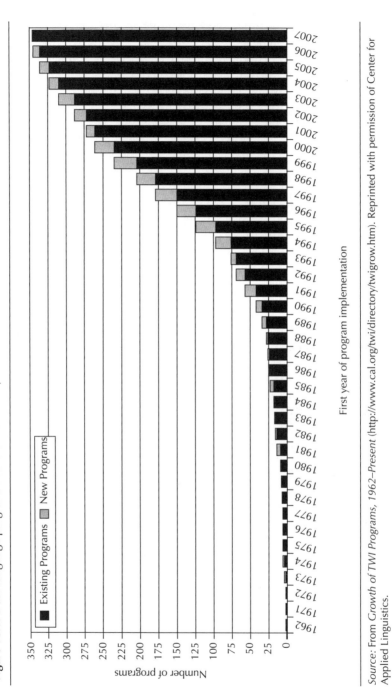

Source: From *Growth of TWI Programs, 1962–Present* (http://www.cal.org/twi/directory/twigrow.htm). Reprinted with permission of Center for Applied Linguistics.

of dual-immersion programs in the state. While fewer than 6% of English learners in California receive bilingual instruction (Gándara, Maxwell-Jolly, & Rumberger, 2008), over 100 new dual-immersion programs have started since 1998. (For a description of the increasing numbers of dual-immersion programs in California after the passage of Proposition 227, see Linton & Franklin, Chapter 11, this volume). This trend may be due to the political viability of these programs, since they serve the educational goals of two distinct populations: linguistic minority students and native English speakers (Christian et al., 2000; Linton, 2006).

THE BENEFITS OF LEARNING IN TWO LANGUAGES

Bilingual education theory and empirical studies indicate that students from minority language groups in the United States benefit both academically and socially from the use of the primary language for instructional purposes (Cummins, 1996). As cited in August, Goldenberg, & Rueda (Chapter 9, this volume), English learners instructed in two languages perform better in English literacy skills than similar students instructed in all-English approaches such as English as a Second Language (ESL) and Structured English Immersion (SEI). August and colleagues (Chapter 9, this volume) further cite the cognitive benefits of learning in two languages, as well as the added benefits of family cohesion and student self-esteem and identity development that can result from bilingual instruction.

In addition to these positive outcomes, the ethnic and linguistic diversity in bilingual education programs can promote positive intergroup relations (Reyes, Laliberty, & Orbanosky, 1993; Whitmore & Crowell, 2006) if equal-status assumptions are met—that is, if both languages and both groups of students are valued equally in the classroom. This, of course, is an outcome that holds increasing importance in today's global society. Interethnic and interracial interactions are an integral part of business and economic relations; thus, learning how to negotiate multicultural settings is an important skill that can benefit students throughout their academic and professional lives. The multilingual and multicultural environment of bilingual and dual-immersion programs can reduce prejudice (Genesee & Gándara, 1999) and promote cross-cultural awareness and friendships (Cazabon, Lambert, & Hall, 1993; Lambert & Cazabon, 1994; Lindholm-Leary, 2001; Reyes et al., 1993; Whitmore & Crowell, 2006).

In a study of social relationships among students in the Amigos program, a two-way immersion program in Cambridge, Massachusetts, findings from surveys and structured observations showed that third-grade students exhibited no racial biases when picking best friends in the class, nor did the Hispanic majority segregate themselves in class (Cazabon et al., 1993; Lambert & Cazabon, 1994). The program was created by the Cambridge Public Schools in a deliberate attempt to integrate language minority students with language majority students through a combination of the best features of transitional bilingual education (for EL students) and language immersion education (for native English speakers). Whitmore and Crowell (2006) also found intergroup relations to be a positive outcome in their study of a third-grade bilingual classroom in a magnet school under a desegregation order in Boston. The authors found that the diverse classroom environment offered, for example, "opportunities to spend the night at each other's houses [which] invited firsthand cross-cultural learning for the girls that widened their views of the world and offered real contexts for hearing and using each other's home language" (Whitmore & Crowell, 2006, p. 279). In interviews conducted by the researchers a decade later, the young adults in the bilingual program conveyed how much they valued their experiences as language learners and expressed an appreciation for the classroom diversity.

Promoting intergroup relations in bilingual programs must be done purposefully; this outcome is not necessarily realized unless explicit attention is paid to it. Problems and prejudice can occur when programs integrate language minority and majority students. Genesee and Gándara (1999) warn that "if bilingual education programs are to provide models for improved intergroup attitudes and relations, teachers working in these programs must understand how to counteract the centrifugal societal forces that act to maintain intergroup prejudice, discrimination, and stereotyping in school" (p. 681). Teacher pedagogy and teacher-modeled peer work can facilitate intergroup relations (Angelova, Gunawardena, & Volk, 2006; Hadi-Tabassum, 1999; Reyes et al., 1993). For example, if teachers employ a "language as resource" (Ruiz, 1984) model in their classroom, peer tutoring and peer work can serve as both an academic and social integration mechanism. Specifically, both English learners and English-speaking students can serve as linguistic resources for their peers and even act as peer teachers to one another when they repeat, translate, echo, clarify, scaffold with cues, code-switch, and paraphrase for each other (Angelova et al., 2006; Reyes et al., 1993). When these peer-teaching strategies are used, all the students are experts in particular areas at one point or another, thus creating a learning environment where the status of Spanish and English is equal.

By raising the status of the target (non-English) language, bilingual and dual-immersion programs aim to raise the status of the individuals who speak the target language. In a study of a Colorado classroom, Reyes and colleagues (1993) noted that students' interactions offered authentic experiences with linguistic and cultural diversity; as a result, "Anglo, Chicano, and Mexican children were brought into constant contact [and] this contributed to a more equitable social status among the three groups" (p. 667). By the end of the year, 44% of the students were classified as highly engaged in cross-cultural language use, friendships, and awareness (and 37% were classified as moderately engaged).

Still, dual-immersion programs in particular face implementation challenges at the middle and high school levels, where less attention is paid to maintaining and using students' primary language. A range of factors can contribute to English hegemony within a school, such as teachers rebuking students' use of Spanish vernacular, a curriculum that focuses on English assessment and low-level language/grammar skills, and peer-group pressure to speak English (Freeman, 2000; McCollum, 1999). These factors can negatively affect the interactions between students from different language groups if one group of students feels subordinate to another.

An example of a school that has grappled with these issues is the Oyster Bilingual School in Washington, D.C., described in Freeman's 1996 ethnography. The school's administrators determined that language planning was an essential program component in order to enact social change for their White, Latino, and African American students. When Freeman found evidence of student self-selected segregation and some tension between ethnic groups, the school "a) recognized discriminatory practices against language minority students in mainstream US society, b) rejected the discourse, and c) collectively constructed an alternative with the goal of socializing language minority and language majority students to see themselves and each other as equal participants in school and in society" (Freeman, 1996, p. 572). The case of the Oyster Bilingual School exemplifies how a school attempted to address issues of prejudice among ethnic groups within the school by confronting societal attitudes and raising the language status of the minority group. When language planning was not enough, the school developed a community council that introduced conflict resolution training for the school and made it part of the standard curriculum. In order for bilingual education programs to foster intergroup relations successfully, school policy and teacher pedagogy must be aligned, and school staff and community members must all be included as stakeholders in the design of the program and be committed to the mission of bilingualism.

PROGRAMMATIC CHALLENGES

Although research on bilingual and dual-immersion programs illustrates the positive effects of these language programs for those individuals who choose to participate in them, each program's success is dependent on the support it garners from all stakeholders, including parents (Miramontes, Nadeau, & Commins, 1997; Smith et al., 2002; Torres-Guzmán, 2002). Even with sufficient support, however, the benefits accrued by participating in these programs are likely to differ for individual students. For example, in a detailed longitudinal study of the long-term academic and linguistic outcomes of a model dual-language program in Florida,

Oller and Eilers (2002) found that native English speakers never acquired the same level of fluency in Spanish as the native Spanish speakers in the program, and the English learners never quite met the same level of proficiency in academic English as their native English-speaking peers. Nonetheless, the gains both groups made were impressively greater than for most other programs serving both English learners and native English speakers.

Sometimes bilingual programs face the challenge of functioning within hostile social and political climates (such as in California, Arizona, or Massachusetts). In these tense environments, programs must grapple with maintaining equal status for the languages taught. When maintenance of the primary language is not emphasized at the same level as English language acquisition, students and communities may receive the message that their language is a problem that needs remediation rather than a resource that will aid them in their academic and career paths. Moreover, it can be challenging to offer bilingual programs to a socioeconomically diverse group of students who not only have diverse needs but also have access to different (and unequal) sets of resources to assist their learning.

Language Status Challenges

Most bilingual programs across the United States are transitional programs in which students are taught in the primary language for a few years and then mainstreamed into English-only classrooms. These programs use the primary language as a tool to transition to English, rather than making maintenance of the primary language a goal. As such, these programs, perhaps inadvertently, promote a greater value and status for the English language than for the minority language.

However, even dual-immersion programs are not without their challenges. Proponents of bilingual education have pointed out that dual-language programs may be designed to serve primarily the native English speakers who enroll in them because of the unequal social power of minority and majority parents (Delgado-Larocco, 1998; Gómez, Freeman, & Freeman, 2005). Moreover, if dual-immersion programs succeed in developing native English speakers into fully proficient bilinguals, the programs may serve to take away the one advantage that ELs have traditionally had: the distinction of achieving a high level of bilingualism (Valdés, 1997).

Fitts's (2006) study illustrated how English hegemony and the White culture of power affected the ways in which students constructed identities as bilinguals in relation to each other. While the school promoted bilingualism and a social justice agenda, attempting to treat all students as equals, the adults in effect undermined the strengths of the native bilingual, mostly Latino, students. By overemphasizing the equality of the students as bilinguals and biliterates, the teachers devalued the literacy skills the Latino students had gained from years of listening, translating, speaking, and writing in two languages.

Also at play in this context of learning in two languages is the politics of language itself, as well as cultural politics among the populations participating in these programs. To this end, one of the biggest questions asked about educational programs is: Who is this program serving? Particularly when a program aims to serve distinct populations of students, questions may arise as to whose interests are being served first and whose voices will be heard when it comes to programmatic decisions. Just as the context matters in terms of student learning, schools also operate in societal contexts where there are hierarchies of race, class, and language. This context may also accentuate the power differences that exist between English-dominant speakers and minority language speakers. This power differential may be especially salient in Spanish dual-language programs, since Latino children and families are usually significantly underprivileged, in comparison to English-dominant students, with respect to socioeconomic status and possession of the social and cultural capital that is most often recognized in school.

Despite these issues, dual-language programs still raise the status of languages other than English; as a result, native English-speaking children and their parents see the value in knowing more than one language (Gómez et al., 2005). Minority language children may become the language models for English-dominant speakers, reversing the broader societal trend in which English speakers and their language are privileged and thus promoting cross-cultural relationships and understandings.

CLASS DIVERSITY CHALLENGES

Many successful dual-immersion programs enroll students who come from socioeconomically advantaged communities, often leading critics of these programs to attribute students' high test scores to their privileged backgrounds rather than to the effects of the program. For this reason, it is imperative that program evaluations include an appropriate control group to test this hypothesis. Of course, even if test scores are no higher for these students in dual-immersion programs, the added value of having acquired literacy in a second language must be considered as an important program outcome.

Another issue arises when a community needs to attract a population of native English speakers to complement the population of English learners. The English speakers who enroll in dual-immersion programs are most often White and middle-class, and questions have been raised about whether these programs would have the same level of success if middle-class students were not enrolled. Of course, inherent in this question is the importance of the middle-class social capital that these students bring and can share with their lower-income peers. One possible answer to these class-based issues is a model developed for dual-language education that is especially well suited for areas with high numbers of ELs, such as near the U.S.–Mexico border (Gómez, 2000). The "50/50 Content Model" was developed in southern Texas and works with a student population that is predominantly Latina/o, with all levels of fluency in both Spanish and English. Although a rigid model, it has been implemented in both Texas and Washington with impressive results on standardized tests (Gómez et al., 2005).

POLICY IMPLICATIONS

School Desegregation

Research related to learning in two languages suggests the need to explore further the manner in which bilingual programs can foster school desegregation. Two-thirds of African American and Latino students in major urban centers attend severely segregated schools where 10% or less of their fellow students are White (Orfield & Frankenburg, 2008). Furthermore, African American and Latino children make up one-third of all children in the United States, yet they account for more than three-fourths of children living in high-poverty neighborhoods (O'Hare & Mather, 2003). Spanish speakers in particular are also isolated from English speakers (Orfield & Lee, 2006; Rumberger, Gándara & Merino, 2006). For poor students also labeled English learners, schools can produce a triply segregated environment, as they are economically, ethnically, and linguistically isolated (Betts, Kim, & Danenberg, 2000).

Since integration has been shown to increase academic outcomes for poor students of color,[1] dual-language programs can offer a number of benefits. They can raise the achievement of EL students, provide enrichment to English-dominant students, and offer much-needed intercultural interaction for all students. Such cross-cultural interaction prepares children to live and work in a global society. In a study of 248 dual-immersion programs, Howard and Sugarman (2001) found that 54% of these programs had no majority ethnic group. In a time when Latino students are often segregated in neighborhood schools where the majority of students are minorities and in English Language Development (ELD) or English as a Second Language (ESL) classes, dual-language programs have the power to attract a more diverse student body and help alleviate ethnic and linguistic segregation of English learners.

The Potential of Dual Immersion

Dual-immersion programs offer a potentially positive educational experience, especially for Spanish-dominant students in anti-immigrant environments where "bilingual education" is misinterpreted as "no English" being taught to English learners. Dual-immersion programs are politically viable because they (1) have proven to be an effective way for English learners to become proficient in English while pursuing an enriched curriculum, (2) serve the needs of at least two distinct groups of students (English learners and native English speakers), and (3) hold great promise as a strategy for diminishing—if not closing—the achievement gap between students of low and high socioeconomic status (SES) in general and between Latino and White students in particular (Linton, 2006).

Considering the demonstrated effectiveness of dual-immersion programs, more schools could adopt them and extend these programs into high school. Currently, the majority of dual-immersion programs are implemented at the elementary school level (Howard, Sugarman & Christian, 2003). Yet some programs that started off in elementary schools have successfully lobbied for continuation into middle schools (Potowski, 2007; Quintanar-Sarellana, 2004). Moreover, these programs could well extend into International Baccalaureate (IB) programs that are already offered at some high schools. The IB program, which incorporates a rigorous internationally designed curriculum, requires competence in two languages and does not privilege either language. Students who are native Chinese or Spanish speakers can pass exams in those languages while they develop their second language, English. IB graduates typically go on to selective colleges.

In our current system, English learners are twice as likely to drop out of high school as all other students (Ruiz de Velasco & Fix, 2000; Rumberger, 2006), in part due to the lack of relevancy of the school curriculum. It is thus imperative to learn from the successes of dual-language programs that currently serve young students from the beginning of their school career and apply these successes to the education of students who come from Spanish-speaking instruction in other countries, particularly at the secondary level. Nonetheless, it must be mentioned that an important consideration in creating K–12 dual-immersion programs is recruiting and training teachers who are equipped to teach in two languages. For these programs to be successful, the preparation and professional development of bilingual teachers needs to become a priority for school districts and states.

CONCLUSION

Looking to the future, if the political and social climate were to change, particularly in states with restrictive language policies, one can envision biliteracy and biculturalism as the instructional goals for all students. Rich academic learning contexts for cultural and linguistic minority children are those that allow them to draw on their multiple linguistic codes and other cultural resources (McKay & Hornberger, 1996; Moll & González, 1994) and that foster cross-cultural relationships and skills that can be utilized throughout their lifetimes.

Restrictive language policies discourage schools from utilizing students' linguistic repertoires in the service of learning. They privilege the language of instruction over content and have limited real opportunities for both English learners and English speakers to access a more enriched education. However, if we look to research and make policy decisions based on empirical evidence, it will inevitably lead us to better models of instruction that incorporate the cultural and linguistic assets that children bring with them to school.

NOTE

1. A 2006 brief to the Supreme Court synthesized the research on integration and found that desegregated schools do in fact produce positive gains. This brief can be found at http://www.civilrightsproject.ucla.edu/research/deseg/amicus_parents_v_seatle.pdf.

REFERENCES

Allport, G. (1954). *The nature of prejudice*. Reading, MA: Addison-Wesley.

Angelova, M., Gunawardena, D., & Volk, D. (2006). Peer teaching and learning: Co-constructing language in a dual language first grade. *Language and Education, 20*(3), 173–190.

Betts, J. R., Kim, S. R., & Danenberg, A. (2000). *Equal resources, equal outcomes? The distribution of school resources and student achievement in California*. San Francisco: Public Policy Institute of California.

California Department of Education. (2006). Two-way bilingual immersion—Title III. Retrieved October 8, 2008, from http://www.cde.ca.gov/sp/el/ip/twowyimmersion.asp

Cazabon, M., Lambert, W. E., & Hall, G. (1993). *Two-way bilingual education: A progress report on the Amigos program* (Research Report No. 7). Santa Cruz, CA: National Center for Research on Cultural Diversity and Second Language Learning.

Christian, D., Howard, E. R., & Loeb, M. I. (2000). Bilingualism for all: Two-way immersion education in the United States. *Theory into Practice, 39*(4), 258–266.

Cohen, E. G., & Lotan, R. A. (1995). Producing equal-status interaction in the heterogeneous classroom. *American Educational Research Journal, 32*(1), 99–120.

Crawford, J. (2004), *Educating English learners: Language diversity in the classroom* (5th ed.). Los Angeles: Bilingual Educational Services.

Cummins, J. (1996). *Negotiating identities: Education for empowerment in a diverse society*. Los Angeles: California Association for Bilingual Education.

Delgado-Larocco, E. L. (1998). *Classroom processes in a two-way immersion kindergarten classroom*. Davis: Division of Education, University of California, Davis.

Fitts, S. (2006). Reconstructing the status quo: Linguistic interaction in a dual language school. *Bilingual Research Journal, 29*(2), 337–365.

Freeman, R. (1996). Dual language planning at Oyster Bilingual School: "It's much more than language." *TESOL Quarterly, 30*(3), 557–582.

Freeman, R. (2000). Contextual challenges to dual-language education: A case study of a developing middle school program. *Anthropology & Education Quarterly, 31*(2), 202–229.

Gándara, P., Maxwell-Jolly, J., & Rumberger, R. W. (2008). *Resource needs for English learners: Getting down to policy recommendations.* Santa Barbara: University of California Linguistic Minority Research Institute.

García, O. (2009). *Bilingual education in the 21st century.* Oxford: Wiley-Blackwell.

Genesee, F., & Gándara, P. (1999). Bilingual education programs: A cross-national perspective. *Journal of Social Issues, 55*(4), 665–685.

Gómez, L. (2000). Two-way bilingual education: Promoting educational and social change. *Journal of the Texas Association for Bilingual Education, 5*(1), 43–54.

Gómez, L., Freeman, D., & Freeman, Y. (2005). Dual language education: A promising 50–50 model. *Bilingual Research Journal, 29*(1), 145–164.

Hadi-Tabassum, S. (1999). Assessing students' attitudes and achievements in a multicultural and multilingual science classroom. *Multicultural Education, 7*(2), 15–20.

Howard, E. R., & Christian, D. (2002). *Two-way immersion 101: Designing and implementing a two-way immersion education program at the elementary level.* Santa Cruz: Center for Research on Education, Diversity & Excellence, University of California, Santa Cruz.

Howard, E. R., & Sugarman, J. (2001). *Two-way immersion programs: Features and statistics* (ERIC Digest EDO-FL-01-01). Washington, DC: ERIC Clearinghouse on Languages and Linguistics. Retrieved November 1, 2008, from http://www.cal.org/ericcll/digest/0101twi.html

Howard, E. R., Sugarman, J., & Christian, D. (2003). *Trends in two-way immersion education—A review of the research.* Baltimore, MD: Center for Research on the Education of Students Placed at Risk, Johns Hopkins University.

Lambert, W. E., & Cazabon, M. (1994). *Students' views of the Amigos program* (Research Report No. 11). Washington, DC: National Center for Research on Cultural Diversity and Second Language Learning.

Lindholm-Leary, K. (2001). *Dual language education.* Tonawanda, NY: Multilingual Matters.

Linton, A. (2006). *Language politics and policy in the United States: Implications for the immigration debate.* San Diego: The Center for Comparative Immigration Studies, University of California, San Diego.

McCollum, P. (1999). Learning to value English: Cultural capital in a two-way bilingual program. *Bilingual Research Journal, 23*(2–3), 113–134.

McKay, S. L., & Hornberger, N. H. (1996). *Sociolinguistics and language teaching.* New York: Cambridge University Press.

Miramontes, O. B., Nadeau, A., & Commins, N. L. (1997). *Restructuring schools for linguistic diversity: Linking decision making to effective programs.* New York: Teachers College Press.

Moll, L. C., & González, N. (1994). Lessons from research with language minority children. *Journal of Reading Behavior, 26*(4), 439–456.

O'Hare, W., & Mather, M. (2003). The growing number of kids in severely distressed neighborhoods: Evidence from the 2000 census. Washington, DC: A Kids Count/PRB Report on Census 2000, The Annie E. Casey Foundation and the Population Reference Bureau.

Oller, D. K., & Eilers, R. (2002). *Language and literacy in bilingual children.* Clevedon, UK: Multilingual Matters.

Orfield, G., & Frankenburg, E. (2008). *The last have become first: Rural and small town America lead the way on desegregation.* Los Angeles: The Civil Rights Project/ Proyecto Derechos Civiles, University of California, Los Angeles.

Orfield, G., & Lee, C. (2006). *Racial transformation and the changing nature of segregation.* Cambridge, MA: The Civil Rights Project at Harvard University.

Potowski, K. (2007). *Language and identity in a dual immersion school.* Clevedon, UK: Multilingual Matters.

Quintanar-Sarellana, R. (2004). ¡Si se puede! Academic excellence and bilingual competency in a K–8 two-way dual immersion program. *Journal of Latinos and Education, 3*(2), 87–102.

Reyes, M. de la Luz, Laliberty, E. A., & Orbanosky, J. M. (1993). Emerging biliteracy and cross-cultural sensitivity in a language arts classroom. *Language Arts, 70,* 659–668.

Ruiz, R. (1984). Orientations in language planning. *NABE Journal, 8*(2), 15–24.

Ruiz de Velasco, J., & Fix, M. (2000). *Overlooked and underserved: Immigrant students in U.S. secondary school.* Washington, DC: The Urban Institute.

Rumberger, R. W. (2006). The growth of the linguistic minority population in the U.S. and California, 1980–2005. *EL Facts,* No. 8. Santa Barbara, CA: University of California Linguistic Minority Institute.

Rumberger, R. W., Gándara, P., & Merino, B. (2006). Where California's English learners attend school and why it matters. *UC LMRI Newsletter, 15,* 1–2.

Smith, P. H., Arnot-Hopffer, E., Carmichael, C. M., Murphy, E., Valle, A., González, N., & Poveda, A. (2002). Raise a child, not a test score: Perspectives on bilingual education at Davis Bilingual Magnet School. *Bilingual Research Journal, 26*(1), 103–21.

Texas Two-Way/Dual Language Consortium. (n.d.). *Texas two-way dual language education.* Retrieved October 9, 2008, from http://texastwoway.org/

Thomas, W. P., & Collier, V. P. (2002). *A national study of school effectiveness for language minority students' long-term academic achievement.* Retrieved July 22, 2008, from http://crede.berkeley.edu/research/llaa/1.1_final.html

Torres-Guzmán, M. E. (2002). Dual language programs: Key features and results. *Directions in Language and Education,* No. 14, 1–16.

Valdés, G. (1997). Dual-language immersion programs: A cautionary note concerning the education of language-minority students. *Harvard Educational Review, 67*(3), 391–429.

Whitmore, K., & Crowell, C. (2006). Bilingual education students reflect on their language education: Reinventing a classroom 10 years later. *Journal of Adolescent & Adult Literacy, 49*(4), 270–285.

Bilingualism for the Children: Dual-Language Programs Under Restrictive Language Policies

April Linton and Rebecca C. Franklin

A SMALL BUT GROWING number of U.S. public schools offer dual language programs (also called two-way immersion, two-way bilingual immersion, or dual immersion). These programs place immigrant children in a position to help native English speakers become bilingual, while the English learners also become biliterate. Language minority (from a single language background, usually Spanish) and English-speaking pupils are grouped together, starting in the earliest grades and extending at least through grade 5. Teachers instruct in both languages, with academic achievement, bilingual proficiency, biliteracy, and multicultural understanding as their objectives. Education researchers and practitioners are interested in dual-language education for several reasons. First of all, it is an effective way for English learners to become proficient in English while pursuing an enriched curriculum. Second, it holds great promise as a strategy for closing the achievement gap between students of low and high socioeconomic status (SES) students in general and between Latino and White students in particular. Dual-language programs also offer cognitive and linguistic benefits to students (see Chapters 9 and 10, this volume). At the same time, dual-language education helps children develop positive self-identities, both in terms of race and ethnicity and as learners (Hawkins, 2005; Reyes & Vallone, 2007).

This chapter reports on the experiences of 12 school districts to explore dual-language educators' and parents' responses to California Proposition 227 and Massachusetts Question 2. Our research is based on fieldwork in schools that offer dual-language programs; interviews with educators, administrators, and parents; and documents, such as reports and news/opinion articles, that reveal the motivations behind school- and district-level decisions. Our coverage of California is much more extensive because dual-language programs are a larger phenomenon there and one we have studied for some time. Unlike Massachusetts, where dual-language education is a stable but rare option under Question 2, in California we see new programs every year, despite Proposition 227. What has motivated the maintenance and further initiation of dual-language programs despite restrictive language policies? And to what ends? We discuss how education professionals and parents have reacted to these laws as well as the reasons why we now observe English immersion policies in some districts whereas in others, restrictive language policies have not impeded the establishment of more dual-language programs.

DUAL-LANGUAGE PROGRAMS AND RESTRICTIVE LANGUAGE POLICIES IN CALIFORNIA AND MASSACHUSETTS

Despite Proposition 227 and Question 2, dual-language education is a growing phenomenon in California public schools and a stable option in Massachusetts. For the 2007–2008 schoolyear, the California Department of Education (2008) lists 201 programs, and we were able to locate 14 in Massachusetts. Figure 11.1 illustrates the growth of dual-language education in California pre– and post– Proposition 227.

Figure 11.1. Dual-language program growth in California, pre– and post– Proposition 227.

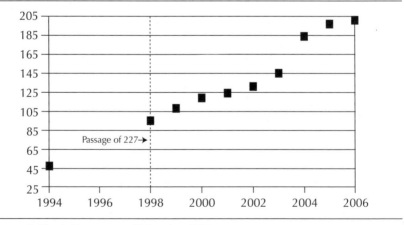

Source: California Department of Education, 2008.

Dual-Language Program Maintenance in California

Some of the older California dual-language programs easily achieved compliance with Proposition 227. For example, in September 1998, the California Board of Education voted to give charter status to Edison Language Academy, then 12 years old, in the Santa Monica–Malibu Unified School District. As of December 2006, there were at least eight California charter schools with dual-language programs. Becoming a charter allowed the school to maintain its dual-language curriculum under Proposition 227, without waivers for English learners. Gates Elementary School in Saddleback Valley Unified School District (Orange County), which has both dual-language and mainstream classrooms, followed suit in 1999. In both cases, the schools' charters were granted on the basis of students' good grades and test scores. Children in the dual-language program were doing better than those in English-only classrooms and performing at or above the district average.

Based on their study of how California schools that provided transitional bilingual education reacted to Proposition 227, education researchers Stritikus and García (2000) categorize educators' responses in three ways: (1) "Outward defiance" was evident where educators who strongly opposed the law on pedagogical grounds sought waivers immediately. (2) "Clarification" occurred in districts that were somewhat opposed to bilingual education. Some teachers saw 227 as a way for them to "clarify their mission" in the classroom by adopting English-only policies. Conversely, Proposition 227 clarified the mission of teachers who strongly believed in bilingual education; they viewed waivers as a way to prevent public intrusion into their classrooms. (3) "Anxiety in the face of climate change," resulting in the greatest confusion, emerged where there was no ideological consistency among districts, school, and teachers.

We find that these classifications apply to dual-language programs as well. For example, the programs in Santa Monica and Saddleback Valley are clear examples of "outward defiance"; however, instead of asking parents of English learners to sign waivers each year, administrators essentially waived their entire schools. We see evidence of "clarification" in Long Beach, where there were two long-established elementary programs when Proposition 227 passed. At Patrick Henry School, which had followed a 90/10 dual-language model in which children first learn reading in Spanish (see Chapter 10 for definitions of program models), administrators felt pressured to add more English early on so that students would meet the district's English reading standard in third grade. As the school's dual-language specialist explained:

> Our children are expected to meet English retention criteria when they've only started transitioning into English at the beginning of third grade. We used to transition them in January. This year we started in September because of that. . . . Even that kills us because [it's not entirely true to the

model]. We didn't have to deal with that before. . . . We're working on how we can retain our program model but accelerate it a little bit for the ELs [English learners]. And that's why we started implementing English sight words in first grade. In second grade we've started doing English phonics.

In the first years after Proposition 227 passed, it became more difficult to recruit English learners into the Long Beach programs, which formerly had waiting lists. This was mainly because of inconsistencies at the district level. Lawsuits ensued because the district was not correctly informing Spanish-speaking parents about their options. For example, parents reported being told that since their children knew English, they had to go into English-only classrooms. This problem has been corrected; there are now six thriving dual-language programs in Long Beach (Long Beach Unified School District, 2007).

Los Angeles and San Diego schools were cases of "anxiety in the face of climate change." By 2001, several of the already scarce dual-language programs in the Los Angeles Unified School District (LAUSD) had been dismantled, and those that remained received little support from the district. Grand View (pre-K–5), Weigand (K–4), and Mark Twain Middle School (6–8) are the only LAUSD dual-language programs that were established before Proposition 227 and still exist today. A bilingual teacher at one school that terminated its program summed up the mood: "Proposition 227 said no more bilingual education. And even though this [dual language] was a separate program that was federally funded, I think the feeling was that it was next. I don't think that there was a lot of district support for our program." This comment typifies LAUSD's initial response to Proposition 227—that dual-language programs were bilingual and therefore undesirable.

Against the odds, Grand View Elementary, located in a low-income, high-immigrant area of Los Angeles, did manage to maintain its dual-language classrooms. In 2000, the principal credited the dual-language program's success at Grand View to a dedicated and stable staff as well as to parents who are "risktakers" and very involved in their children's schooling. He also expressed concern about how the anti–bilingual education climate in LAUSD might impact his school. Four years later, a new principal praised the teachers who started the program, noting that its survival is a testament to their "fortitude and the strength." He is still working to obtain magnet status for the school, which would give it a higher profile in the district and attract more Spanish learners to the dual-language program because students get free transportation to magnet schools.

Dual-language education was also rare in San Diego Unified School District (SDUSD) prior to Proposition 227. There were only three programs: Fremont Elementary (now closed), Longfellow Elementary (no dual-language program there now), and the Language Academy–San Diego. But there were many transitional bilingual programs, and to preserve them school district administrators initially tried to find as much flexibility in Proposition 227 as was legally possible. SDUSD was among the 38 California school districts that applied for a blanket waiver from Proposition 227. In July 1998, an attorney for SDUSD stated that, under the law, "students who speak limited English may be able to attend sheltered English immersion courses for longer than a year before transferring to mainstream classrooms. What's more, parents who request waivers may be able to keep their children in traditional bilingual education courses until they fully grasp English" (quoted in Mendel, 1998). But SDUSD was not granted a blanket waiver, and the ensuing situation was somewhat chaotic. For example, during the 1998–1999 schoolyear, only four parents of the hundreds of English learners at Knox Elementary School had signed waivers. But at Central Elementary School, "students whose parents signed waivers filled 23 classrooms, and only 11 parents wanted their children to continue mostly English instruction" (quoted in Moran, 1998).

SDUSD administrators prepared "flexible" guidelines for complying with Proposition 227 that aimed to inform parents of their choices. The guidelines were emulated by the San Diego County Department of Education and other California school districts. Meanwhile, the district was held up as an example of one that came "close to subverting the intent of the law" because the guidelines encouraged school personnel to inform parents of English learners about the available options for their children, including waivers and bilingual education. Critics such as political scientist Christine Rossell claimed that by telling parents about Proposition 227's waiver provision, rather than automatically placing English learners in English-only classrooms unless parents asked for a waiver, San Diego schools were breaking the law (see, e.g., Rossell, 2003). The district transitioned toward predominantly English as a Second Language (ESL) programs (usually pull-out instruction for English learners who spend most of their time in mainstream classrooms).

Then, in 2004, a group of parents and educators who favored bilingual education filed a complaint against SDUSD, contending that the district had denied parent requests for waiver forms, had failed to inform parents of their right to appeal waiver denials, and had not adequately publicized mandatory meetings where forms are available (Gao, 2004). These issues are still unresolved. In a 2006 parent forum with former Superintendent Carl Cohn, lack of bilingual education came up three separate times on the list of concerns expressed by the parents in attendance (Parent Voice for Education in San Diego, 2006).

An important outlier, the Language Academy–San Diego, was never enmeshed in the turmoil around Proposition 227. The school's staff supplied waivers to Spanish-speaking parents, who were eager to sign them. This did not attract negative attention, most likely because the Language Academy is a magnet school that offers French immersion in addition to the well-established dual-language program. Language Academy students consistently score above district and state averages on standardized tests. According to a longtime school administrator, Proposition 227 was "no big deal."

Dual-Language Program Maintenance in Massachusetts

Among the Massachusetts dual-language programs established before Question 2's passage, we also see evidence of "outward defiance" (most obviously in educators' successful campaign to exempt dual-language programs from the law), "clarification," and "anxiety in the face of climate change." In Brockton, a dual-language program opened at Dr. William Arnone Community Elementary School in the fall of 2002—right when the "English for the Children" campaign was in full swing. School and district staff had spent 2 years planning for the program and engaged in considerable community outreach efforts. For example, they placed announcements in the Spanish language media and held information/orientation meetings in Spanish and English. The school had no trouble recruiting Spanish or English speakers. Today, admission is by lottery.

In Framingham, where students can pursue a dual-language education through high school, Question 2 and its aftermath stimulated educators to reflect on their practices and how to improve them. This self-study enhanced staff cohesion because teachers, principals, and support personnel collectively decided on and implemented changes. For example, it was evident that some native English speakers in the dual-language program were not becoming fluent and literate in Spanish. This led to a switch from a differentiated teaching model in which children first learned to read in their native languages to an 80/20 model in which all kindergarten and first-grade students learn together, in Spanish, 80% of the time.

A new principal arrived at Nathaniel Bowditch School in Salem the same year that Question 2 passed. The school's dual-language program was struggling; students were not performing at grade level, and there was very high attrition among the Anglo students. The principal is a firm believer that every child should be educated in two languages, so instead of terminating the failing dual-language program, she initiated a process of "clarification" that led to substantial reforms to the program's eclectic structure and pedagogy. Test scores rose, and parents started to come back; the school now has a waiting list for both native English and Spanish speakers.

Despite their exemption from Question 2, some dual-language programs have floundered since the law's passage, and no new ones have been established. This is largely because of superintendents who do not support the programs, turnover in the leadership of bilingual programs, and the general political climate in Massachusetts—negative toward immigration in general and bilingual education in particular. According to Ester de Jong (personal communication, December 17, 2007), who has extensively studied the Massachusetts case, dual-language programs were always outliers in an education community that generally favors English-only instruction.

An ongoing, more general challenge is that public education funding in Massachusetts is extremely limited. In fiscal year 2004, state and local spending on education was 4.2% of total revenues, putting the state in 35th place nationally (Berger & McLynch, 2006, p. iii). New dual-language programs require funds for planning, training, and materials. There is no state money for this, and most districts provide only limited (if any) grant-writing support to educators seeking federal funds. Established dual-language programs do not incur substantially higher expenses than their English-only counterparts, but dual-language educators do sometimes have to scrape for professional development resources. This has always been the case. When asked about the impact of Question 2 on resources, the principal of one of the oldest dual-language schools in the country, Rafael Hernández Two-Way Bilingual School in Roxbury, remarked: "Support is limited, but it has always been limited. What makes the difference is that we are successful in passing the state exam Massachusetts Comprehensive Assessment System (MCAS) at more than acceptable levels, so they can't criticize the work we do."

New Dual-Language Programs in California

A fourth reaction to Proposition 227, unique to dual-language education in California, has been innovation. New, carefully researched, and proactively funded programs have emerged, even in Los Angeles. Despite major disincentives such as a highly standardized curriculum, a teacher shortage, and high teacher and student mobility, dual-language programs are spreading across LAUSD, albeit slowly. In 2007–2008, there were 24 Spanish–English programs, eight Korean–English, and one Mandarin–English (Los Angeles Unified School District, 2007). The primary reason for this turnaround is renewed district-level support. With one superintendent as an outspoken advocate for dual-language education, Spanish–English programs have come under the wing of the Asian Pacific and Other Languages Office (APOLO). A standardized reading curriculum is still required, but now it is available in Spanish and students must meet high standards in both languages. APOLO has reserved federal government funds for an in-house, competitive grant to schools that want to start dual-language programs, and the APOLO staff helps schools apply for other grants.

What renewed the energy for dual-language education in LAUSD? Sometimes a push came from the local district, sometimes from principals, sometimes from parents. But in 2004, APOLO's director firmly noted that "in the end, everyone has to buy in: local district and superintendent, staff, the APOLO office, the school community. They are all stakeholders." The coordinator of an emergent dual-language program at Meyler Street School in Torrance said that in order to start she "had to look out of the district to see what other districts are doing in dual language. Now, dual language in the district is getting more organized. There is much more support, and direction and training. . . . It's a lot better now. LAUSD panicked at 227."

Two schools in the Montebello Unified School District implemented dual-language programs in 1999, after 2 years of grant-funded preparation. Interviewed in 2001, the coordinator and professional development specialist (both former transitional bilingual teachers) said they felt that the new law created an opportunity to do something better than what they were doing before. To draw attention to what the new Montebello program offers native English speakers, it is called "dual-language enrichment." This terminology is "totally political. It makes it an equal-access program. Sometimes people are under the impression that these programs are remedial; this helps mitigate that feeling." Early on, it was necessary to actively recruit Montebello parents, but now they learn about the dual-language programs via word of mouth.

In Ventura, the dual-language program at Montalvo School began in 2000. The principal explained that the program emerged because the school board and superintendent did not want Proposition 227 to mean English-only in Ventura. With their support, the district's director of bilingual programs actively sought an alternative. This individual saw dual-language education as one step better than transitional bilingual education and Montalvo as the best school site for implementation. Like the newer programs in Los Angeles and Montebello, this one began with assiduous research and planning. It has become so popular that admission is by lottery.

In Chula Vista, as in Montebello and Ventura, educators view the district's seven new dual-language programs as a step up from the old transitional models. A new crop of dual-language programs has emerged on the east side of Chula Vista. Prior to this time, there was one dual-language charter school, Chula Vista Learning Community Charter (CVLCC) on the city's west side, in place since 1997. On the east side, the oldest dual-language strand started in 2001, the newest in 2004. All together, they include Heritage, Hedekamp, Liberty, Salt Creek, Arroyo Vista, Valle Lindo, and Veterans. Many of these programs, all of which are strands within larger schools, were initiated in brand-new schools, part of the new development and construction in East Chula Vista.

Why are new dual-language programs burgeoning in East Chula Vista? We note two trends. In the first scenario, the "consumer-maintained" design, the school convinces a few key parents to support the program, they subsequently recruit other parents, and once all the parents are committed, they become extremely active and influential in the development and maintenance of the program. In the second scenario, the dual-language program exists because of parental preferences and active solicitation and application of these preferences by the school. This innovation is the result of a "consumer-driven" school design, in which schools cater to the educational preferences of the community. The construction of each new school in the area was preceded by a community forum and the completion of "interest lists" by prospective parents. In some East Side schools, parents were very vocal about their wish to help create dual-language programs. In other schools, parents were initially hesitant, but once convinced by administrators, they played a vital role in recruiting other parents and in supporting the program. Because Chula Vista is a decentralized district, schools have limited autonomy under the district's guidance, making dual-language innovation much easier. Moreover, the school district is supportive of the dual-language strands and provides assistance through the Office of Language Acquisition and Development.

The dual-language programs within East Chula Vista continue to be popular. Prospective parents do not have to be recruited, and there are often waiting lists. The demand was aptly described by one district officer: "There have been some parents, for example, last year at Heritage, that camped out all night, just to be the first on the waiting list." Parent activism and ties are very strong in many of these school communities. Parents talk to one another and recommend the dual-language programs in their school to others. In Chula Vista, the old stigma surrounding bilingual education has almost entirely been erased by the new dual-language programs: "In the beginning there was more recruitment than now. Now it seems that parents know about the program; the program has been around for 6 or 7 years now. The community knows about it, and the newer families get interested in it." While there are still traces of stigma, parents currently involved in dual-language programs seem to disregard the old negative notions about bilingual education. In 2007, the assistant principal of Salt Creek Elementary noted that her parents are well educated about the issue and do seem to know the difference between the "old" bilingual programs and the new dual-language programs. Parents seek out the dual-language strands because they see the value of knowing two languages.

Despite restrictive language policies, new dual-language programs have emerged in some districts, but not in others with similarly appropriate demographics. As is evident in the discussion above, program maintenance and long-term success require support from both parents and educators (and usually school district administration). But we observe two different patterns in regard to initiation of dual-language programs, both of which relate to the innovation we observed above. Most commonly, educators who believe that dual-language programs will best serve the needs of their student populations (or some subset thereof) take the lead. But sometimes programs are in place because parents asked for them. We discuss these in the following section.

EDUCATORS AND PARENTS AS DUAL-LANGUAGE ADVOCATES

Educator-Driven Programs

In many of the schools and districts we studied, the existence of a dual-language option is due to the work of dedicated educators at the school and/or district level.

This was clearly the case in Los Angeles, Montebello, Ventura, and throughout Massachusetts. For example, in Brockton, the dual-language program at Arnone got started because the district's Department of Bilingual/ESL services advocated for it. District staff chose a school that already had support structures in place because there had been a transitional bilingual program there. There were bilingual teachers, staff, and materials.

Asked how a dual-language program emerged at Daniel Webster School in Long Beach, the principal replied, "Well, three principals ago, there was a principal who wanted to do it. And he was the driving force. Then there was a good group of LEP [Limited English Proficient] students and families and a lot of English speakers, too. So they had both groups to draw from." In Santa Monica, the Edison Language Academy, established in 1986 with support from the California State Department of Education and the Center for Language Education and Research at the University of California, Los Angeles (UCLA), initiated a dual-language program as part of the district's desegregation effort. The population in the school's neighborhood was primarily Latino, according to a 2001 comment from district personnel: "The numbers of enrollment were dropping. We needed some incentive to start adding numbers to our schools. So a way of selling them was with a dual language program. . . . What it attracted was students from all over Santa Monica into the program—specifically, students who were wanting to learn Spanish as a second language." Santa Monica's dual-language program and others in California that emerged at approximately the same time were well supported by the California Department of Education and the Center for Language Education and Research (CLEAR), mainly in terms of funding for considerably more teacher training and evaluation.

Parent-Driven Programs

The following is an excerpt from an interview with the Title VII coordinator at Gates Elementary School in Orange County, California:

> LINTON: Do you know much about how the program got started here?
> GATES: It started because of the parents. . . . It was just different parents that wanted to expose their children—not just to expose them, to have them grow up to be biliterate. Seeing the changes that are occurring in the state, and knowing that was a good ticket to a good future.
> LINTON: With "ticket to a good future," are they talking about cultural awareness, economic rewards?
> GATES: I think economic is the main one, with the change in demographics.

A key reason for Gates parents' success is that they were able to garner support from the school district administration. One administrator in particular helped establish the program, wrote the Title VII grant for it, and served as a critical liaison between the school and the district. Later on, Gates's dual-language parents formed a nonprofit organization called Advocates for Language Learning. Their main activity is fund-raising—to buy more Spanish books or "anything to help out the immersion program." One English-speaking parent reported a fringe benefit: "They say they can't help but learn Spanish because they have to help with the homework. They get the Spanish–English dictionary, and get started."

Another example of a parent-driven program with district support is Patrick Henry School in Long Beach, California. As explained in 2004 by the district's bilingual coordinator:

> There was a group of parents from the LA County Office of Education. She was in the ELD [English Language Development] department. It was her along with a group of other parents who wanted a dual-language program for their children. So they went to the district and said, "This is really what we want. There isn't a school in Long Beach that offers it." At that point the superintendents went to a principals' meeting and basically opened it up to the principals in the district and said, "There are some parents who are interested in a program like this. Is there anyone out there who would like this at your school?" And the principal here said yes. That's why it's here at Henry. It wasn't necessarily the neighborhood parents at Henry that demanded it, it was this group of parents that said, "We just want it somewhere," and this principal was the one who responded. And that's a really crucial part of starting a program. Whoever the administrator is has to be someone who believes in it and really wants it there.

As noted in the previous section, parents were also pivotal players in the implementation and maintenance of dual-language programs in East Chula Vista. Administrators consistently point out the high level of parental contribution toward the programs, characterizing the parents as very dedicated and active within the schools: "Generally what we find is that our dual-immersion parents tend to volunteer a lot in the classrooms." Parent assistance both inside and outside the classroom is a key component in the success of the students, as learning in two languages can require much more work from both the child and the parents. Many schools in East Chula Vista host activities to assist English-speaking parents with children in dual-language programs. The support ranges from quarterly meetings for dual-language parents to parent education nights, after-school help centers for both native Spanish- and English-speaking students, and an initial information session for parents new to the programs.

In one East Chula Vista school, English- and Spanish-speaking parents are paired up to help each other with language issues in the homework. But the

Spanish-speaking parents lead. The majority of the Spanish-speaking parents in the program speak at least some English, and in this school the Spanish- and English-speaking parents are on even socioeconomic levels. Both the Spanish- and English-speaking parents say that the parents work together well in the "dual-immersion parent group." A number of the parents indicated that they were initially fearful of putting their kids in the program, but after 3 or 4 years, they feel very pleased with the results. The leadership of the Spanish-speaking parents, in conjunction with the cooperative work occurring with the English-speaking parents, was very important for the success of this program, according to district personnel.

Parents who participate in dual-language programs in East Chula Vista are very committed. Administrators believe that these parents understand the value of multi-lingualism and of multiculturalism, especially the long-term economic advantage these skills offer: "There's a push for multilingualism, and I think they see a more global society. They also see that the families are going to travel, it's good for business. This is about their long-term professionalism and just enrichment. So I think they see this huge picture about how we fit into our global society."

While multiculturalism is important for many parents, the everyday utility of language is also important. Just as reading and writing need to be made relevant to young students, so do language and culture. Thus, the proximity of Chula Vista to Mexico, with its downtown located about 9 miles from the border, and the daily use of Spanish and English that goes on in this border region make bilingualism a locally salient and important skill: "Others just see we want to learn Spanish and English, it's just two languages, because it's very local." Spanish is used every day in Chula Vista, and many parents are involved in businesses that straddle the Mexico–U.S. border: "In the eastern part of Chula Vista there are affluent families from Mexico, many times it's their second home. They have businesses that cross the border. . . . We have a lot of families that are leaving Tijuana due to the safety issues." Both native Spanish- and English-speaking parents are involved in commerce and business in their local area and know first-hand the relevance of bilingualism and biculturalism to their children.

INITIATING AND MAINTAINING DUAL-LANGUAGE PROGRAMS: CHALLENGES AND OPPORTUNITIES

Who Is Being Served?

In some of the parent-driven programs we studied (all in California), there is concern that—because the parents who push for and are most active in the programs tend to be better educated and informed as well as wealthier than other parents who are recruited by school staff—the first group of parents will exert undue influence on how a program is run. A Chula Vista administrator said, "I think there are parents that go out and seek out things, and they tend to be more affluent or more educated parents. In that way again, the dual immersion becomes a program for children from very affluent families, and they may not be very [financially] affluent, but they tend to be culturally affluent." This administrator was concerned that East Chula Vista's dual-language programs could become elitist, even if this was not intended at the outset. For example, if schools require a 7-year commitment from families entering a dual-language program, students from disadvantaged or less affluent families might not qualify for entry. Those excluded could include military families, families who are not homeowners and/or are of a low socioeconomic background (and as a result, are possibly more mobile), and families who do not have the time to support their children academically outside of the school—a very important piece in dual-language programs.

Another concern is the representativeness of the dual-languages programs: Are these programs truly representing and serving the community? One administrator opined in 2007 that East Chula Vista's programs were for English-dominant children, not for the entire community:

It's really a second-language program. So we're not really a dual immersion, we're a Spanish immersion. We start with Spanish and move up. It would be quite interesting to find out what the ethnicity of the all the children in our Spanish immersion is [as compared to the rest of the school population]. I know there's African American and White; I do have some Hispanic. Is it representative of our community, or is it a White program? I don't think it would be a White program; it's not that obvious.

For this reason, the administrator voiced the idea that more study was needed to find out who these programs are serving in the school and neighborhood community.

The principal of a Los Angeles school where affluent, mostly White parents were influential in starting a dual-language program (although now dismantled) echoed this concern:

Unfortunately, what we have seen here is that it doesn't serve our EL population well because—and this is just my supposition—the EL population is not coming from as high of an SES background. I think it's a literacy issue and a socioeconomic issue, not an EL issue. Because what they did was they recruited kids who didn't live in our attendance area, so then you have a disadvantage. These [English-speaking] parents have a lot of advantages; these other [Spanish-speaking] parents are working two or three jobs to survive. So those are the kids who are failed by the program. That's unfortunate. For some of the teachers here, this has become a political issue. They brought the program in to serve those children, but in fact what we've done is not serve those children well.

While it is certainly not always the case that parent-driven dual-language programs end up primarily serving the children of the most empowered parents, this possibility does exist and educators should be aware of it and of the need to maintain balanced numbers of native English and Spanish speakers.

Maintaining a Balance

Demographics can challenge educators trying to maintain a dual-language program. Even with adequate numbers of native English and Spanish speakers in a district, keeping a program balanced can be difficult due to differential mobility between the groups and/or transportation issues. Where transportation is provided as part of a district's school choice policy, parents are more likely to be able to consider the dual-language option for their children.

In Chula Vista, administrators noted that it has been more difficult to attract students from Spanish-dominant families. These families emphasize the need to learn English, and some do not want their children in dual-language programs. As one administrator described in 2007, "Our English learner parents are hesitant: Is this program really going to work? My child is being instructed in his or her primary language: Is this really for his or her benefit? So there is anxiety and doubt from our English learner parents." An assistant principal concurred that Spanish-speaking families often require more information about the dual-language program so they can make an informed decision for their child. According to an official in the district office, "We still have the majority English-only students participating in these programs versus English language learners." Latino families who are English-dominant or who are bilingual themselves are much more apt to put their children into dual-language programs. In these cases, the goal is often to maintain or increase the child's knowledge of Spanish, according to district personnel.

Similarly, as noted by a staff member from the district's Department of Bilingual/ESL Services, Spanish-speaking families in Brockton "got the Question 2 message" and were hesitant to put their children in a dual-language program, whereas "for the native English population, this is a prestige program." Now that the program is well established, there is a waiting list for both groups of students, but it is much longer for English speakers. Spanish-speaking parents who choose the program tend to be very active in the community and politically savvy. Once one child gets in, their siblings do, too, so some of the program's Spanish-speaking kindergarteners arrive almost automatically.

Increased Workload

No dual-language educator has ever told us that what they are doing is easy. Dual-language programs require a huge effort from all involved, especially school-level professionals. In the words of one principal in 2001:

> It is a lot more work. But you don't even stop to get off the merry-go-round or the roller coaster to think about it. You just keep going. I have to ensure that their children will get—not just regular education—but better. And I have to know that they're going to get it because I'm promising the parents that their children will be successful, not just in terms of what the state demands of us, but all that in two languages. So I'm promising them more than any other school in this county's promising them. I have to make sure I have the right staff. You know, even if we didn't have money or materials, if I have the right teachers, they're going to do it.

We observe differences in program implementation and success based on the level of autonomy allowed to school administrators by their districts and state governments as well as on how districts reward competent educators.

DISCUSSION

Dual-language programs enrich the students and parents they serve. Yet there are limits to how widespread they can become. Some challenges stem from restrictive language policies, such as Proposition 227 and Question 2, and the political climate that provoked their passage. The discussion above illustrates how these challenges have been met—or not. Just 10 miles north of Chula Vista in San Diego, where foreign-born Latinos are 11% of the city's population according to the 2005–2007 American Community Survey estimates for San Diego County, there is still only one dual-language program.

Our analysis raises the concern that parent-driven dual-language programs can end up serving English-speaking or bilingual families more than English learners. We do not wish to caution against implementing parent-instigated programs but rather to alert educators about this issue and encourage them to proactively address English learners' needs. Dual-language education will continue in California and Massachusetts because of educators and parents who are committed to it. As more and more studies document dual-language students' academic success, parents' demand and educators' advocacy and support for the programs is likely to grow.

To the extent that the public is able to differentiate dual-language education from transitional bilingual education designed solely to serve English learners, the dual-language option is not politically contentious. Our California narratives provide several examples of educators who saw Proposition 227 as an opportunity to promote bilingualism for everyone rather than to teach English-only. Negative public discourse about bilingual education contributed to the spread of dual-language programs by increasing parent and teacher creativity and activism.

We have seen that new dual-language programs in Chula Vista are results of "consumer-driven" school design, in which schools actively solicit and respond to parent preferences for school programs. Demand and support for dual-language programs in U.S. schools is also a response to growing numbers of Latino Americans and the increasing opportunities to use Spanish in the economic and political spheres. As Spanish speakers disseminate more fully throughout the nation, we expect increased demand for dual-language programs.

Finally, the growth of these programs corresponds to a change in the degree to which non–Latino Americans value Spanish and cross-cultural understanding, but parents often expressed the values of multilingualism and multiculturalism in terms of their being potential moneymaking instruments, not simply as cognitive or cultural goals. This reflects a parental emphasis on their children's long-term careers. A globalizing world presents opportunities and challenges that cannot all be met in English. Dual-language programs are one way to preserve and enhance our linguistic resources while doing right by our nation's English learners.

POLICY RECOMMENDATIONS

Our analysis suggests several policy recommendations. First, it is clearly important to have explicit—or at least implicit—school-district collaboration and support. Planning and outreach should start 2 years ahead of implementation; school districts and administrators need to work with parents to inform and prepare them as well as to offer them appropriate services and volunteer opportunities. When parents are the initiators of a dual-language program, school districts should listen to their needs. The most successful programs are strict about maintaining a balance between native Spanish and English speakers. District-provided transportation is valuable in this regard because it makes it easier for children to attend schools outside their neighborhoods.

Second, it would obviously be helpful if California were to copy Massachusetts's example and exempt dual-language programs from the state's anti–bilingual education law (or overturn the law altogether).

Finally, favorable federal policies could abet the spread of dual-language education. For example, increased funding to support early foreign-language learning for native English speakers would likely promote the initiation of more dual-language programs, even if first-language maintenance and English acquisition for the children of immigrants were not a stated objective. Dual-language programs must be presented as a valuable academic and cultural opportunity for all students.

NOTE

We are grateful to Tim Allen, Cheryl Forbes, and Olga Vásquez for consultation regarding the San Diego case and to Briana Abrams for research assistance. Four anonymous reviewers provided insightful comments that helped us refine our work.

REFERENCES

Berger, N., & McLynch, J. (2006). Public school funding in Massachusetts: Putting recent reform proposals in context. Massachusetts Budget and Policy Center. Retrieved January 25, 2008, from http://www.massbudget.org/Public_School_Funding_in_MA.pdf

California Department of Education. (2008). California two-way immersion programs directory. Retrieved January 25, 2008, from http://www.cde.ca.gov/sp/el/ip/ap/directory.aspx

Gao, H. (2004, November 8). Fight over bilingual education continues. *San Diego Union Tribune.* Retrieved January 26, 2008, from http://www.signonsandiego.com/uniontrib/20041108/news_1m8biling.html

Hawkins, M. R. (2005). Becoming a student: Identity work and academic literacies in early schooling. *TESOL Quarterly, 39*(1), 58–81.

Long Beach Unified School District. (2007). *LBUSD's many foreign language options help students prepare for a global society.* Retrieved December 11, 2007, from http://www.lbusd.k12.ca.us/Main_Offices/Curriculum/Areas/Foreign_Language/whats_new.cfm

Los Angeles Unified School District. (2007). 2007–2008 dual language programs directory. Faxed to the authors upon request.

Mendel, E. (1998, July 16). Curbs on bilingual education ruled valid. *San Diego Union Tribune.* Retrieved January 26, 2008, from http://www.onenation.org/0798/071698a.html

Moran, C. (1998, October 12). Schools differ on Prop. 227. *San Diego Union Tribune.* Retrieved January 26, 2008, from http://www.onenation.org/1098/101298b.html

Parent Voice for Education in San Diego. (2006). Forum summary. Retrieved January 31, 2008, from http://www.parentvoicesforeducationsd.org/Feb06.htm

Reyes, S. A., & Vallone, T. L. (2007). Toward an expanded understanding of two-way bilingual immersion education: Constructing identity through a critical, additive, bilingual/bicultural pedagogy. *Multicultural Perspectives, 9*(3), 3–11.

Rossell, C. H. (2003, Fall). The near end of bilingual education. *Education Next,* pp. 44–52.

Stritikus, T., & García, E. E. (2000). Education of Limited English Proficient students in California schools: An assessment of the influence of Proposition 227 on selected teachers and classrooms. *Bilingual Research Journal, 21*(1&2), 1–11.

PART IV

Charting the Future of Language Policy in Education

Challenging Limitations: The Growing Potential for Overturning Restrictive Language Policies and Ensuring Equal Educational Opportunity

Daniel Losen

OUR EDUCATION policy initiatives for language acquisition have historically been closely linked to issues of immigration, the right to education, and civil rights. Congress has long recognized that English learners (ELs) need measures to ensure that they have equal educational opportunity and can meet high academic standards. However, the policies that have been put into place to guide and regulate the instruction of these students have not always been informed by sound research or knowledgeable practitioners. Recent policies that severely restrict the use of primary language for instructional purposes are a case in point. Data revealing large gaps in academic performance and the slow progress of EL students, along with subtle shifts in the law and policy landscape toward higher standards and greater accountability for their academic performance, suggest a growing potential for overturning restrictive English-only language policies in court or eliminating them through new educational policy. Challenging restrictive language policies is critically important, but just one of several needed steps to improve educational outcomes for English learners.

This chapter begins by reviewing the contours of ELs' right to education under federal civil rights law. Serious questions are raised about the legality of restrictive language policies in light of these legal contours when considered alongside the most recent achievement data from the National Assessment of Educational Progress for ELs. The suggestion that these restrictive policies may be susceptible to legal challenges given the new evidence raises the deeper question of whether the needs of EL students are being met in any state. The chapter then explores what other state and federal law and policy changes, including removing restrictive language policies, might be needed to better support EL students' right to equal educational opportunities.

CIVIL RIGHTS LAW AS A FOUNDATION FOR ENGLISH LEARNERS' RIGHT TO LEARN

Most Americans regard our system of public education as a strong example of how a democratic and egalitarian society provides opportunities for advancement to all of its members. In significant respects, the historical record since 1964 supports these beliefs. In fact, despite the high level of anti-immigrant sentiment throughout our history, at various times since 1964 all three branches of government have bolstered the rights of English learners to receive an adequate education. (The definition of what constitutes an "adequate" education is explored through the description of court rulings and legislation that follows, as there is no singular definition of the term.) Through the combined effects of Supreme Court decisions, legislation by Congress, and regulation by the executive branch, EL students have been provided protection from discrimination. State and local educational agencies have been mandated to meet their educational needs, and federal assistance has been provided to improve their educational outcomes. Rights, however, are not self-enforcing, and significant struggles have been waged to try to ensure that the benefits associated with these rights were realized.

The Civil Rights Act of 1964 and Its Results

Many of the legal protections for English learners evolved out of the civil rights movement. After Congress passed the Civil Rights Act of 1964, regulations were promulgated under Title VI of that act that specifically addressed educational issues relating to national origin minority students. The regulations connected limited English proficiency and the prohibition of discrimination on the basis of national origin (U.S. Commission on Civil Rights, 1997). In 1974, the Supreme Court upheld a challenge to these regulations in a landmark case, *Lau v. Nichols*. The Court ruled that the failure of the San Francisco school system to provide instruction to Chinese-speaking children that allowed them to access the same curriculum as their English-speaking peers had the effect of denying their meaningful participation in the system of public education and therefore violated Title VI. Within weeks of the *Lau* decision, Congress passed the Equal Educational Opportunities Act (EEOA), which further imposed on state and local educational agencies an "affirmative duty" to take "appropriate action to overcome language barriers that impede equal participation by its students in the instructional program."

Following the *Lau* decision and the passage of the EEOA, the Office of Civil Rights (OCR) attempted to provide more guidance to school districts on how to fulfill their obligations toward students with "limited English proficiency," pursuant to Title VI (OCR is not responsible for enforcing the EEOA). For example, in 1975, the agency issued a very prescriptive draft guidance document, commonly referred to as the "Lau Guidelines" (U.S. Commission on Civil Rights, 1997). Many school districts relied on these unpublished guidelines, while other districts and states resisted. The dispute over the correct implementation of *Lau* was partially resolved when the U.S. Court of Appeals for the Fifth Circuit decided *Castañeda v. Pickard.* Even though the case interpreted section 1703(f) of the EEOA, not Title VI, OCR explicitly adopted the three-pronged test in *Castañeda* to guide the agency in the enforcement of Title VI (U.S. Commission on Civil Rights, 1997).

In 1981, the *Castañeda* plaintiffs, Mexican American children and their parents, alleged that the Raymondville, Texas, school district had engaged in policies and practices of racial discrimination that deprived plaintiffs and their class of rights secured for them by the Constitution and various federal statutes. Even though the court of appeals partially overturned the lower court's decision for the plaintiffs, this decision continues to form the basis for the enforcement guidance for Title VI of the Civil Rights Act of 1964 as well as the EEOA. To determine whether an entity is fulfilling the requirements of 1703(f) of the EEOA or of Title VI, courts must look at (1) whether the educational program in question is supported by at least some experts in the field (prong one); (2) whether steps were taken to implement the program effectively (prong two); and (3) whether the program can be shown to be successful in overcoming the language barriers confronting students with limited English proficiency (prong three).

ELs' Potential Vulnerability to Restrictive Educational Policy

Court decisions in the 1990s illustrate how vulnerable the rights of English learners are, especially when they are in tension with the rights of states to set "local" educational policy. When put to the test initially, the EEOA and other civil rights protections pertaining to EL students did not prevent the passage of restrictive language laws in California or Massachusetts, despite predictions that the measures would restrict the range of resources for EL students. The initial challenges to restrictive policies were not found to meet the criteria set out in *Castañeda,* despite a substantial body of research that argued against such restrictive pedagogy. Even in 2001, insufficient evidence was presented to convince the court that reducing instructional options to English-only would be harmful to English learners (Myhill, 2004). If English-only programs, or particular implementations of those programs, had been proven to be harmful, it is unlikely they would have survived judicial scrutiny. According to Hakuta and Gutiérrez (cited in Myhill, 2004):

> The limits of our knowledge regarding effective practices for ELL students has contributed to the courts' reluctance to strike down state laws constraining the range of ELL programs and exposure in favor of English Immersion programs and requiring English-only exit exams. (p. 393)

Although a solid body of research has accumulated based on sophisticated analyses of EL instructional practices with small samples of students, the field is lacking conclusive proof that one instructional method is superior to another. Past attempts at such proof have been confounded by high EL student mobility and a diversity of circumstances that influence learning. Moreover, programs' emphases, faculty, and instructional practices have been characterized by inconsistency (see, e.g., Ramírez, Pasta, Yuen, Ramey, & Billings, 1991). Unfortunately, EL programs, students, and faculty lack sufficient stability and fidelity to allow for sufficient long-term tracking of student outcomes.

THE QUESTIONABLE LEGALITY OF "ENGLISH-ONLY" LIMITATIONS ON EDUCATIONAL OPPORTUNITY: MEETING THE *CASTAÑEDA* CRITERIA

The ruling in the *Castañeda* case required that to fulfill the provisions of the EEOA and Title VI, entities must show that programs are research-based, well implemented, and successful in overcoming the language barriers that English learners encounter. Courts have interpreted the EEOA as allowing for some degree of experimentation as well (see, e.g., *GI Forum v. TEA*, 2000). Thus, English-only programs have been viewed as protected under the provision of being "experimental." However, given that *Lau* explicitly forbade schools to immerse English learner students into English without other instructional modifications, it is crucial to continually evaluate whether the imposition of similar circumstances after just 1 or 2 years meets the *Castañeda* criteria. Although many researchers have argued that English-only has not been proven to be superior to bilingual instruction and predicted that the policy would be harmful, courts have contended that they were mired in a battle of "experts."

Without conclusive evidence of pending harm, courts followed the well-established deference to education policymakers and referendum voters and allowed states to restrict EL program options. William Myhill (2004) points out that in the first challenge to Proposition 227, *Valeria G. v. Wilson* (1998), the plaintiffs were not able to meet the first prong of *Castañeda* (that the program lacked expert support) and that there were also no data to bring to bear on the third prong (that the program was not effective). However, in the three states with English-only policies, there are now more than 5 years' worth of outcome data to analyze, and more than 10 years' worth in California, making it appropriate to revisit the question of the policies' effectiveness and potential harm under the third prong of *Castañeda*.

New evidence may justify revisiting EEOA-based challenges. Even without conclusive evidence that English-only programs harm students, stronger arguments might be made that English-only policies deny EL students access to the full range of effective programs and thereby unlawfully deny equal "educational opportunity."

A slightly different, yet highly relevant conceptual argument regarding the review of a federal court's remedy pursuant to the EEOA was recently explored in a decision handed down by the Supreme Court on June 25, 2009, in the case of *Horne v. Flores*. At issue was the adequacy of resources for English learners provided by the Nogales School District and the State of Arizona. Pursuant to the EEOA, in 2008, in *Flores v. Arizona*, the U.S. Court of Appeals for the Ninth Circuit had reviewed a district court's ruling against the state. The Court of Appeals held that the district court "did not abuse its discretion" in finding in-adequate a proposed legislative remedy that used a weighted system of financing to provide extra money, but that also "cut funding to children who had not yet learned English after two years of instruction. . . ." As part of the holding, the Court of Appeals had also affirmed the district court's rejection of the argument that this legislation, and other factors, sufficiently "changed circumstances" to justify ending the earlier court order to provide larger amounts of additional funding for ELs.

In *Horne v. Flores*, the Supreme Court, in a narrow 5-4 decision, reversed the Ninth Circuit's affirmation of the district court's review of "changed circumstances," and remanded the more substantive questions back to the district court to produce a new ruling based on a more comprehensive review of the evidence. While the Supreme Court's reversal is important, it neither limited the rights of ELs to use the EEOA for injunctive relief nor reversed the original holding that the district of Nogales and the state had violated the EEOA by failing to provide ELs with adequate resources.

The Court's remand of the case to the district court called for "a proper examination of at least four important factual and legal changes that may warrant the granting of relief from the judgment: the State's adoption of a new EL instructional methodology, Congress' enactment of NCLB, structural and management reforms in Nogales, and increased over-all education funding" (*Horne v. Flores*, 2009, p. 23). Of these four areas, the first is the most relevant to our discussion of English-only policies. Specifically the Supreme Court has asked the federal district court to decide "whether Nogales' implementation of SEI methodology—completed in all of its schools by 2005—constitutes a 'significantly changed circumstance' that warrants relief" (*Horne v. Flores*, 2009, p. 25).

The Supreme Court ruling suggests that the change from bilingual educa-tion to the English-only policy may have benefited ELs sufficiently to satisfy the EEOA, but left it to the district court to decide the matter. On remand, the federal district court could determine that the change to the English-only policy consti-tutes "appropriate action" pursuant to the EEOA and is sufficient grounds for ending the prior court-ordered remedy to the funding inadequacy. However, if this or other changes cannot be shown to have improved outcomes for ELs in Nogales (or Arizona), or are associated with lower achievement, they would not count as "appropriate action." It is important to note that the Supreme Court re-jected the assertion by the challengers that the implementation of the federal No Child Left Behind Act automatically satisfied the requirement of "appropriate action" under *Castañeda*. However, the Court's majority called for further review of the impact of NCLB in Nogales, stating that "through its assessment and re-porting requirements, NCLB provides evidence of the progress and achievement of Nogales' ELL students." Similarly, upon review, the district court could find that Nogales's new NCLB-driven EL programming is effective and constitutes "appropriate action" sufficient to warrant ending the court-ordered funding rem-edy. On the other hand, the district court could determine that NCLB's implemen-tation in Nogales or Arizona is insufficient to constitute the "appropriate action" required by the EEOA, in which case the court's order to increase funding for ELs may survive the review.

Additionally, because a review of the evidence could lead the district court to conclude that Arizona's restrictive language policy is an obstacle to ELs' achievement and is contributing to a continuing violation of the EEOA, it is con-ceivable that the district court could issue an order stemming from this remand that would require the state to rescind Arizona's English-only policy.

If nothing else, the *Flores* decision has elevated the importance of evaluat-ing academic progress to the "appropriate action" analysis required by the EEOA. Arguably, the remand has transformed a case about how to remedy Arizona's failure to provide adequate educational resources to ELs into a case about the adequacy of new policies and practices, including English-only, based on the academic results linked to such changes.

Given the importance of demonstrating academic progress to EEOA litiga-tion, and given that enough time has passed to allow a longitudinal results analy-sis under the results-oriented third prong of *Castañeda*, an important additional source of evidence for the argument against English-only instruction, pursuant to the EEOA, is suggested by the following analyses of national data collected on English learners. The National Assessment of Educational Progress (NAEP) tests students from all 50 states in fourth and eighth grade reading and math (as well as some other subjects periodically). A review of the NAEP data suggests that English-only programs may not be more effective than the bilingual programs that are blocked by restrictive language policies. The *Castañeda* decision, in fact, held that "a state violates the EEOA if even an adequately-funded program fails, after being employed for a period of time sufficient to give the plan a legitimate trial" (see *Castañeda v. Pickard*, 1981, p. 1010). In addition, a review of national academic performance data combined with the data being generated from individual states (see Chapters 3, 4, and 5) suggests that stronger grounds for mounting a challenge to English-only on the basis of *Castañeda*'s third prong may be close at hand, especially in Arizona and California.

The National Assessment of Educational Progress, also known as the "Nation's Report Card," provides an excellent source of information for state comparisons because of the uniformity and consistency of the assessment instrument over time and among state administrations. The NAEP evidence is examined here in two ways. The scaled scores in reading and math are presented to give the most accurate representation of actual score increase or decrease over time.[1] The scaled scores are grouped by range into proficiency categories, and the changes for ELs in the category of "at or above proficient" give a better sense of changes in the overall level of academic achievement for ELs over time.

These scores show a disturbing pattern of growing gaps between English learners and their English-speaking counterparts on the national NAEP assessment when these two student groups are compared. (See Chapter 6, this volume, for additional NAEP comparisons.) Since the passage of Proposition 227 in 1998, which severely restricted bilingual education in California, the scaled scores of California's ELs have declined in reading in grade 8 from 8 points above the national average to 3 points below. And in grade 4 reading and math, where average scaled scores did rise, the national average scores increased at a higher rate, resulting in a larger gap between California's English learners and the nation's. Arizona's EL scores in reading rose and then fell to their initial level at grade 4 and show an overall decline at grade 8 (see Figures 12.1 and 12.2).

The comparison to the national data on reading scaled scores suggests that English-only instruction did not benefit students in Arizona and California (see Figure 12.2). Massachusetts's data are more difficult to explain. English learners in that state made a 12-point gain in grade 4 reading between 2003 and 2005, during which time national scores went up only 5 points. Some explanation for this increase may be found in Chapter 5 of this volume, where the authors show the dramatic shift in numbers of students being identified as EL in Boston, the city with the bulk of the state's English learners and the most disadvantaged students, after the passage of Question 2. The authors of Chapter 5 also point out that Massachusetts has a very different English learner population than California and Arizona. In California and Arizona, at least 85% of ELs are Spanish speakers and most are low-income, whereas in Massachusetts, only 56% are Spanish speakers and more than 15% are Asian, with a more diverse socioeconomic composition. Moreover, Massachusetts made an exception in its law for dual-language programs, allowing these generally strong programs to continue providing

Figure 12.1. Average scores for English learners on the NAEP reading scale, grade 4.

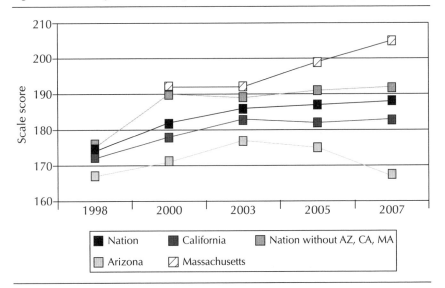

Notes: Scale scores are on a scale of 0 to 500. Author's calculations used the Advanced NCES data tool to exclude Arizona, California, and Massachusetts. Compression of a national average was calculated with instruction from NCES personnel. According to NCES, the compression of new national average using the Web tool automatically adjusts for sample size. For consistency, Arizona and Massachusetts were excluded from the national averages in 1998 even though English-only policies were not yet in effect.

Source: Data compiled from National Center for Education Statistics, 2008.

bilingual education. It is not known to what extent these programs contribute to the difference in patterns of achievement for Massachusetts's ELs. Further, between 1998 and 2007, EL students in grade 8 reading in all three states with restrictive language policies never scored higher than the national average for EL students, and all had extraordinarily low rates of academic proficiency (see Figure 12.3).

In math, Arizona and California's EL scores first rose after the implementation of the restrictive policies, but then began declining, while the national average showed consistent increases. As with reading, however, Massachusetts's EL scores do show an increase since English-only became law (see Figures 12.4 and 12.5).

The third prong of *Castañeda* looks for proof of success. These data cast serious doubt on any claims that English-only is providing significant benefits compared to other forms of EL instruction. While further analyses are required, these data suggest that the English-only initiatives have not improved the reading performance of either fourth- or eighth-grade students in the states where the policy has been in place the longest and is most restrictive (see Figures 12.3 and 12.6).[2]

Figure 12.2. Average scores for English learners on the NAEP reading scale, grade 8.

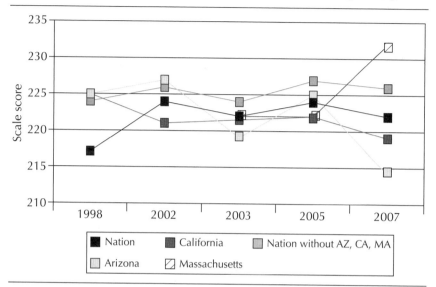

Note: Scale scores are on a scale of 0 to 500.

Source: Data compiled from National Center for Education Statistics, 2008.

Moreover, this finding is consistent with the other studies included in this volume, as well as several other studies published over the last several years (see for example Grissom, 2004; Parrish et al., 2006).

LIMITATIONS OF THE DATA

There are several limitations on data, both at the state and national levels, when it comes to drawing conclusions about the performance of English learners over time. At the state level, tests and standards vary; each state constructs and gives its own tests, and both the tests and standards are modified and vary over time. When state-created assessments change, as they have in Arizona, Massachusetts, and California since the implementation of English-only policies, the task of measuring increases and decreases in achievement based on such unique measures becomes difficult, if not impossible. At the state level, researchers have also been unable to control for changes in the composition of cohorts of students being examined. At the national level, the metric (NAEP) has remained the same, but there are known problems with the exclusion of some English learners from the analyses, with

Figure 12.3. Percentage of English learners scoring at or above proficient on the NAEP reading scale, grade 8.

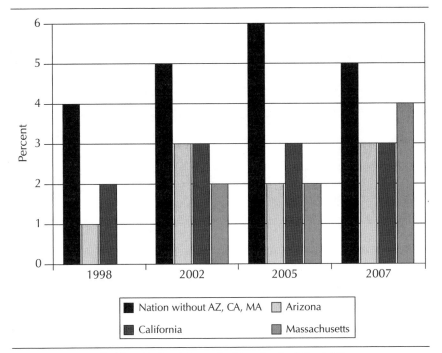

Source: Data compiled from National Center for Education Statistics, 2008.

different states setting different standards for who is included and who is excluded. The ideal analysis would track cohorts of students over time. Even though NAEP data reveal how students are achieving at a given grade level, and the measurement itself remains the same over time, the students who take the NAEP in grade 4 are not necessarily the same students who are assessed 4 years later in grade 8. While the NAEP is likely the best indicator of progress available and certainly the most accurate measure for comparing states, the fact that it does not track cohorts of students means that more definitive conclusions about outcomes in any given state should include additional data.

Thus all of these longitudinal studies suffer from certain limitations. The strength of the arguments, however, rests in good part on the accumulation of evidence from different sources that all point in the same direction. There has been no study at either the state or national level that has shown a significant or sustained closing of the academic achievement gap between English learners and English speakers in the states that have enacted English-only policies. On the

Figure 12.4. Average scores for English learners on the NAEP math scale, grade 4.

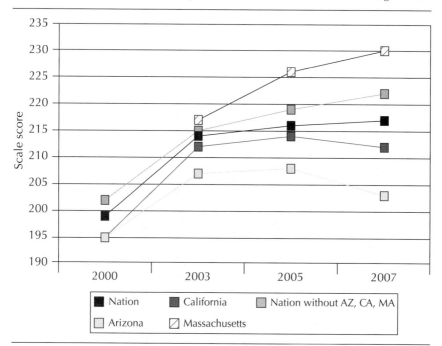

Note: Scale scores are on a scale of 0 to 500.

Source: Data compiled from National Center for Education Statistics, 2008.

contrary, the data all point in the direction of either increases in the gaps or no change.

LEARNING WHAT WILL WORK

These findings leave us with the more important question: If not English-only, what will work? In a statewide analysis of California's programs, researchers (Parrish et al., 2006) suggest that an analysis that pits English-only against bilingual, English as a Second Language, or dual-language programs is insufficient. The data from that evaluation show (1) statewide achievement gains for all students across grades and language classifications but (2) performance gaps between native English speakers and English learners that have not closed in most subject areas and grades. Even more relevant to the current discussion, the researchers state:

Figure 12.5. Average scores for English learners on the NAEP math scale, grade 8.

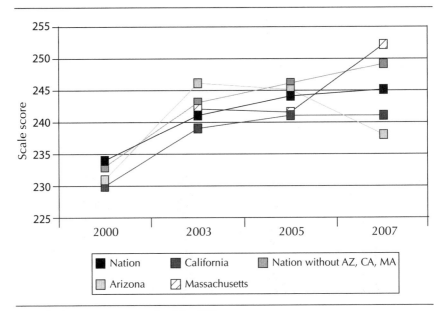

Note: Scale scores are on a scale of 0 to 500.

Source: Data compiled from National Center for Education Statistics, 2008.

The factors identified as most critical to their success were staff capacity to address English learners' linguistic and academic needs; schoolwide focus on English language development and standards-based instruction; shared priorities and expectations in educating English learners; and systematic, ongoing assessment and careful data use to guide instruction. (n.p.)

Civil rights law has provided a basic and defensible foundation for protecting English learners' rights to the same public education offered to other students. The criteria laid out in *Castañeda* and codified in the EEOA must be pursued as new conditions and programs emerge. Ultimately, the efforts to provide an adequate education to ELs must evolve from preventing harmful policies to devising a remedy that improves academic outcomes for ELs.

THE RESULTS PRONG OF EEOA MAY STILL HAVE GREAT UTILITY

Even considering the Supreme Court's remand in *Flores*, another recent case pursuant to the EEOA may bolster the prospects for challenging substandard and

Figure 12.6. Percentage of English learners scoring at or above proficient on NAEP reading scale, grade 4.

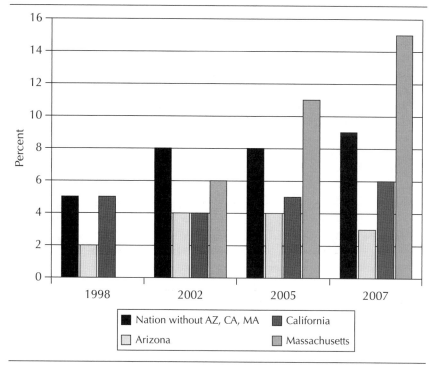

Source: Data compiled from National Center for Education Statistics, 2008.

inadequate education provided for ELs generally. The example comes from Texas, where restrictions on bilingual programs have never succeeded by way of referendum, but where the quality of EL instruction has still suffered as a result of failed programs and poorly implemented policy, especially at the secondary level. In contrast to the primary grades, where bilingual instruction is the default, few bilingual options exist at the secondary level.

In *United States v. Texas*, one of the core questions before the court was "whether Defendants' administration of the state's chosen program for educating LEP students violates the Equal Education Opportunity Act" (*U.S. v. Texas*, 2008, p. 726). Citing to *Castañeda*, the court reiterated that the question of the sufficiency of the state's actions was reviewed pursuant to the "results" prong (*U.S. v. Texas*, 2008, p. 759).

Most noteworthy is that a pattern of reduced success among secondary school ELs similar to that presented in the national NAEP data was found with regard to both Arizona's and Texas's statewide achievement tests. In *Texas*, the court found these data especially relevant to its ultimate conclusion that the Texas Education Agency (TEA)'s program of instruction violated the EEOA. Specifically, the court reasoned that it was "compelled to consider the 'panoptic results' of LEP students in all grades rather than considering the achievement of primary and secondary students separately" (*U.S. v. Texas*, 2008, p. 762).

The *Texas* ruling suggests that unless programs for ELs demonstrate clear achievement and outcome gains by students in grades K–12, they are particularly vulnerable to challenge with the passage of time and the accumulation of longitudinal data. The court stated that it would

> not attempt to broadly define the standard of causation, if any, for failures of LEP programs under prong three of *Castañeda*. Instead, the Court holds, consistent with precedent, that sufficient evidence of student failure sufficiently proves program failure. But as discussed *infra*, the evidence of prolonged failure of secondary LEP students is so overwhelming on a multitude of indicators that it narrows potential causes of student failure to the educational program's failure. Based upon the same evaluative tools used by TEA, the clear failure of secondary LEP students unquestionably demonstrates that, despite its efforts, TEA has not met its obligation to remedy the language deficiencies of Texas students. *Castañeda*, 648 F.2d at 1009. (*U.S. v. Texas*, 2008, p. 773)

The *Texas* case has been appealed to the Court of Appeals for the Fifth Circuit, and could prove to be an even more important decision than the Supreme Court's ruling in *Flores*.

After all, the *Flores* case remanded most of the substantive questions to the district court. The primary question answered by the Supreme Court in *Flores* was whether the district court, "abuse[d] its discretion" when it found inadequate a proposed legislative remedy" (*Flores v. Arizona*, 2008, p. 1156). Perhaps the most damaging aspect of the Supreme Court's ruling is the direct rejection of the argument that limiting funds for ELs beyond two years necessarily violated the EEOA. There is no question that the Supreme Court's reversal of the Ninth Circuit Court of Appeals on this issue raises new obstacles for advocates seeking to use the federal EEOA to challenge a state's provision of resources.

Essentially, the Court's majority opinion expressed a strong judicial preference for limiting a federal court's ongoing involvement in matters of state and local governance. The ongoing *Flores* litigation is an excellent illustration of the complex interplay of state and federal law and policy regarding the resources needed to ensure adequacy for English learners. As the next section will demonstrate, where resource deficiencies are at issue, even if *Flores* ultimately results in diminished EEOA utility, other legal challenges will remain available to those seeking adequate resources for ELs pursuant to some state laws and constitutions.

RIGHTS OF ENGLISH LEARNERS IN THE CONTEXT OF THE RIGHT TO EDUCATION UNDER STATE CONSTITUTIONAL LAW

What the *Flores* litigation does suggest, albeit indirectly, is that a challenge to a restrictive language policy could be brought in state court, pursuant to state constitutional law, either independently or in the context of an adequacy lawsuit. Thus English-only policies may be vulnerable to legal challenges on behalf of EL students, pursuant to state constitutions where the policy can be linked to restricted or seriously diminished resources for ELs. A critical new development is that state courts have increasingly acknowledged that ELs have greater resource needs, as evident, for example, in the recently decided school resource case, *Montoy v. Kansas* (2006).[3]

State courts might acknowledge that some ELs do need more than 1 or 2 years of specialized instruction, as the Ninth Circuit stressed in *Flores*. The restriction of resources resulting from a restrictive language policy would arguably violate the ELs' right to an education under the state constitution. The failure to meet the educational needs of ELs has arisen as explicit evidence of inadequacy in the context of more comprehensive school finance/adequacy litigation, and with some positive results. Therefore, depending on the state, advocates seeking to break down barriers to opportunity for EL students, should consider challenges under state laws to the adequacy of educational resources provided to ELs.

San Antonio Independent School District v. Rodriguez and the Concept of Adequacy

In 1973, in the landmark ruling *San Antonio Independent School District v. Rodriguez*, the poorer residents of the Edgewood district of the metropolitan San Antonio area, who were approximately 90% Mexican American and had substantially lower income and property values than many of the surrounding districts, challenged the state's unequal funding system of public schools on behalf of students in poor districts throughout Texas and almost won. In reversing the district court's ruling, the U.S. Supreme Court clarified that there was no federally guaranteed right to an education under the U.S. Constitution. The plaintiffs had argued that the school funding system in Texas violated the Constitution's Equal Protection Clause and had convinced the district court by showing that with property taxes as the primary source of school funding, even if they taxed themselves at substantially higher rates than wealthier districts, and despite some state support, they could only generate about half the per-pupil revenues (*Rodriguez v. San Antonio Independent School District*, 1971).

However, in reversing the district court, the Supreme Court introduced the adequacy rationale into the legal discourse with its suggestion that the Constitution might be violated if education expenditures fell short of "some identifiable quantum of education," if the Court conceded that such was a necessary "prerequisite to the meaningful exercise" of either the right to speak or the right to vote (*San Antonio Independent School District v. Rodriguez*, 1973, pp. 36–37). After *Rodriguez*, advocates were frustrated with the *de minimus* concept of adequacy under the U.S. Constitution and began an ongoing effort to define what level of resources was adequate to achieve that "identifiable quantum of education" in state constitutions.

Recently, as national and state expectations for student performance have both clarified and increased, plaintiffs, their lawyers, and expert witnesses have shifted their arguments from a focus on equal inputs to the adequacy of the resources students require to reach high, common outcomes. As a result, there have been increasingly explicit discussions of what English learners need to succeed in the context of school finance/resource litigation. These highly detailed courtroom explorations make the need for high-quality evidence all the more important and raise the risk that what courts deem to be "adequate" outcomes will veer away from equal educational opportunity in a race to a bare minimum.

The *Williams* Case and the Right to Adequate Educational Resources

In *Williams v. State of California* (2000), a broad coalition of expert witnesses (see Gándara & Rumberger 2002; Hakuta, 2002; Oakes, 2002) revealed students' limited access to effective instruction: high teacher–pupil ratios, including the lack of specialists available to serve English learners, and disparities in access to experienced and certified teachers (see "Decent Schools for California," n.d., for the complaints filed, expert testimony, details of the settlement, and developments in legislation and enforcement). The case has served as a prominent vehicle for public discourse and educational advocacy around inadequate resources in California and the nation.

The case also brought to the fore the inadequate opportunities experienced by English learners, who were, for example, almost twice as likely as students statewide to have a teacher who was not fully credentialed (25% compared to 14%) (Hakuta, 2002). The evidence also suggested that students who were receiving or had received bilingual instruction made the greatest gains in reading achievement between grades 2 and 5, while students with no exposure to bilingual instruction made the smallest gains.

Beyond these simple disparities, court testimony delineated inequalities in more sophisticated resources, such as the different levels of training available to teachers working with EL students. Thus, the testimony openly addressed the importance of resources that are hard to quantify, supporting the conception of fiscal equity focused on the effective use of dollars for instructional outcomes rather than dollars per se (Grubb & Goe, 2002).

Cases challenging the adequacy of education may or may not entail a close or particularly powerful analysis of what the prerequisites are for adequate instruction. An analysis of the likelihood of school equity cases to provide the kind of education resources children most need concluded that the most the effective resources for improving educational outcomes can be defined in "complex" and "abstract" terms (Grubb & Goe, 2002, p. 102). "Complex" resources include professional development and pedagogical practices, including constructivist and "hybrid" approaches, and "abstract" resources involve curriculum coherence and staff and student stability (Grubb & Goe, 2002). Because research suggests that these resources matter most, remedies should be more specific and go beyond increases to per-capita funding. Of course, when resources are wholly inadequate, such as the complete absence of funding for EL students after 2 years, a remedy requiring access to resources is a necessary prerequisite.

Whatever the vehicle, it is apparent that delivering equal opportunity to ELs requires more carefully structured resources. In the meantime, federal policy under No Child Left Behind (NCLB) is up for reauthorization soon. The reauthorization of this law holds potential for remediation of both the current federally imposed restrictions and inadequate resources. Should the Supreme Court curtail the potential utility of the EEOA, pressure will mount on Congress to either restore the EEOA or to transform NCLB into a true vehicle for meeting the needs of ELs.

NO CHILD LEFT BEHIND AND ENGLISH LEARNERS

It deserves mentioning that much can be accomplished through federal legislation to end restrictive language policy short of declaring English-only to be discriminatory or an outright violation of the EEOA. The Elementary and Secondary Education Act (ESEA, now NCLB) is known for the many requirements that states must fulfill in exchange for an infusion of federal funds. It is conceivable that in reauthorizing the ESEA, states that maintain restrictive English-only policies could have those funds frozen or restricted for a variety of reasons. Research might soon provide enough evidence for members of Congress that they would decide that English-only restrictive policies undermine the efforts to offer the full spectrum of best practices in educating ELs. Congress could deny or restrict federal education funding to states that maintained such policies purely as a matter of policy.

Alternatively, Congress might find that English-only policies, by requiring more EL students to be tested in English before they are ready, contribute to higher rates of invalid testing of EL students and put additional conditions or restrictions on ESEA funds to states that maintain such policies.

Either legislative initiative would be a striking change in federal policy because in 2001, No Child Left Behind added language restrictions. Besides the full participation of English learners in the NCLB accountability scheme, the law created a new requirement that EL students must be tested annually to assess their level of English language proficiency as well as their academic progress. Pursuant to Section 1111 (b) (3) (C) (ix) (III) of the law, students' academic progress is to be assessed "in a valid and reliable manner" and "to the extent practicable, assessments in the language and form most likely to yield accurate data on what such students know and can do in academic content areas." Moreover, the law provides for a standard moratorium of 3 years, and up to 5 years, on testing in English on a case-by-case basis. However, English-only states simply ignore these provisions and test EL students in English only, whether they can understand the language of the test or not. Nonetheless, accountability consequences attach both to the assessment of achievement in reading and mathematics and to the assessment of language proficiency.

NCLB requirements have placed the status and progress of English learners squarely in front of educators, policymakers, and families. However, as the law has been implemented, several major issues have arisen. One is that most statewide assessments administered to ELs are not valid for accountability purposes. More fundamentally, the system is flawed because in most states these assessments, as administered, are not accurate measures of achievement.

The most recent Government Accounting Office (GAO) report (2006) illustrates clearly that in most states serious problems regarding the test validity have been raised but not remedied. Thus NCLB is categorizing districts and schools using questionable tools. But without good measures of EL achievement, educators are left not knowing how to meet their instructional needs. The knowledge gaps occur on a number of levels (Hakuta, 2002). Most important, Standard 11.22 of the AERA/APA/NCME Standards for Educational and Psychological Testing requires that tests be investigated for validity with EL populations, something that has not been done in California, Arizona, or Massachusetts. Time limits for English assessment contained in NCLB and many state laws do not mesh with the research. Poor test practices, such as tests normed on native English speakers, yield invalid data and thus confound the evaluation of programs and practices. Similarly, the inappropriate use of these dubious test results for EL students to evaluate schools and districts creates perverse incentives to "game the system" in ways that harm children. Finally, federal and state laws and policies further contribute to the confusion by using different definitions of English learners and by varying the way program evaluations and school system assessments treat students who appear to have gained English proficiency.

CONCLUSION

As of 2009, No Child Left Behind is overdue for reauthorization and could prove to be an important vehicle for improving the educational outcomes of EL students. Improved resources, assessments, teacher preparation, and pedagogical strategies would lead the list of reforms that need to be included in the reauthorization. However, the challenge for advocates, lawyers, researchers, and educators is to apply historic tools (e.g., the Civil Rights Act, the Equal Education Opportunities Act, fiscal equity cases, and the process of reauthorizing the ESEA) to gain a more equitable education for these students. This chapter has outlined three areas where such work is needed immediately: (1) building the policy-relevant research base to challenge state initiated restrictive language policies; (2) using the reauthorization of the ESEA to develop better and more valid measures of long-term achievement for ELs; and (3) using the courts and Congress to eliminate restrictive policies and drive deeper shifts in policy and resource distribution, especially instructional resources, to improve our capacity to meet the needs of these students. These are not, by any means, exhaustive of the many improvements that will be needed, but rather the first steps to bring effective resources to ELs.

NOTES

This chapter developed out of a paper that was commissioned by ETS through the Annenberg Institute for School Reform at Brown University. The original paper for Educational Testing Service (ETS) was co-authored by Mary Helen Ybarra, Erica Frankenberg, and Dennie Palmer Wolf. The author is deeply grateful for them. The original research, opinions, and conclusions presented in this chapter are solely those of the author.

1. Most academic researchers prefer the more detailed scaled score information, as proficiency categories can artificially enhance or diminish actual score changes. This discrepancy happens because the categories have set ranges, and differences on the edges of those ranges of 1 point may appear to be more substantial than the actual data reflect. Both types of reporting are used in this chapter.

2. These are preliminary indicators only. More conclusive findings will require further analyses accounting for factors such as the redesignation of successful students out of English learner programs and the capacity to examine their continued progress through the system on a number of indicators.

3. In *Montoy v. Kansas* (2006), the legislature passed a bill that redistributed finances using a formula that provided significantly more funds to ensure EL students and others receive an adequate education. See 2006 Slip Opinion, *Montoy v. Kansas*, 112 P.3d 923, 2006 WL 2088176 (Kan.) (July 28, 2006). "This court considered each component of the formula, . . . and held that . . . it still failed to provide constitutionally suitable funding for public education because the changes were not based on considerations of the actual costs of providing a constitutionally adequate education and exacerbated existing funding inequities" (pp. 839–840). Specifically, this court found that the increases in the bilingual weighting and special education funding all varied substantially from the cost information in the record and that the state had failed to provide any cost basis to support the amount of funding provided.

REFERENCES

Castañeda v. Pickard, 648 F.2d 989 (5th Cir. 1981).

Decent schools for California: *Williams v. State of California*. (n.d.). Retrieved October 15, 2008, from http://www.decentschools.org/index.php

Equal Educational Opportunity Act, Pub. L. No. (93-380), 88 Stat. 515 (1974).

Flores v. Arizona, 516 F.3d 1140 9th Cir. (2008).

Gándara, P., & Rumberger, R. (2002, October 1). *The inequitable treatment of English learners in California's public schools*. UCLA's Institute for Democracy, Education, & Access. Williams Watch Series: Investigating the Claims of Williams v. State of California. Paper wws-rr005-1002. Retrieved October 30, 2008, from http://repositories.cdlib.org/idea/wws/wws-rr005-1002

General Accounting Office. (2006). No Child Left Behind: Assistance from education could help states better measure progress of students with limited English proficiency. Retrieved September 14, 2008, from http://www.gao.gov/products/GAO-06-815

GI Forum et al. v. TEA et al., F.Supp., 1 (W.D. Tex. 2000).

Grissom, J. B. (2004). Reclassification of English learners. *Education Policy Analysis Archives, 12*(36). Retrieved January 27, 2008, from http://epaa.asu.edu/epaa/v12n36/

Grubb, W. N., & Goe, L. (2002). *The unending search for equity: California policy and the "new" school*. Los Angeles: UCLA's Institute for Democracy, Education & Access (IDEA).

Hakuta, K. (2002). English language learner access to basic educational necessities in California: An analysis of inequities. Retrieved from http://www.decentschools.org/experts.php?sub=per

Horne v. Flores, 557 U.S. 289 (2009).

Lau v. Nichols, 483 F. 2d 791 (9th Cir. 1973), *cert. granted*, 412 U.S. 938 (1973), *rev'd* 414 U.S. 563 (1974).

Montoy v. Kansas, 279 Kan. at 839-40, 112 P.3d 923 (WL 2088176 Kan. 2006).

Myhill, W. N. (2004). The state of public education and the needs of English language learners in the era of "No Child Left Behind." *Journal of Gender, Race & Justice, 8*, 393.

National Center for Education Statistics. (2008). *The nation's Report Card. Background questionnaires*. Retrieved September 14, 2008, from http://nces.ed.gov/nationsreportcard/bgquest.asp

Oakes, J. (2002, October 1). *Education inadequacy, inequality, and failed state policy: A synthesis of expert reports prepared for Williams v. State of California*. UCLA's Institute for Democracy, Education, & Access. Williams Watch Series: Investigating the Claims of *Williams v. State of California*. Paper wws-rr016-1002. Retrieved October 30, 2008, from http://repositories.cdlib.org/idea/wws/wws-rr016-1002

Parrish, T. B., Merickel, A., Perez. M, Linquanti, R., Socia, M., Spain, A., Speroni, C., Esra, P., Brock, L., & Delancey, D. (2006). *Effects of the implementation of Proposition 227 on the education of English learners, K–12: Findings from a five-year evaluation*. Palo Alto, CA: American Institutes for Research and WestEd. Retrieved September 10, 2008, from http://www.wested.org/cs/we/view/rs/804

Ramírez, D., Pasta, D., Yuen, S., Ramey, D., & Billings, D. (1991). *Final report: Longitudinal study of structured English immersion, early-exit and late exit transitional bilingual education programs for language minority children.* San Mateo, CA: Aguirre International.

Rodriguez v. San Antonio Independent School District, 337 F. Supp. 280 (W.D. Tex 1971).

San Antonio Independent School District v. Rodriguez, 411 U.S. 980 (1973).

Title VI, Civil Rights Act of 1964, 42 U.S.C. Sect. 2000(e) *et seq.*

U.S. Commission on Civil Rights. (1997). *Equal educational opportunity and nondiscrimination for students with limited English proficiency: Federal enforcement of Title VI and Lau v. Nichols, Equal Educational Opportunity Projects Series, Vol. 3.* Washington, DC: Author.

United States v. Texas, 572. F. Supp.2d 726 (E.D. Texas 2008).

Valeria G. v. Wilson, 12 F. Supp.2d 1007 (N.D. Cal. 1998), *aff'd sub nom* Valeria v. Davis, 307 F.3d 1036 (9th Cir. 2002), *pet. for reh'g en banc denied,* 320 F.3d 1014 (9th Cir. 2003).

Williams v. State of California, No. 312236 (Cal. Sup. Ct. 2000).

CHAPTER 13

Moving from Failure to a New Vision
of Language Policy

Patricia Gándara and Gary Orfield

N O ONE WOULD WANT their medical treatment decided by a poll or a referendum, particularly one in which the question was written by someone who was completely unknowledgeable about medicine and was trying to force the professionals who know something about treating the condition to abandon the treatment they believed to be best. Yet that is exactly the way we have decided policy about educating children who are learning English. The idea of making public policy by referendum was part of a package of political reforms in the early 20th century designed to permit the public to decide a policy when the public will was blocked by one of the corrupt political machines that exercised so much power at that time. It was expected to be a vehicle for progressive causes, and sometimes it was. The process evolved, however, into one that too often framed distorted questions and then created the semblance of public will by spending a great deal of money to hire workers to gather signatures for a misleading policy with a beguiling name. "English for the Children" was such a distorted issue. In a situation such as this one, it is all too easy to appeal to prejudice for a victory. The idea that a rich businessman with no educational expertise who had failed in a run for political office could use his money to control the educational rights of large groups of extremely disadvantaged students in three states is extraordinary. The result was a political coup and an educational failure.

The claims made by the advocates of restrictive language policies have not been seriously examined by policymakers, in part because they fear to challenge what they see as public beliefs on the subject. And not without reason. While 85%

of respondents in a recent Gallup poll (2007a) said they thought teaching a second language in school was either "important" or "very important," and a large majority thought it should start in elementary school, much smaller percentages believe that bilingual education is a good idea. Perhaps this is because of the way that pollsters typically frame the question as either/or. Respondents are asked if they think children should be in bilingual education or learn English, as though the two were mutually exclusive. For example, a 2007 Gallup poll asked if students should learn English first or if public schools should be required "to provide instruction in the students' native languages." Put this way, it sounds as though the schools would provide instruction in any number of other languages, *except* English. Not surprisingly, 61% opted for English first. Almost 20% thought that children should have to learn English at parents' expense in special classes (Gallup, 2007b).

The media, too, have fueled views of bilingual education that contradict actual research findings. McQuillan and Tse (1996) found that while the great majority of studies reported in the academic literature found bilingual programs to be successful, the majority of op-eds and other newspaper articles described them as failures. This kind of reporting creates erroneous beliefs among the public that then convert into votes at the ballot box.

THE EFFECTS OF RESTRICTIVE LANGUAGE POLICIES

Most of the data collected, and most of the attention by researchers who have studied the effects of restrictive language policies in California, Arizona, and Massachusetts, have been directed at student outcomes. However, none of these states had large percentages of their English learners in strong bilingual programs to begin with. As noted, California had only 29% of its EL students in any kind of bilingual program (and no doubt some programs were stronger than others) in 1998, when Proposition 227 was passed. Arizona had unknown percentages of its EL students in these programs. But as in California, most students were in some form of English immersion instruction, or simply mainstreamed into regular classrooms. It is not surprising, then, that the impact on test scores and other quantifiable student outcome measures was modest at most. Few students were actually subjected to a substantially different program after the passage of these laws. But teachers *were* affected in sometimes dramatic, and often very discomfiting, ways. Teachers who had prepared themselves with the additional coursework and practica required to obtain a bilingual credential or certification were told they could not use the skills that they had acquired and that they believed had been effective with their students. For many teachers this was frustrating, confusing, and even frightening since the legislation allowed them to be sued if they stepped over a poorly defined line of using "too much" primary language in attempting to communicate with their students. The impact of restrictive language policies has probably been felt less on students than on the erosion of teacher capacity in these states.

In the immediate aftermath of the passage of Proposition 227, several studies were conducted to assess its impact. Both Gándara and her colleagues (2000) and Maxwell-Jolly (2000) found that schools and districts responded in ways that were largely consistent with the attitudes and philosophies they held before the law was passed. If they had resisted bilingual instruction, they were happy that they would no longer have to engage in it or seek reasons for why they did not; if they supported it, they were distressed and resentful, and many, at least initially, tried to seek waivers to avoid the full impact of the law. However, regardless of which programs or instructional strategies they preferred, most schools and districts still felt they both wanted and needed bilingual teachers. They understood that these teachers could communicate with families to gather information and support, and with students to motivate and encourage them; that they could informally assess students' understanding and help to discriminate between learning problems and second-language issues; and that they were a critical resource for other teachers in the school who lacked these skills. Not surprisingly, Gándara, Maxwell-Jolly, and Driscoll (2005) found a linear relationship between the amount of training that teachers of English learners had received and the amount of confidence they had that they could serve these students well. Teachers with bilingual credentials were the most confident of their skills, those with ESL or other English-only instructional preparation were less confident, and those with little or no training were the least confident of all. Studies have shown that teachers' confidence in their skills is indeed related to their effectiveness in the classroom (Berman & McLaughlin, 1978; Rosenholtz, 1985; Rutter, 1989). Yet fewer and fewer teachers are seeking to prepare themselves with bilingual competencies under the new laws.

In 1998, the year that Proposition 227 passed in California, 1,829 teachers had received a bilingual credential or certification through either a teacher preparation program or a rigorous state examination. In 2008, only 1,147 teachers had sought these credentials—a decline of more than one-third, in spite of a growing English learner population (California Commission on Teacher Credentialing, 2005, 2009). Although earlier data are not available for Arizona, in the short period between 2006 and 2009, there was a 16% drop in the number of credentialed or certified bilingual teachers in that state, from 2,955 to 2,479 (Arias, 2009). With few or no rewards and substantial additional burdens in schools where they are called upon, for no additional remuneration, to aid the staff who lack their skills, not many prospective teachers want to go through the added time, trouble, and expense to become a bilingual teacher. The research suggests that the losers in this scenario are the students, who increasingly encounter teachers who have no idea how to teach them, much less the ability to communicate with them.

The passage of these propositions has also had a broader effect of encouraging a movement to abandon bilingual instruction in other parts of the country. This campaign, led by an organization with the title "English for the Children," also popularized beliefs that bilingual education was not only ineffective but harmful for children's educational development, that learning English would happen rapidly and easily once these destructive programs were removed, and that there was a self-serving conspiracy of bilingual educators and researchers who were only concerned with preserving their own livelihood. Such attitudes influence support for bilingual programs even in states that do not have prohibitions against them. In 2003, Zehler and colleagues found a steady increase over the prior decade in instruction being provided in English only, from 37% of all English learners (ELs) in 1992 to 59% in 2002. Increasingly, primary-language instruction is being shelved in favor of English immersion. New York, a state that has consistently supported multilingualism and developed assessments in the major languages spoken in that state so that English learners' academic progress can be tracked, has nonetheless seen a consistent decline in bilingual education programs, particularly since the 2002 passage of No Child Left Behind (NCLB) (Menken, 2008). Figure 13.1 shows the decrease in enrollment in bilingual programs in New York City from 2002 to 2006 (from approximately 40% to 31%) and the corresponding increase in English-only programs (from approximately 53% to 67%). Menken (2008) argues that these programmatic changes are evidence that NCLB is a language policy in and of itself. To be sure, the combined effects of English-only legislation in several states and the accountability requirements of NCLB are devastating for EL students across the nation who had been learning in their primary language while they acquired English.

In a country with the largest immigration in its history, where Latino and Asian students have increased fourfold in the last 40 years and many are having severe problems in the schools, the referenda campaigns blamed the educational problems of the students on the programs that were intended to help them. Proponents appealed to a public belief that their ancestors had learned English without any special programs and that today's immigrants could as well. The campaign reflected the common conservative tendency to blame the problems of highly disadvantaged groups not on the society or its policies but on the programs and the people who are trying to help them. Some leading politicians joined these campaigns. Whatever one might say about the campaigns on these measures, there was certainly no serious debate on the actual evidence on bilingual programs, and decision makers were not well informed. Yet these policies quickly eliminated what had been the largest effort to respond to these children's needs. They also disregarded the Supreme Court's 1974 decision in *Lau v. Nichols*, which held that simply instructing children in a language they did not understand did not meet the basic requirements of civil rights law. Surely the first principle in education, as it is in medicine, should be "above all, do no harm." The research reviewed in

Figure 13.1. Program enrollment of New York City English learners by school year, 2002–2008.

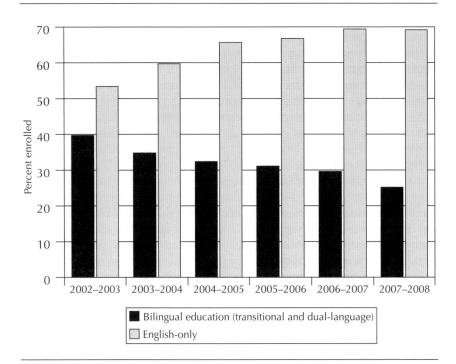

Source: Reprinted with kind permission from Springer Science + Business Media: *English Learners Left Behind: Standardized Testing as Language Policy*, 2008, Kate Menken, copyright © 2008 by Multilingual Matters, Ltd.

this volume suggests that restrictive language policies may not meet the test of this principle.

In terms of their assumptions and promises, restrictive language policies have not worked. There is no evidence that the students who were excluded from bilingual education have done any better and no evidence for the proposition that they would rapidly acquire a high level of English ability if only the shackles of bilingual programs were removed. The studies reported in this volume for Arizona, California, and Massachusetts show no overall closing of achievement gaps between English learners and their native English-speaking peers and no more rapid progress toward ELs' fluency in English. Moreover, national assessments suggest that EL students in states with restrictive language policies may be fairing more poorly than EL students in states without such policies. But concerns have been raised that more students may be improperly placed in special education, more may be dropping out of school altogether, and many qualified and experienced bilingual teachers may be leaving the classroom. One of the ironies of the anti-bilingual instruction movement is that the vast majority of English learners were already in English-only instruction *before* the measures were passed, and so it is not surprising that we did not see wild shifts in academic outcomes or test scores. Only a small percentage of English learners were actually removed from bilingual classrooms, but the new laws did cause chaos and misunderstanding in schools; frustration and embarrassment among many parents; and the movement of many students into English mainstream classes where teachers were unprepared to teach them.

KEY FINDINGS ON RESTRICTIVE LANGUAGE POLICIES

The research that was commissioned and conducted for inclusion in this volume was designed to answer the question: Have restrictive language policies delivered on their promise? We wanted to examine the evidence on what had happened to English learners as result of being placed in Structured English Immersion classrooms in the states that imposed these policies. We also wanted to know how such policies had affected schools, classrooms, teachers, and communities. Unfortunately, the focus of most studies related to these policies has been almost exclusively on student academic outcomes; there has never been any large-scale research on the affective outcomes for students—their engagement with school, their self-concept as learners, or their likelihood of wanting to continue on with their studies beyond high school. Similarly, there has been relatively little written about the impact of these policies on teachers. Has it affected their motivation to teach these students? How much has it increased the likelihood of such teachers leaving the teaching profession or at least leaving the classroom? We do not know the answers to these questions because the data are not available or the studies have not been conducted.

As Ester de Jong, M. Beatriz Arias, and María Teresa Sánchez point out in Chapter 8 of this volume, these policies directly affect the work of teachers and their ability or inability to adapt their instruction within the narrow parameters of an English-only regime, which in turn directly affects the quality of instruction that EL students receive. De Jong and her colleagues show how teachers worried about reducing the pace and content of what they were teaching and how they were concerned about their students' comprehension of their instruction, as it was delivered in a language they barely understood.

Although many of the answers we sought remain unknown, the research compiled in the preceding pages does come to a series of strong conclusions: (1) No, the restrictive language policies imposed in the three states—Arizona,

California, and Massachusetts—have not delivered on their promise. (2) Yes, teachers have felt confused and disheartened by these policies. (3) There is an urgent need to study other outcomes of these policies, such as whether they are increasing misplacement in special education and encouraging students to drop out of school and whether they are affecting teachers' preparation and skills as well as their likelihood of staying in the field. Daniel Losen (Chapter 12, this volume) also suggests that by removing a set of tools from teachers that have been shown to be effective at least with some of their English learners, while prescribing a method that has not produced superior results, the principles of the *Castañeda* decision (1981) and the Equal Educational Opportunity Act may have been violated, which could possibly provide the bases for a legal claim to overturn these policies.

MOVING AWAY FROM RESTRICTIVE LANGUAGE POLICIES

Whether or not states and locales choose to take a legal route to redress the failure of the restrictive language policies, it is clear that something more must be done to help EL students achieve at levels that will provide the opportunity for success in American society. This effort is not happening now; the data show overwhelming failure for these students. To consider what can be done in this increasingly anti–bilingual education environment, several researchers outline what has been shown to be effective. Diane August, Claude Goldenberg, and Robert Rueda (Chapter 9, this volume) summarize the research on teaching English learners to read. They find an unequivocal advantage to teaching EL students to read in their primary language whenever possible, an important conclusion as well in a major National Academy of Sciences report on reading research. They also report on a host of other cognitive and noncognitive advantages to being educated bilingually. Their conclusions, drawn in part from a state-of-the-art meta-analytic study published in 2006, are supported by the most prominent researchers in the area of second-language acquisition and reading instruction in the nation.

If bilingual education was unable to defend itself in the campaigns against it, and the new Structured English Immersion programs have shown no greater propensity to close the achievement gaps between English learners and English speakers, then what is at the root of the problems English learners experience in school? Gándara and Rumberger (2003) conducted an extensive study of the schooling conditions of ELs in California for the California state court hearing the *Williams* case, a case examining the massive inequality in California's public schools that was settled by Governor Arnold Schwartznegger. The study's investigators found that English learners received a demonstrably weaker education along seven different dimensions than even other poor children in the state. They were more likely than all other children (except special education students) to have teachers who lacked the qualifications to teach them; they were more likely to be housed in inadequate facilities—schools infested with vermin and without working toilets, for example; they had less actual learning time available to them with fewer adults to help them; they had inadequate materials to meet their instructional needs; their teachers were provided inadequate professional development to learn how to teach them; they were more segregated and isolated with other low-income and non-English-speaking students; and they lacked valid assessments of their skills and abilities and insufficient counselors to advise them and their families of available career paths. It was clear from this research that gaining an adequate education was a virtual impossibility for most of these children. In the settlement of *Eliezer Williams v. State of California* in 2004, the state agreed to provide funds to upgrade classrooms, books, and certain other aspects of unequal schools to the extent permitted by settlement funds.

While some states do, indeed, do a better job of educating English learners than California—national test (National Assessment of Educational Progress [NAEP]) data suggest that Texas may offer more positive learning opportunities for its elementary-age ELs, and New Jersey spends a lot more money on its EL students—many states do as meager a job or worse. Russell Rumberger and Loan Tran (Chapter 6, this volume) show wide gaps between EL students and English speakers, even in high-performing states. They also find that the segregation and isolation that many of these students encounter in their schools probably contributes significantly to their depressed academic achievement. But EL students' academic outcomes are not just the product of inadequate education. For most of these students, it is also the product of a social system that provides no safety net for them or their families.

Most English learners are not immigrants; they are native-born American citizens. But most have at least one parent who is an immigrant. And America does not treat its immigrants, or its poor, very well. These are families who struggle with high levels of poverty even when both parents work full-time, live in neighborhoods with profoundly unequal schools and other conditions, often have no health care coverage for their children, have marginal dead-end jobs, and frequently face prejudice in the community. The immigrant members of these families came seeking opportunity, believing that the schools were the key to their children having better lives. Given the extraordinary hurdles that students who are English learners must face in this country, and in our schools, what kind of schooling policy would make sense for these students and how should we go about creating it?

Forbidding the children's language in their schools has failed. Bilingual education, where it was available, was often better, but not good enough to create equal opportunity for most English learners. Those who gain English still face many other problems that deeply impact their school opportunities and performance. If we reject the restrictive language policies—and the evidence presented in this volume indicates that they should surely be rejected—it will not be for the goal of going back to what there was before these initiatives. It has to be about something better, akin to the strategies discussed in the later chapters in this book.

Dual-Language Programs

P. Zitlali Morales and Ursula Aldana (Chapter 10, this volume) point out that while restrictive language policies attempted to ban, or at least severely restrict, bilingual instruction, there was little discussion in the debates leading up to these initiatives or in the aftermath of their passage about just how primary language has been used to instruct students. They note that there are several variations of "bilingual" programs, and some of these are eagerly endorsed by large portions of the electorate. Morales and Aldana explain that the students' primary language can be used across a continuum—from merely using it to explain specific concepts to providing full-day instruction in two languages. The outcomes appear to be stronger for the programs that truly teach in two languages over long periods of time, and April Linton and Rebecca Franklin (Chapter 11, this volume) describe the efforts that have been made, largely spearheaded by English-speaking parents, to bring about more of these kinds of programs. It is an irony that in a period when bilingual programs have come under severe attack, there has been a simultaneously steep growth in dual-language programs. These programs mix English learners with native English speakers with the goal of achieving biliteracy for both groups. Is there something in a name? Or is it just *who* they are serving that makes the great difference? Is it more palatable to the American public to educate middle-class youngsters in two languages than to educate immigrant students in the same way?

Morales and Aldana also report that dual-language programs have an added advantage of confronting one of the great social and educational scourges of our time—the continuing, and in some cases increasing, segregation of students in our schools. Dual-language instruction has shown great promise for bringing low- and middle-income, Black, Latino, Asian, and White students together in equal-status contact where they not only learn in two languages, but also learn to like and respect each other's cultures. Given that these programs tend to demonstrate among the highest academic achievement outcomes of all interventions for English learners, they must be seen as a viable alternative to current programs where it is feasible to implement them.

Teacher Training

There must also be a focused effort to determine what the skills are that make a teacher highly qualified to teach English learners. Evidence suggests these skills are not what are being taught in many credentialing or certification programs. Many programs attempt to train teachers to take on the extremely complex task of teaching EL students in a matter of 45 to 90 hours or in some of the "infused" programs in which instruction of English learners is embedded in routine teacher preparation curriculum. Unfortunately, it appears that it is often so embedded in the curriculum, it cannot be found at all. And while research strongly recommends that students be given the opportunity for instruction in their primary language whenever possible, especially as they are learning to read, there is a desperate need for teachers from the same language communities as the students—teachers who know the students' challenges and assets, understand their communities, and can communicate directly with them and their parents. In our study of 5,300 educators of English learners in California (Gándara, Maxwell-Jolly, & Driscoll, 2005), the single greatest challenge reported by most elementary school teachers was the inability to communicate with children's parents and thereby enlist their support in the education of their children. Even when the curriculum is not a bilingual curriculum, bilingual teachers are a major asset to any school. Any policy that erodes the supply of well-trained bilingual teachers or discourages new teachers from preparing themselves in this way should be reconsidered. It deprives the teaching force of some of its most important resources.

BEYOND THE CLASSROOM

We need a much broader educational and social policy initiative to educate parents, improve working and income conditions, create access to better neighborhoods and schools, address children's health care needs, respect their culture, and help them be welcomed into the mainstream of a society where they are a very large part of the next generation. In short, we must receive these immigrant and minority language families as the assets they are to our nation. The first step will be to cast aside the seductive but erroneous idea that forbidding their language is the shortcut to that dream. That policy has wasted years on what turns out to be a dead end, something that has too often served to compound inequality. There is no shortcut to educational equality. Language, properly used, is not an obstacle, but a potentially important asset in a society destined to have more than one hundred million residents of Latino descent, as well as many other vibrant language groups, by mid-century.

REFERENCES

Arias, B. (2009). Unpublished data based on Arizona Department of Education data.

Berman, P., & McLaughlin, M. (1978). *Federal progams supporting educational change: Vol VIII. Implementing and sustaining innovations.* Santa Monica, CA: RAND Corp.

California Commission on Teacher Credentialing. (2005). [Years 1988–2004]. Unpublished data compiled by S. Porter.

California Commission on Teacher Credentialing. (2009). [Years 2005–2008]. Unpublished data compiled by M. Suckow.

Castañeda v. Packard, 648 F.2d 989, 5th Cir. (1981).

Gallup (2007a). 39th Gallup Poll, September 2007, *Phi Delta Kappan, 89*(1). Retrieved March 9, 2009, from www.pdkintl.org/kappan/k_89/k0709pol.htm

Gallup (2007b). *Growing diversity translates into classroom challenges.* Retrieved March 9, 2009, from http://www.gallup.com/poll/20425/Growing-Diversity-Translates-Into-Classroom-Challenges.aspx?version=print

Gándara, P., Maxwell-Jolly, J., & Driscoll, A. (2005). *Listening to teachers of English language learners: A survey of California teachers' challenges, experiences, and professional development needs.* Santa Cruz, CA: The Center for the Future of Teaching and Learning.

Gándara, P., Maxwell-Jolly, J., Stritikus,T., Curry, J., Garcia, E., Asato, J., & Gutiérrez, K. (2000). *The initial effects of Proposition 227 on English learners.* Santa Barbara, CA: University of California, Linguistic Minority Research Institute. Available on line at http://www.lmri.uscb.edu

Gandara, P., & Rumberger, R. (2003, October 1). The inequitable treatment of English learners in California's public schools. *Educational Policy Analysis Archives.* Retrieved February 2, 2009, from http://epaa.asu/epaaV71n36

Lau v. Nichols, 414 U.S. 563 (1974).

McQuillan, J., & Tse, L. (1996). Does research really matter? An analysis of media opinion on bilingual education, 1984–1994. *Bilingual Research Journal, 20*(1), 1–27.

Maxwell-Jolly, J. (2000). Factors influencing implementation of mandated policy change: Proposition 227 in seven northern California school districts. *Bilingual Research Journal, 24*, 37–56.

Menken, K. (2008). *English learners left behind: Standardized testing as language policy.* Clevedon, UK: Multilingual Matters.

Rosenholtz, S. (1985). Effective schools: Interpreting the evidence. *American Journal of Education, 93*, 352–388.

Rutter, M. (1989). School influences on children's behavior and development. *Pediatrics, 65*, 208–220.

Zehler, A. M., Fleischman, H. L., Hopstock, P. J., Stephenson, T. G., Pendzick, M. L., & Sapru, S. (2003). *Descriptive study of services to LEP students and LEP students with disabilities* (Vol. I). Washington, DC: U.S. Department of Education, Office of English Language Acquisition, Language Enhancement, and Academic Achievement of Limited English Proficient Students (OELA).

About the Editors and the Contributors

Patricia Gándara is a professor of education at the University of California, Los Angeles. She is also the co-director of The Civil Rights Project/Proyecto Derechos Civiles. Her research focuses on educational equity and access for low-income and ethnic minority students, language policy, and the education of Mexican-origin youth.

Megan Hopkins is a doctoral student at the Graduate School of Education and Information Studies at the University of California, Los Angeles. She is author and co-author of several publications related to English learners, teacher education, and education policy. She holds a BA from Indiana University and an EdM from Harvard University. She is a former bilingual teacher.

Ursula S. Aldana is a doctoral student at the Graduate School of Education and Information Studies at the University of California, Los Angeles. Her research interests include dual-immersion programs, models of education for urban school contexts, and the education of English learners. She received a B.S. from Georgetown University and an M.A. in education from Loyola Marymount University.

M. Beatriz Arias is an associate professor of language and literacy in the Mary Lou Fulton College of Education at Arizona State University. Her research focuses on the impact of restrictive language policy on teacher education and educational policy and equity for English language learners. Her work on language policy and teacher preparation is in *Structured Immersion Implementation in Arizona* (Multilingual Matters, 2009) and in *Coming to Voice: Preparing Teachers for ELs* (Roman Littlefield Press, 2009).

Alfredo J. Artiles is a professor of special education at Arizona State University. His research examines disability identification practices and professional learning as windows into schools' cultural constructions of difference and their implications for educational equity. He has published extensively in the general, special, and bilingual education fields. He is the vice president of AERA's Division G (Social Contexts of Education).

Diane August, Ph.D., is currently a senior research scientist at the Center for Applied Linguistics as well as a consultant located in Washington, D.C. Her research focuses on the education of language minority children, particularly their literacy development. She has published widely in journals and books.

Ester J. de Jong, Ed.D., is an associate professor in ESOL/bilingual education, School of Teaching and Learning at the University of Florida. Her research interests include two-way immersion and other integrated approaches to bilingualism and second-language learning, language policy and discourses, program effectiveness for language minority students, and teacher preparation for English learners.

Virginia Diez is a doctoral candidate at Tufts University's Eliot-Pearson Department of Child Development and a research assistant at the Mauricio Gastón Institute for Latino Community Development and Public Policy at the University of Massachusetts, Boston. Her research examines the interaction of individual and sociocultural factors in the development of children and adolescents living in predominantly Latino communities.

Edward G. Fierros is an associate professor in the Department of Education and Human Services at Villanova University. His major research interests are in the placement of minority students with learning disabilities, charter school policy, Native American education, and the theory of multiple intelligences. He has written numerous journal articles and is co-author, with Mindy Kornhaber and Shirley Veenema, of *Multiple Intelligences: Best Ideas from Research and Practice* (Allyn & Bacon, 2004).

Rebecca C. Franklin is a graduate student at the University of California, San Diego.

David García is an assistant professor at the Mary Lou Fulton College of Education at Arizona State University. His research interests include school choice, school accountability, and policy implementation across levels of the education system. He received his doctorate from the University of Chicago.

Claude Goldenberg is a professor in the Stanford University School of Education. He received his Ph.D. from the Graduate School of Education and Information Studies at the University of California, Los Angeles. His research focuses on literacy and academic achievement among English learners.

M. Cecilia Gómez is a sociolinguist and a doctoral student in the School of Education at the University of California, Davis. Originally from Argentina, she has worked in teacher education and bilingual education in Latin America and the

United States. Her research interests include the schooling of bilingual students, language policy, second/third and heritage language acquisition, teacher education, and the teaching of Spanish in the United States.

Kenji Hakuta is the Lee J. Jacks Professor of Education at Stanford University. He is the author of many publications, including *Mirror of Language: The Debate of Bilingualism* (Basic Books, 1986). He has testified to Congress and other public bodies on language policy, the education of language minority students, affirmative action in higher education, and improvement of the quality in educational research.

Tom Haladyna, professor emeritus at Arizona State University, has been an elementary school teacher, researcher, test director, and university professor in teacher education. He specializes in designing and evaluating testing programs. He has authored or co-authored 12 books and hundreds of journal articles, conference papers, technical reports, white papers, and evaluation reports.

Janette K. Klingner is a professor of education specializing in bilingual multicultural special education at the University of Colorado at Boulder in the Department of Educational Equity and Cultural Diversity. She was a bilingual special education teacher for 10 years before earning a Ph.D. in reading and learning disabilities from the University of Miami. To date, she has authored or co-authored more than 80 articles, books, and book chapters. In 2004 she won AERA's Early Career Award for outstanding research.

Nicole Lavan is a doctoral candidate in public policy at the John W. McCormack School of Policy Studies at the University of Massachusetts, Boston. She has been a researcher at The Mauricio Gastón Institute for Latino Community Development and Public Policy since 2005. Her research is focused on school dropouts.

April Linton is an assistant professor of sociology at the University of California, San Diego. She studies immigration, particularly in relation to language issues. Her recent publications include "Contexts for Bilingualism Among U.S.-Born Latinos" (*Ethnic and Racial Studies 28*(4), with Tomás Jiménez) and "Language Policy and Politics in the United States: Implications for the Immigration Debate" (in *International Journal of the Sociology of Language*).

Daniel Losen, J.D., M.Ed., is a senior education law and policy associate with The Civil Rights Project and lecturer on law at Harvard Law School. His work concerns the impact of federal, state, and local education law and policy on students of color; addressing the school-to-prison pipeline; and implementation concerns related to No Child Left Behind.

Jeff MacSwan is a professor and program director of the Applied Linguistics Ph.D. Program at Arizona State University. He received his Ph.D. from UCLA in 1997. His research focuses on education policy related to English learners in U.S. schools and on the linguistic study of bilingualism. He has served as associate editor of the *Bilingual Research Journal* and currently serves on five scholarly editorial boards.

Kate Mahoney is an assistant professor in the Department of Language, Learning, and Leadership at the State University of New York (SUNY) at Fredonia. Her current research addresses the validity of using achievement and language proficiency test scores for English learners, program evaluation, and meta-analysis. She teaches classes in bilingual education, assessment of ELs, and research methods courses and also serves as thesis director for graduate students conducting master's thesis research.

P. Zitlali Morales is a doctoral candidate at the Graduate School of Education and Information Studies at the University of California, Los Angeles. Her dissertation work focuses on the academic identity development of linguistic minority students in a Spanish–English dual-immersion program in the Los Angeles area. She received a B.A. from Stanford University and formerly worked as a school partnership director for Partners in School Innovation, a school reform organization in the San Francisco Bay Area.

Gary Orfield is the professor of education, law, political science, and urban planning at the University of California, Los Angeles. He was co-founder and director of the Harvard Civil Rights Project and now serves as co-director of The Civil Rights Project/Proyecto Derechos Civiles at UCLA. His research interests are in the study of civil rights, education policy, and minority opportunity.

Nathan Pellegrin is a research analyst for the California Partnership for Achieving Student Success. He has provided data management and data analysis services to education institutions and research organizations for over 10 years. He holds a B.A. from the University of California, Berkeley, and an M.S. in Statistics from California State University, East Bay.

Robert Rueda is a professor in the area of psychology in education at the Rossier School of Education at the University of Southern California. His research has centered on the sociocultural basis of motivation, learning, and instruction, with a focus on reading and literacy in English learners as well as students in at-risk conditions. He also teaches courses in learning and motivation.

Russell W. Rumberger is a professor of education in the Gevirtz Graduate School of Education at the University of California, Santa Barbara. A faculty member at

UCSB since 1987, he has published widely in several areas of education: education and work; the schooling of disadvantaged students, particularly school dropouts and linguistic minority students; school effectiveness; and education policy.

María Teresa Sánchez is a research associate at Education Development Center (EDC). Her experience is in conducting mixed-methods, quantitative, and qualitative research studies in areas such as the implementation of English-only educational language policies and their impact on teachers, state-level initiatives that support data-driven decision making in districts and schools, and the associations between student achievement and individual and school characteristics. She holds a B.A. from Pontifical Catholic University of Peru, an M.Ed. from Northeastern University, and a Ph.D. from Boston College.

Amanda Sullivan is the co-director of research and evaluation for the Equity Alliance and a doctoral candidate at Arizona State University. Her research addresses issues of diversity and equity in school psychology and special education, with attention to the ways in which systemic factors, educational policy, and professional practices shape the experiences of diverse students.

Karen Thompson is a doctoral student in educational linguistics at the Stanford University School of Education. Prior to her time at Stanford, she worked for more than a decade in California public schools as a bilingual teacher, school reform consultant, and after-school program coordinator.

Loan Tran is currently a postdoctoral fellow at the University of California, Riverside, working on topics such as learning disabilities and response to intervention of poor readers. She received her Ph.D. in research methodology from the University of California, Santa Barbara, in 2008. During her graduate study, she worked on several topics ranging from access to preschool to the achievement gap of English learners. She has an M.Ed. from the University of Pittsburgh and a B.A. from the University of the Pacific.

Rosann Tung, Ph.D., is the director of research at the Center for Collaborative Education in Roxbury, Massachusetts, an education advocacy organization whose mission is to create and sustain equitable, high-performing public schools. She has used qualitative and quantitative methods to study school change, effective practices, and student outcomes, including producing a biannual report on Boston pilot school student engagement and performance.

Miren Uriarte, Ph.D., is an associate professor of sociology at the College of Public and Community Service and the director of the Mauricio Gastón Institute for Latino Community Development and Public Policy at the University of Massachusetts, Boston. She conducts research and policy analysis focused on the differential impact of education and social policy on minority communities in general and on Latinos in the United States specifically as well as program development and evaluation research in education, health care, and human services.

Laura Wentworth is a doctoral student at Stanford University. Her doctoral work focuses on administration and policy analysis and covers topics such as school and district reform as well as education policies affecting English learner achievement. To date, she has co-authored a number of other publications, including "Assessment for Learning Around the World: What Would It Mean to Be Internationally Competitive?" (Phi Delta *Kappan*, December 2008, with Linda Darling-Hammond). She worked for 7 years as an elementary school teacher.

Index